Advance Praise for *Arrow to the Heart*

"The Bureau of Land Management raided Mr. Kortlander like he was Scarface. Using force to go after drug dealers or violent criminals is understandable, but somebody in a hot, sultry part of Montana, in a trading post where people are wandering around buying blankets? Come on."

—*Penelope Strong*, Criminal Defense Attorney

"This story can be described as a defense lawyer's dream. Christopher Kortlander suffered the slings and arrows of the federal government with courage and integrity. He is truly a dedicated American citizen."

—*Charles "Timer" Moses*, Criminal Defense Attorney

"In 2009, at the end of its criminal investigation, the United States had a duty to return the items or institute forfeiture proceedings if it believed the items were contraband. It has done neither; therefore, as a matter of law, the property must be returned."

—*William Perry Pendley*, President, Mountain States Legal Foundation

"*Arrow to the Heart* gives a raw, behind-the-scenes account of federal overreach into the lives of private individuals and corporations alike. This has now become commonplace in our nation. It is important that citizens like Chris Kortlander stand up for what is right and to stop federal tyranny."

—*Lance Tobacco*, Former DOI Law Enforcement Officer

Arrow To The Heart

The Last Battle at the Little Big Horn
The Custer Battlefield Museum vs. The Federal Government

Christopher Kortlander

Foreword by
Ammon Bundy

A POST HILL PRESS BOOK

Arrow to the Heart
The Last Battle at the Little Big Horn:
The Custer Battlefield Museum vs. The Federal Government
© 2018 by Christopher Kortlander
All Rights Reserved

ISBN: 978-1-68261-709-0
ISBN (eBook): 978-1-68261-710-6

Cover design by William C. Reynolds
Interior design and composition by Greg Johnson, Textbook Perfect

No part of this book may be reproduced, stored in a retrieval system, or transmitted by any means without the written permission of the author and publisher.

About the front cover: The arrow pictured on the front cover is an authentic arrow from the Battle of the Little Big Horn. It was given to the author by Presidential Medal of Freedom recipient Dr. Joseph Medicine Crow, a former board member at the Custer Battlefield Museum. Dr. Medicine Crow was given the arrow by his maternal step-grandfather, White Man Runs Him. White Man Runs Him was a scout for Custer. Oral history states that this arrow was picked up on the Custer Battlefield at Last Stand Hill, where Custer and his command were killed, on June 25, 1876.

Post Hill Press
New York • Nashville
posthillpress.com

Published in the United States of America

Dedication

This book is dedicated to Dr. James Redd, Steven Shrader, and Robert Weaver, who took their own lives because they were not able to endure the wrath, verbal abuse, threats, intimidation, and bullying by federal agents during armed raids by the Bureau of Land Management.

Author's Note

Robert "Bob" Weaver's death by suicide occurred on December 31, 2016 in Cody, Wyoming, only three hours from Garryowen, Montana. Weaver's death was the final straw that compelled me to tell my story. Andrew Turck, Editor of the Big Horn County News, wrote about this tragedy on March 16, 2016 in an article titled "Four Suicides Involved: Custer Battlefield Museum director seeks to 'terminate' BLM law enforcement function." Weaver, known by many Cody residents as "Bob the Geologist," died of a self-inflicted gunshot wound three days after investigators from the BLM and Office of Inspector General arrived at his trailer with search warrants. These warrants were served regarding his allegedly illegal activities collecting rocks and fossils on public lands.

Contents

Foreword by Ammon Bundy ix
Introduction xvi

 1 Custer Was Just the Beginning 1
 2 Enemy in Our Midst 22
 3 I Knew There Was a Woman Involved in This Somewhere 40
 4 Button, Button, Who's Got the Button? 56
 5 The Bones of Little Girls 76
 6 The Smoke Clears 93
 7 The Investigation That Never Happened 108
 8 The Nine Firings 120
     Photo Gallery 129
 9 Lost Freedom 145
10 A White Bird 160
11 Government Tan 180
12 Federal Revelation 189
13 Threats, Intimidation, and Bullying 200
14 One Nation Under God 209
15 Redemption 219
16 Looking Back to the Future 229

Epilogue 236
Resources 241
Endnotes 253
Acknowledgments 265

Foreword

by Ammon Bundy

Having a gun pointed at you can affect you in several unusual ways. To some, it is terrifying and takes years to overcome; to others it's just alarming. At the age of 18, unfortunately I had such an experience.

While in the southern Nevada desert, a man came up to my pickup truck and put a pistol in my face. He told me to leave the area and said, "I've killed before, and I would do it again." Not knowing what had provoked him, those who were with me and I calmly got into my truck and drove away. We were approximately 30 miles south of Mesquite, Nevada, at the northern tip of Lake Mead on the Bundy Range. After contemplating the event, I concluded that the man had claimed his camp nearby and simply did not want us around.

Although it did not cause me to fear much, it was alarming to experience how willing he was to use a gun to get us to leave. A few days later, I heard how the sheriff's department was searching for a man hiding in the desert and considered him dangerous. Being certain it was the same man who had pointed his gun at me, I gave the information to a deputy. I believe they arrested him, and I never heard any more about him again.

Before this incident, in all the time my family has run cattle in the desert, for five generations, since 1877—140 years—I had never heard of a person on our range using a gun to force or intimidate another. Then the Bureau of Land Management (BLM) came to town in early 2014.

Just like the man in the desert, some BLM law enforcement agents, pointed guns at people's heads and threatened deadly force simply because the BLM personnel did not want us there. Through its Office of Law Enforcement and Security, the BLM functions as a federal law enforcement agency of the U.S. Government. It is hard to describe the overwhelming force used by the BLM upon our community and family. The best way for me to describe it is that it was like a scene out of the Hollywood movie *Red Dawn*. Helicopters, more than 200 agents, full battle gear, loudspeakers, checkpoints, attack dogs, armed convoys, surveillance aircraft with night vision and infrared capabilities, assault after assault, snipers on the hill, missions, and misinformation campaigns, just to mention a few elements.

In an explanation of a campaign on the Bundy family and community, the BLM states, "This is a military-type operation," and that the Intelligence Collection Program command procedures used were "military model." Steve Myhre, U.S. attorney for the district of Nevada, in defense of the BLM admitted in court records that "the BLM was a military-type force of some sort." It was reported that the BLM spent close to $6 million to move in and start this operation.

During the 10 days the teams took setting up their base of operation, a BLM "crisis negotiator" contacted my family by phone and told us, "If you resist in any way, this will be another Waco or Ruby Ridge….We will kill you."

The operational plans and the Memorandum of Agreement (MOA) report show that multiple sniper teams were surveilling my family's home "24 hours a day with 360-degree surveillance" and that "lethal force" may have been "imminent."

You may be asking, "Why such a show of force? Are the Bundys such terrible people?" As a Bundy myself, I will not try to defend the character of my family and myself. Whether we are just a simple American ranching family or not is for you to answer for yourself, if you so desire.

However, I will say this: the armed-to-the-teeth paramilitary force used by the BLM[1] upon our community and family was not over a $75 Indian bead the size of the end of my pinkie—the bead used by BLM officials to justify sending special agent in charge of the BLM in

Nevada and Utah, Dan Love, and over 120 BLM agent operators to raid homes and terrorize families in Blanding, Utah.

Neither was the force upon my family over Indian Wars–period relics. A buckle and buttons were used by the BLM to justify having BLM agents in full tactical gear and with assault rifles bust through doors to raid a local museum in Montana, terrorizing employees and interns who had never heard of the Bureau of Land Management before.

Nor was my family stormed by the armed law enforcement division of the U.S. Fish and Wildlife Service over legally obtained exotic wood used for making guitar parts.

No, the force upon my family was not over antiques. The millions of dollars spent, hundreds of tactical agents converging, helicopters flying, farm vehicles rolling, and so on were because my father's cattle were eating what the BLM said was their grass, a claim the Bundy family and many others constitutionally dispute.

But still the same, the excessive force upon my family used by the BLM was over cattle eating grass. Of course, I could go into the details and talk about how my family had grazed our cattle on that land since 1877, for 140 years, before Las Vegas had even one tent in it, and seventy years before the Bureau of Land Management existed. I could talk about how our water infrastructure is over a hundred years old and, without it, much of the wildlife would not be able to survive in parts of that desert.

I could point out the constitutional violations of the BLM by controlling over 89 percent of the land in the state of Nevada, and how Nevada's rural economy has been devastated by the BLM land control. I could continue to go on about the many injustices by the BLM and other federal land control agencies, and even show how detrimental these types of actions are to the fundamental liberty of each American, violating our most basic rights—most notably the Fourth Amendment, which ensures "the right of the people to be secure in their reasons, houses, papers, and effects" and protects citizens from "unreasonable searches and seizures."[2]

But, putting all that aside, putting the dispute out of view, what you have left is a military-type force, funded by American taxes, coming down upon American families with such terrifying force that lives were being taken. For what? An Indian bead? Old buttons and a buckle? Some wood? Cows eating grass? I know I'm not the only one who finds this ludicrous, and I'm sure that this insult to everything that is American is one of the reasons Chris has written this book.

One of the ironies of this whole matter is, when Congress established the Bureau of Land Management in 1946, combining the U.S. Land Office with the U.S. Grazing Board, the directive from Congress was to dispose of the land and give it to the people, and encourage ranchers to graze cattle on the land. That is what Congress organized the BLM to do. So why the use of excessive force? Maybe I can best explain it this way through a short, and true, story.

When I was around nine or 10 years old, my family visited Lehman Caves in central Nevada. After going through the magnificent underground chambers, my brothers and I were intrigued by some little birds that had built their nests with mud under the canopy of the visitors' center. I climbed the railing to get a peek into the mud nest, when a park ranger came up and strictly reprimanded me for disturbing the birds. He said, "How would you like it if I came and frightened you in your home?" My intention was not to harm or frighten the birds in their homes. I was just curious. Embarrassed, I quickly jumped down. The park ranger continued to rail on us about our intrusion into the birds' habitat, how the birds had a right to be secure in their homes, how getting too close to them would cause them to feel danger, and how now they might move to another location. In shame, we accepted the reprimand. Then the ranger turned on his heels and, with a straight back and head up, he walked away.

My point in telling you this story is not in the irony of the ranger's question, "How would you like it if I came and frightened you in your home?" The point I would like to make is that the park ranger was a stuffy man in a uniform with a goofy hat who knew a lot about birds. He did not wear a gun. He did not have a radio. He was not wearing a protective vest or armor plates or a helmet. He did not wear a star on his chest, and his vehicle did not have red and blue lights on it. He did not threaten to arrest us or use force upon us in any way. In fact, I do not think the use of force was in his nature. He was someone who loved the birds and looked after them. He did his job, stopped our intrusion, educated us with a little shame, and then walked away.

Many years later I became aware that at the time, if this park ranger had wanted to have me arrested, he would have had to call the county sheriff. He held no policing or arresting power. In fact, the park ranger not only had no policing or arresting power, but he would have had no jail to take me to. If I had been put in the county or state system, the judge would have had the case thrown out, because no state or county law had been violated. You see, that stiff park ranger in his goofy hat held very little power, just as the Constitution intended. Unless I had broken a local law, voted upon by the representatives of the local people and enforced by an elected local sheriff, who received policing and arresting powers from the local people, I was protected.

As extreme environmentalist and socialist groups began to take over federal agencies like the Bureau of Land Management, constitutional checks and balances became very frustrating for them. They connived a way to create color of law without legislation by implanting their policies in the federal registry, making them appear as laws. But what good was their so-called law if the sheriff would not enforce that law and they had no enforcing powers themselves or jails to punish people with? These extreme environmentalists knew the local people, in general, would never pass their radical policies as local law. So, they began to devise another means to force their ideologies upon the American people. They simply would create their own law enforcement structure.

Like the picture of an ape evolving into a man, peaceful park rangers in goofy hats, over 35 years, have evolved into terrifying soldiers with training to equal their gear. Federal law enforcement training centers were established, where all the training and gear are available to any agency that wants a force. Federal jails were built, and administrative judges were hired. Local checks and balances were broken down through federal funding and MOUs (Memorandums of Understanding). Local law enforcement departments were given federal funding to purchase needed equipment if they would accept federal agents, such as park rangers, as authorized law enforcement with policing and arresting powers.

The constitutional protections afforded to people regarding voting and delegating their policing and arresting power were deceptively bypassed. Now, all a federal agent must do to obtain policing and arresting power is go to the federal training center and get certified. The solemn and sacred power to take life, liberty, or property through the law once came from the local people by delegation, through elections and deputizing. This has all been usurped by federal agents through certification.

The once constitutionally frustrated extreme environmental bureaucrats, with no mechanism to enforce their own policies, have, for over 35 years, developed a system to create their own laws, enforce those laws, and interpret those laws with no checks and balances and no local interference. There is no way to hold them accountable. There is no way to indict them. You cannot vote them out, and if the local representatives stand in their way, like San Juan County commissioner Phil Lyman did, they arrest them, prosecute them in their own system, and punish them like all the others. The word to describe this is "despotism."

As appalling as it is for the Bureau of Land Management to justify raiding families in Utah over an Indian bead, or a museum in Montana over an old buckle and some buttons, or a guitar factory for using some exotic wood, or waging a full military-type campaign in Nevada over cows eating grass, the real reason for the shows of force has nothing to do with beads, buckles, buttons, wood, or grass. You do not have to look far back in time to see how unchecked power attracts those who thrive on force and intimidation. Men like Dan Love and his once loyal team of military-like operators thrive on this force.

Men and women excited to use the color of law in taking life, liberty, and property are turning once peaceful little communities into places of terror and mourning. Add to this the ideology of extreme environmentalists who believe it is their divine right to force all people, by any means, to align with their far-flung beliefs. Then add federal agents who believe they are above the law, and lives will continue to be lost over items such as beads, buckles, buttons, wood, and grass.

There is nothing we can do about the past except learn from it. The future is entirely different. We can change what is happening. I suppose we must keep learning the same lessons repeatedly because humans live only so long. Future generations forget what once was common knowledge—knowledge such as ultimate power ultimately corrupts. Men and women in power must have checks and balances, or they will abuse it. The best way to prevent power from being abused is to keep it distributed among all the people and not allow it to be consolidated into one body. There will always be more overzealous federal agents in the world.

So, if we desire to end the destruction of life, liberty, or property over beads, buckles, buttons, wood, or grass, then we must reinstall the strict constitutional checks and balances once held by the local people, their sheriffs, and their representatives. Thank you.

Written while in solitary confinement at the federal detention center in Pahrump, Nevada.

Introduction

Most Americans are aware of the "innocent until proven guilty" meme. We think about it as the way of law and order in this country. However, in federal law enforcement, the more likely lesson on the law would be "the end justifies the means." Modern experience has provided evidence that federal prosecutors and federal agents extend vague and esoteric federal criminal laws into people's daily conduct that would not be readily seen as criminal.

The rules of criminal law deal with the rights of the accused after an arrest. It is only after one is formally charged with a crime that most constitutional protections come into play (for instance, the right to a speedy trial). It may be that in the eyes of the federal agencies, including the Bureau of Land Management, the maxim is "no charge, no harm."

Law enforcement agents can utilize assumed identities, controlled operations in which criminal activity is allowed, and intrusive surveillance without a warrant. Seizure of property arguably for evidence is a common practice. But even if no criminal activity is prosecuted and no charges are ever filed, the government's targeted victims face an uphill battle to get their private property returned. Frequently, seized property disappears into the government bureaucracy down a dark hole where the public cannot follow. Furthermore, the financial devastation arising from persecution by the federal government is daunting and insurmountable.

"*Malum in se*" is a Latin phrase meaning "wrong or evil in itself." The phrase is used to refer to conduct (such as rape and murder) assessed as sinful or inherently wrong by nature, independent of regulations governing the conduct. *Malum prohibitum* is a "prohibited wrong," whether by statute, regulation, or rule. This latter class of crimes generally results in no direct or immediate injury to a person or property, but merely creates the danger or probability of it. Increasingly, you can be guilty of a crime that you did not even know was a crime and for which you never knew or suspected there was a rule. Intent associated with a guilty mind when committing the criminal act is no longer necessary. In criminal law, intent (or *scienter*) is one of three general classes of *mens rea* (guilty mind) necessary to constitute a conventional, as opposed to a strict liability, crime.

Harvey Silverglate writes and documents prosecutorial abuses in his book *Three Felonies a Day*. He tells how our individual liberty is threatened by zealous crusades by the Department of Justice. Even the most intelligent and informed citizens, he says—including lawyers and judges—cannot predict with any reasonable assurance whether a wide range of seemingly ordinary activities might be regarded by federal prosecutors as felonies.

This problem is not fundamentally based upon the political party of the agent or prosecutor. It is the product of a judicially centrist bureaucracy that rewards convictions over justice, a system that allows federal prosecutors immense power without independent oversight and accountability.

Being a former law enforcement officer who was around prisoners, I would constantly hear them claim, "I'm innocent! I pled guilty because I couldn't take the interrogation anymore." I blew it off as "jailhouse talk." Now I know it was much more than that. The justice system in the United States is flawed to a point where we have innocent citizens pleading guilty just to avoid further abuse, with no end in sight.

As you read through this narrative, you will come to find that in some cases, instead of pleading guilty to a crime they did not commit, some people resorted to taking their own lives because the threats, intimidation, and bullying by federal agents of the Bureau of Land Management were insufferable.

1

Custer Was Just the Beginning

"What's that he says?" asked General George Armstrong Custer.

Bloody Knife, Custer's most trusted Arikara Indian scout, repeated his fears to translator Frederic Gerard.

"He says we'll find enough Sioux to keep us fighting [for] two or three days," Gerard interpreted.

Smiling, Custer replied, "I guess we'll get through them in one day."[1]

In the early morning of June 25, 1876, in the southern Montana Territory, the United States 7th Cavalry, along with several Crow and Arikara scouts, dined on a breakfast of boiled pork and crackers.[2] Bewildered by exhaustion from having marched a great distance in the days prior, the men knew they had to prepare their bodies and minds for the battle that was looming on the horizon. Mounting his steed, the steely-blue-eyed "Boy General of the Golden Lock" rode throughout the encampment issuing orders, telling his soldiers they would begin their march at 8:00 a.m.[3]

Custer, who forged a sterling reputation as a rapacious warrior during the American Civil War, eventually rose to the rank of brevet major general during that great conflict. He furthered his status by displaying his military prowess as a fierce Indian fighter following his successful campaign against Black Kettle's Southern Cheyenne at the Washita River in Oklahoma in 1868. Although Custer did not know it, his gallant ride into this glorious fight, known as the Battle of the Little Bighorn, not only would define his life as a soldier but would cement his historic legacy.

As the enigmatic Custer galloped ahead with several scouts to survey the enemy encampment, the column he had just aroused rose behind him. It is said that many of the men began to joke with one another about the coming fight. In fact, one confident soldier even declared, "The campaign will soon be over once we catch Sitting Bull."[4]

In response, another soldier piped up and said, "If that is all, the campaign will soon be over and Custer will take us all with him to the Centennial." A third chimed in, "Of course we will take Sitting Bull with us." The confident men all erupted in much laughter.[5]

Sitting Bull, the Hunkpapa Lakota chief whom the men joked about, was a peerless leader and a fearless warrior. With long, flowing black hair tied into braids that hung over his shoulders and deep, almost black, piercing eyes set into a weathered face, the Lakota medicine man was every bit as fearsome and noble as he appeared to be. Originally, he was named Jumping Badger. After he counted his first coup at age 14, by participating in a battle against his traditional enemy, the Crow Indians, his father named him Tatanka-Iyotanka (Sitting Bull). From then on, he built his reputation as a great warrior and soon was named the supreme war chief of the entire Lakota Nation around the age of 45.[6]

As the United States 7th Cavalry and their Indian scouts prepared for battle, so too did Sitting Bull's combined force of Lakota, Northern Cheyenne, and Arapaho Indians. They were holed up in a large village with inhabitants from 1,500 to 2,500 strong, entrenched along the banks of the Little Bighorn River. Custer, with five of the 7th Cavalry's 12 companies in tow, prepared to attack with little knowledge of the size of this formidable village.

Custer's troops, unbeknownst to him, were operating under incorrect assumptions as to the number of Indians they were about to encounter. The army's suppositions were based on inaccurate information provided by Indian agents who wagered that no more than

800 hostiles were in the area. The Indian agents based that number on the number of Lakota Indians led by Sitting Bull and other leaders off the reservation in protest of U.S. government policies. This was an accurate estimate until several weeks before the battle, when the "reservation Indians" joined Sitting Bull's ranks for the summer buffalo hunt.

The Indian agents did not account for the thousands of "reservation Indians" who had unofficially left their agencies to join their uncooperative nonreservation counterparts led by Sitting Bull. Thus, Custer unknowingly faced thousands of Indians in addition to the 800 nonreservation hostiles he was aware of.[7]

There are several versions of just how "Custer's Last Stand" played out, but most are conjecture because all of Custer's men were wiped out and no witnesses were left to tell the tale. In the end, the hilltop was probably too small to accommodate the survivors and wounded. Enemy fire from the southeast made it impossible for Custer's men to secure a defensive position around Last Stand Hill, where the soldiers put up their most dogged defense. According to Lakota accounts, far more of their casualties occurred in the attack on Last Stand Hill than anywhere else. The extent of the soldiers' resistance indicated they had few doubts about their prospects for survival. According to Cheyenne and Sioux testimony, the command structure rapidly broke down. Many of the most reliable accounts say the combined Indian forces destroyed Custer and his men around an hour after the battle began.[8]

Recent archaeological work at the battlefield indicates that officers on Last Stand Hill restored some sort of tactical control during the desperate fight. E Company rushed off the hill toward the Little Bighorn River but failed, resulting in its destruction, leaving behind some 50 to 60 men.[9] The remainder of the battle took on the nature of a running fight. Modern archaeology and historical Indian accounts indicate that Custer's force may have been divided into three groups, with the Indians attempting to prevent them from effectively reuniting.

Several Indian accounts described the battle as warriors running up from the village to wave blankets to scare off the soldiers' horses.

One 7th Cavalry trooper claimed to find several stone mallets, each consisting of a round cobble weighing eight to 10 pounds (with a rawhide handle, which he believed had been used by the Indian women to finish off the wounded). Fighting after being dismounted, the soldiers were overwhelmed. As individual troopers were wounded or killed, initial defensive positions would have been abandoned as untenable.[10]

Under threat of attack, the first U.S. soldiers did not return to the battlefield until three days later, and then they hurriedly buried the troopers in shallow graves where they had fallen. A couple of years after the battle, markers were placed where men were believed to have fallen, so the placement of troops has been roughly reconstructed.

As Custer's name was etched into the history books that fateful day, so too were the names of many of the brave Indian leaders who opposed him. The likes of Gall, Crazy Horse, and of course the unflappable Sitting Bull would make a lasting mark in this last great battle of the Indian Wars.

In the decades following, historians, both amateur and professional, have debated what happened on that hot June day in 1876. The facts that we know for certain are that the U.S. 7th Cavalry, a force of around 700 men led by George Armstrong Custer, suffered a severe defeat. "Five of the 7th Cavalry's twelve companies were annihilated; Custer was killed, as were two of his brothers, a nephew, and a brother-in-law. The total U.S. casualty count, including scouts, was 268 dead and 55 wounded."[11]

Famous Old West historian Robert Utley once wrote, "More words have been written about the Battle of the Little Bighorn than any other battle in American history outside of Gettysburg." It is no surprise that an event of this magnitude continues to draw thousands of people every year to the historic battlefield. These tourists want to follow the trail that Custer took, to survey the land as the Crow scouts saw it, to stand where Sitting Bull's camp once stood, and most of all, to get a sense of history from a place that holds so much meaning for America's past.

As I stand on the back porch of my property in the early hours of an unusually brisk summer morning, I look down upon what was once Sitting Bull's encampment. The sun shines brightly through the trees, and a light pink hue accentuates the sky. The mild chill of the day's morning air fills my lungs and heightens my senses. If I close my eyes, I can almost see the 7th Cavalry soldiers as they unknowingly march in columns towards their destiny.

Focusing inward, I can hear the echoes of the Indian's war whoops and the steady beat of the drums as the entire Sioux Nation rises to meet its invading enemy. Surrounded by these ghosts from the past, I believe this piece of land retains a certain sacred magic found in few other places.

I am not alone in my reverence either. Many find it sacred, from the Native American tribes that inhabit the reservation lands on and surrounding the battlefield to the tourists passing through with a casual interest in history, and the folks affectionately referred to as "Custer Crazies." This last group has spent a good portion of their lives devoted to the minutiae of the battle, dwelling over the decisions made by the commanding officers during it, and to the details of the lives of the people who fought it. These three groups make up the literally hundreds of thousands of people who pass through the battleground every year.

With all the numerous interested parties, it is no wonder that those who find the land sacred also find the artifacts left behind from the battle sacred as well. These items stand, to many, as a reminder of this country's not-so-distant past and as a physical symbol of that bygone age. My personal interest in the battle and its artifacts dates back to the late 1970s, when I purchased the saber of Sergeant James Butler, who perished at the Little Bighorn.

Butler was the first sergeant for 7th Cavalry lieutenant James "Jimmi" Calhoun. Calhoun was also George Custer's brother-in-law through marriage to Custer's sister, Margaret.[12] By all accounts, Butler fought furiously for his life during the battle. Captain William Frederick Benteen, Thomas Weir, Charles DeRudio, Henry Nowlan, and their guide, James Bradley, were the first to find Butler's body. Near the sergeant's corpse were the bloated remains of a bullet-riddled horse and several spent shell casings. The casings all belonged to Butler, who was known as a crack shot.[13]

I bought the saber from a dealer named Putt Thompson, a man whom I would eventually come to call a good friend. Putt is a tall man with a long braid of golden blond hair running down his back; he accentuates this look with a cowboy hat and sharp Western wear. His Southern drawl, a result of being raised on a Texas dairy farm, adds to his authentic Western appearance. His immense knowledge of Crow Indian tribal culture, from his being adopted by a prominent Crow family, gives him a unique knowledge of tribal culture and allows him to sell his antiques without much question as to their provenance.

When Putt offered to sell me the Butler saber, I was energized by the opportunity to get my hands on a piece of the past from the most famous battle in American history. Embellishing the blade's provenance a tad, Putt told me the sword had been mysteriously found in a cave in eastern Montana. After hearing the story, I was smitten with the item and purchased it for $5,000.

While researching the item, I found it was indeed the genuine article but that the finding of it in the cave was completely bogus. Even so, with an authentic piece of history in my hand, I turned around and sold the item for $15,000 to an equally enthusiastic collector. After that one transaction, I was hooked. I decided from that point on that I would focus on making my living dealing in historic artifacts, especially on Western Americana.

So, in 1980 I founded and incorporated Historical Rarities Inc. Through this business, I have successfully brokered acquisitions of historical ephemera, autographs, rare and desirable manuscripts, signed books, first editions, Western Americana, native art, early Native American beadwork, and period photographs of Western peoples and historic locations for private and public collectors around the world. In some regards, my collection of Native American artwork and Western Americana is unparalleled.

When I established this business, I made it a point to gain a reputation for being a dealer who treated clients fairly and with respect and never, ever tried to swindle, con, or cheat any of the people who purchased artifacts from me. I acquired this hard-earned reputation over two decades of transactions and dealings, and then the dawn of the internet allowed me to expand and strengthen my business through the online auction site eBay. Presently, my rating on the auction site is A-class, which stems from over 5,500 reviews and over 10,000 completed auctions; I've been a valued member since 1998. The history behind many of the pieces I have collected and sold over the years, like that of the saber, makes them something much more than artifacts. They almost are living entities with stories to tell.

My first contact with Montana and the history of the Little Bighorn came in 1976 after high school, when I decided to visit my good friend Jeff Robertson who had moved from California to Big Sky Country that same year. Although he was three years my senior, Jeff and I became good friends, as he had been my church counselor in North Hollywood, California. In fact, our friendship flourished to the point where he eventually asked me to be a groomsman in his wedding. Jeff was familiar with Montana because his father owned a ranch in the state and was a turquoise dealer there. His father had often taken us on road trips to the mountainous state during the summer, and continued this even after I graduated high school. Jeff had always encouraged me to visit him and his family on their ranch. So, after graduation I made a three-week trip to visit Jeff. That short visit turned into a 12-year stay.

After going on a hunting trip with Jeff and seeing the seasons change, something I had never experienced growing up in Southern California, I fell in love with Big Sky Country and decided it was where I wanted to live. Without much hesitation, I moved all my possessions to Billings in 1977. The following year I married my childhood sweetheart, Kim, in Southern California and she moved to Billings with me. Our son was born in 1983, and Kim and I would live in Billings until our divorce in 1988.

In 1989 I met my second wife, Karan, while in the city of Billings. I had to have oral surgery on a tooth that had chipped and was in desperate need of a root canal. Karan was the surgical assistant assigned to me, and we hit it off almost immediately. After dating for about two years in Billings, we married in 1990 in Malibu, California, so that our friends and family could attend the ceremony.

California is one of the places my obsession with Western history can be traced back to. When I was growing up, my father, John Kortlander, owned about 50 head of beef cattle on a plot of land in Lancaster, California. He had his own brands, was his own veterinarian, and gave me a strong sense of the past and the history of the land. I remember him so vividly standing tall with a Stetson hat and an almost self-sufficient John Wayne demeanor. He was a great influence in my life, and I will never forget the lessons he taught me and the love he gave me.

My father, being an extremely intelligent man, eventually designed an anti-noise disposable earplug and patented it for the Lockheed Corporation (which later became the Lockheed Martin Corporation). He branched out on his own with the approval of Lockheed and supplied these earplugs to the company as a private manufacturer. His business ambitions eventually made him a global manufacturer of the earplugs.

Like many Westerners, John Kortlander had ties to the history of the land. I inherited those ties. I also inherited the responsibility of being the caretaker for my great-uncle Henry Kortlander's historic hunting lodge, the oldest home still standing in Malibu, built in 1906. My uncle owned more than 600 acres in Malibu. Eventually, my father inherited the lodge along with the acreage. My father was something of a philanthropist. He felt that he should preserve the Malibu virgin hills and protect the land from any type of mass development. He found out that the U.S. Department of the Treasury had something called a "donative sale."

In a donative sale, half of a parcel of land is donated and half is sold. My father knew that the California Conservancy, a quasigovernment nonprofit agency, was acquiring private land for a state park system in Malibu. Much of the Kortlander parcel encompassed incredible mountain peaks, lush cliffs and arroyos, and flowing water from the High Sierras straight through the property, dumping into the Pacific Ocean below. It also had beautiful portions of forestland. A good deal of the land became what was known as the Santa Monica Mountain Conservancy.

The Santa Monica Mountain Conservancy is an agency of the state of California established by the state legislature in 1980. It is dedicated to the acquisition of land for preservation as open space, for wildlife and California native plants, and for public recreation activities.[14] The land, before the Mountain Conservancy took over, had around 20 spots of actual buildable property. This land was eventually developed into some of the most expensive and luxurious properties in the country. Eventually, the conservancy merged our family estate with the Santa Monica Mountains National Recreation Area, the jurisdiction of which lies with the Department of the Interior's National Park Service.

It is interesting to note, my uncle Henry Kortlander also owned the Western Lithograph Company in downtown Los Angeles. He became well known for printing large calendar tops depicting romantic Old West scenes and landscapes painted by famous Western artists such as Frank Tenney Johnson, Frederic Remington, and Charlie Russell.

The hunting lodge that I inherited and was fortunate enough to make my home was an exquisite structure. The small, quaint, 1,100-square-foot home, built of brick and eucalyptus wood beams, was constructed at the base of two canyons on a Chumash Indian ritual ground. Today, it would be considered an early Arts and Crafts design before the style became prevalent in the following decades. Located at the junction of Little Las Flores Creek and Las Flores Canyon, the home stood like something out of a dream in this immaculate location. The land was shrouded in a canopy of lush green vegetation with a quite rustic feel, accentuated by a large amount of scrub brush encircling the canyon and a small waterfall that gave it the sound of paradise.

In 1988, I decided to move back to Malibu from Billings. I wanted to renovate the lodge in the hope of having the home listed on the National Register of Historic Places. I thought it would make my great-uncle and my mom and dad proud, plus I love a historical challenge. After my divorce from Kim, I found I had a good deal of time to oversee the remodel, which also helped me to keep my mind off the failure of the marriage. Over nearly a year and a half, I gutted the entire home and transformed it into a quaint and quite lovely petite domicile filled with original antique Stickley oak furniture.

One evening in 1990, Karan and I hosted a dinner party in the lodge with no more than 15 people. Our dinner guests included family members and our closest friends. After we finished the main course, right before dessert, there was a knock on the door. Karan and I nervously looked at each other. We knew who was at the door—it was the pastor we'd invited to drop in on our party. While everyone was enjoying their dessert wine, I answered the door and announced to our family and friends that this was no ordinary dinner party—we had chosen to get married that night in the hunting lodge with our nearest and dearest by our sides. The shocked looks on everyone's faces were priceless. They were floored. The ceremony took only about 15 minutes, and we spent the next few hours tipping champagne glasses.

In 1991, during this period of my home renovation, U.S. House of Representatives member from Colorado Ben Nighthorse Campbell authored a bill to change the name of the Custer Battlefield National Monument to the Little Bighorn National Monument. The Little Bighorn National Monument is in southern Montana. Campbell is a Northern Cheyenne Indian, and his great-grandfather had fought alongside Cheyenne chief Two Moons to defeat Custer in that most famous battle.

The bill quickly passed both the House of Representatives and the Senate, and in December of that year the bill was signed into law by then president George H. W. Bush. With that single action, the name "Custer Battlefield" was abandoned. I happened to view this live on CNN. I called my Montana attorney and instructed him to incorporate the name Custer Battlefield Museum. He filed with the Montana secretary of state the next day, securing the name as soon as it became available. This was the very same month the bill was signed into law.

By October 1993, following the home restoration, I returned to Montana to visit my friend and future business associate Putt Thompson. As he and I sat down to breakfast early one morning, Putt tossed his daily mail onto the dining table. Wedged in amongst the bills and usual junk was the monthly *Custer Battlefield Association Newsletter* he subscribed to. Pulling it out of the stack as Putt poured both of us some freshly brewed coffee, I noticed an article. The piece proclaimed that the town of Garryowen, Montana, was up for sale.

Intrigued by this, I asked Putt, "What's Garryowen?"

"It's where the battle began."

"What's down there? I mean, are there any real significant structures or what?"

Putt informed me that the only structures on the seven-acre parcel were an unmarked tomb of an unknown soldier, a post office that was falling in on itself, a ramshackle house, and a pit of a gas station.

Founded in 1895, the town of Garryowen served as a water stop for the Chicago, Burlington, and Quincy Railroad. Garryowen was the drop-off point for mail, supplies, and troops bound for Fort Custer. It is located outside present-day Hardin, Montana, which is about 18 miles to the north.[15] The town is also just three miles from the Little Bighorn National Monument, and sits directly along the I-90 route followed by tourists traveling to and from Yellowstone Park, the Black Hills of South Dakota, and Mount Rushmore.

As the only town located within the boundaries of the site of the Battle of the Little Bighorn, Garryowen has the distinction of being the spot where the first shots of the battle were fired.[16] This site was Sitting Bull's camp, and before Custer's men engaged fully in the battle three miles downriver, some of his men initiated a fight with Sitting Bull's braves at the end of the huge Indian encampment. Garryowen sits in the middle of the Crow Indian Reservation.

After hearing what Putt knew about the town, I insisted that we drop our preplanned historical trading session and go there. So, by 10:30 a.m., we hit the road and drove to the town. As we approached, taking the I-90 off-ramp marked "Garryowen," a truly depressing sight lay before me. The historic parcel of land had obviously never been taken care of or brought up to showcase its true potential. My God, let's keep in mind there is a tomb of a United States unknown soldier on the property! After parking, Putt and I exited the vehicle and were quickly greeted by sheets of trash lifted by the swirling Montana winds and sent flittering into our path.

As I sidestepped the bags of garbage and kicked through piles of rubbish, I approached the gas station. It was a 1960s-style structure; the gas pumps were fitted with glass globes and dial gauges but had not been in operation for nearly 40 years. Looking at the dingy, dismantled heap of a building, I immediately conjured up memories from my youth watching the now classic television series *The Twilight Zone*. Letting my mind wander, I imagined if I stepped inside the rusted hulk of a station I would see a Martian standing behind the convenience store counter and Rod Serling reciting his usual monologue.

With that image burned into my brain, I decided against going into any of the buildings and followed Putt to the unmarked grave of the unknown soldier. It, much like the gas station and post office, had seen better days. It had been left to decay over the years, and I felt a kind of injustice sweep over me for the man inside the tomb. He had given his life in service of his country, and his final resting place was in shambles.

The remains of the unidentified trooper buried there were found in 1926, just a few months prior to the 50th commemoration of the Custer battle. Presumed to have been one of Major Reno's men and one of the first 7th Cavalry members killed in the opening phase of the battle in the river valley near Garryowen, the soldier was decapitated when he encountered the massive Sioux and Cheyenne forces. Apparently high water in the spring following the famous battle caused the soldier's body to be buried, and it was not found until the road crew building U.S. Highway 87 uncovered it.[17]

The 50th commemoration of the battle in 1926 saw Chief White Bull of the Lakota Sioux and then Brigadier General Edward S. Godfrey of the United States 7th Cavalry, two men who had fought during the battle, shake hands at the end of a ceremony in front of 50,000 people. The tomb was constructed to not only commemorate the men on both sides who had lost their lives during the battle, but to stand as a symbol of peace between the United States and all Indian nations.[18]

At the dedication of the newly erected monument tomb that same year, representatives of both the U.S. government and the Indian tribes took part in a burying-of-the-hatchet ceremony, placing a hatchet below a trap door in the tomb. The hatchet was buried along with 19 other artifacts, including an original letter from Elizabeth Custer stating why she could not attend the ceremony, a jeweled 7th Cavalry crest, battlefield maps, and historical photography, just to name a few of the items.[19] All the artifacts remain inside the tomb today. This was the largest gathering ever for a burying-of-the-hatchet ceremony, and it helped to give the phrase "burying the hatchet" its popularity today.[20]

I'm not sure if it was my love of history or my sense that I would be preserving something for future generations, or if I just saw it as a unique business opportunity, but in the hours after visiting Garryowen I decided to purchase the town. I called the person acting for the owners, Larry Martin, around noon that day. He seemed glad to speak with me, and we arranged a time to meet.

Martin was a white man whose wife had been a full-blooded Crow Indian. She and her family owned the land Garryowen sat upon. Apparently, she had died on the property from a severe alcoholic condition, which was one of the reasons Martin was looking to sell. Martin, after his wife's death, eventually transferred the land from being an Indian federal trust property to being a fee simple property. Through this process, I purchased a 12-month option to buy the town of Garryowen. After funding the option in full, I left Billings and headed for Malibu. On my return trip, I felt confident I had made the right decision to purchase Garryowen. What person can say that he or she owns a town in the middle of one of the most historic battlefields in America? Not only that, but I would be involved in taking care of the tomb of a United States unknown soldier. What an honor! At least that's what I thought.

Karan blew a gasket. "You're out purchasing real estate and not having me involved with the decision-making process? Are you insane? That was very rude of you to do, Chris," she said.

My justification was, I'm in the historical rarities business. This was an opportunity not only for me to be involved in preserving history, but to place it in the right hands of a future caretaker. I didn't even think of Karan or her opinion when I pulled the trigger and decided to legally tie the property up. Not only that, but I was never planning to move there. My plan was to find a philanthropist to protect and preserve this site in perpetuity for future generations. So, I had a justifiable explanation for Karan— at least I thought—only to find out later she did not feel the same way.

Nine days after I bought the option to purchase Garryowen, a pair of arsonists set a fire in the hills above my historic Malibu lodge in Topanga Canyon on the famous Mulholland Drive. The Old Topanga Fire, as it would come to be known, began on Tuesday, November 3, 1993, and burned for 10 days. The swath of destruction left 359 homes— including mine—in ruins and 18,000 acres of Malibu charred, caused $375 million in damage, and left three people dead.[21] In the following years, the Los Angeles County District Attorney's Office suspected two firefighters were the culprits for the blaze. Unfortunately, the district attorney did not have enough evidence to prosecute them.

Driven by the infamous Santa Ana winds gusting up to 60 miles per hour in the canyons, the fire raced from Mulholland Highway and Old Topanga Canyon across the Santa Monica Mountains to the Pacific Coast Highway in a matter of hours. Allegedly, the two firefighters' motivation for igniting the blaze was selfishness. Apparently, the men felt if they extinguished the fire, they would be heroes. Unfortunately for me, the fire they started engulfed everything I had; destroyed my collection of rare coins, manuscripts, watches, photography, firearms, and Indian artifacts; and nearly ended my life.

It was a normal morning for me on November 3, 1993. I drove down the Pacific Coast Highway, looking to the right and seeing *Baywatch* being filmed, which was a regular occurrence on my morning commute. I arrived at my office in Marina del Rey to catch up on some work concerning my Historical Rarities Inc. business. I had not been in my office for more than a few hours when the phone rang. Snatching the phone from its cradle and placing it to my ear, I was met by the frantic voice of my ex-wife, Kim.

"Chris!" she shrilly shouted. I could hear her voice trembling.

Surprised to hear her voice so early in the morning, I answered, "Good morning, Kim. How are you?"

Before I could say anything else, she told me a fireball was cresting Old Topanga Canyon, just a canyon over from the family home. I no sooner hung up with Kim than I quickly dialed an employee of mine named John Bottenfield. Sputtering and nervously choking out the words, I frantically informed John of the situation. He agreed to leave his home in the San Fernando Valley and meet me at my historic family home.

Nearly flying down the office steps, I hopped in my car, backtracking to where I had just come from a few minutes earlier; I went toward Las Flores Canyon and sped down the Pacific Coast Highway. While driving, I switched on the radio and spun the dial to find a local news station. It was only a moment until I heard reports of a flood of fire washing through the canyon and claiming everything in its path. Through my car's windshield, as I approached my home, I could see a dark, thick plume of ominous smoke rising in the distance, filling the Malibu sky. The embers and stench of the burning forestland seeped into the car and choked me, nearly closing my throat.

Approaching the canyon, I was met by a bevy of police officers, barricades, firefighters, and emergency personnel. They had shut down the Pacific Coast Highway with a massive roadblock staring me in the face. I frantically pleaded with them to let me access the canyon road, showing them my local ID. After I negotiated with them for what seemed like an eternity, they eventually let me pass and I raced into the very heart of the firestorm.

I flew through the canyon as quickly as I could. John, who also negotiated to get past the police barricades, came a few moments later in a large white Econoline van. Sparing few words, I instructed him to follow me into my home. We wasted no time and quickly began priming the pumps leading from the creeks to a 5,000-gallon in-ground concrete cistern. I had recently constructed the cistern in the hills above my home for this very reason. As we worked, we were assaulted by vicious superheated air rushing down the ravine, blasting us with waves of 50- to 70-mile-per-hour oxygen-eating heat. The place was becoming a supercharged furnace. Realizing the bleakness of the situation, I commanded John to get in his van and get to safety.

The collection of art and artifacts I had in my home was valued at over half a million dollars. It was full of memorabilia, such as signed Abraham Lincoln documents, Western artist Charlie Russell's family photographic archive, Plains Indian war shirts, an antique gun collection, and some extremely rare Lewis and Clark materials. I loaded the Lewis and Clark artifacts and a few other items into John's van, then screamed at him to hit the road. As I watched him leave, I could see the flames beginning to crest and, like a molten hand, they reached out to engulf the forest surrounding my home.

The fire department was not able to react quickly to the blaze because they had an extremely difficult time getting to the Malibu community. The Rambla Pacifico Road, which had been closed since 1984 because of a landslide, was really the main road into the canyon.[22] I believe, as do many of my former Malibu neighbors, that if the road had been made passable before that fire-drenched day, many homes and much of the Las Flores watershed would have been salvaged from the consuming blaze. Over the years, before this fire, the Malibu community argued on several occasions that the road should be open, but the city never followed up on the citizens' complaints.

But in that moment, the Rambla Pacifico Road was the farthest thing from my thoughts. With all the chaos raining down upon me, the fire department crew that was now in my driveway foaming the lodge began to cut the hoses they were using to control the inferno. I heard somebody scream over the fire truck's PA system, *"Code red! Code red!"* I looked at the firefighter foaming my residence. He said, "We're leaving now—immediately!" As firefighters rushed down my staircase to their truck, a firefighter screamed at me, "Are you coming? We're cutting the hoses now!" Much to my surprise, I saw a firefighter take a sharp knife and slice the hoses from the fire truck. Without much hesitation, I jumped onto the back of the truck.

Cresting the top of my driveway, I saw my neighbor Gus Uhlner out of the corner of my eye. He was trying to fight off the firestorm bearing down on his home. Gus, who was about 70, stood with a garden hose in one hand spraying his burning home while sweat poured down his aged, craggy face. He looked exhausted, and I noticed that the little shock of white hair perched on the top of his head had been tinted a muddy gray from the ash raining down.

I screamed at him, "Gus, you coming!?! They're cutting off the hoses, and the whole place is going to hell!"

"I ain't leaving!" he blurted out over the crackling wood and engulfing flames. "I can't find my cat!"

"Well, shit," I said. "If you're staying, then I am too!" I hopped off the fire truck and waved the firefighters on so I could run to help him. As they sped off, one of them yelled, "You damn fool, you're gonna get killed!"

I paid them no mind and approached Gus. He was in the process of dousing a wet rag with water. Twisting the cloth with a free hand, Gus fashioned it into a makeshift bandana and wrapped the drenched rag around his face. I followed suit, soaking another cloth he gave me and slapping it on my face to combat the intense heat and smoke bearing down upon us.

"Zoey!" he cried, yelling for his pet.

"Gus," I said, "I don't think she's going to be able to hear us over the firestorm!"

The inferno swirling around had become so powerful and destructive because of the eucalyptus trees surrounding our homes. These trees are very oily, and when set ablaze they burn like gasoline. The trees had been brought from Australia and introduced to the California landscape to be used in building the Transcontinental Railroad. Though they were quite useful in the 1860s, the burning trees in this moment were threatening to destroy my life and everyone in it.

"We need to protect the house!" I screamed at Gus. "If we don't do something to protect the home, we'll both die!"

Gus nodded in agreement and ran for the back of the home toward a large lap pool containing thousands of gallons of water. He then engineered it with a propane pump that connected to two-inch fire hoses. Once we had the water pump primed, I saw the hose become hard as concrete with water pressure. I grabbed the red nozzle, and with the hoses in tow, we began to soak the roof and frame of his home. As we did, I thought I saw steam rising from the freshly soaked shingles. Gus and I worked our way around one corner of the home, then eventually to the other.

Circumnavigating the back of the home by myself, I saw Gus running around the far side of the building heading directly toward me. He was waving his arms frantically. As I turned to face my elderly friend, his lips were moving but what he was screaming was lost on me, as the deafening sound of saplings bursting drowned out all other noise. I made a motion with my hand toward my ear to let him know I could not hear, but it did no good; he just continued to yell. As he came closer, I could see the terror etched on his aged face and the horror swimming in his sharp blue eyes.

Grabbing my arm, he nearly yanked it from the socket. "The fire's on us, Chris!" he screamed into my face. "We've gotta get inside or we'll be killed!"

Without hesitation, I dropped the hose and ran after Gus, who was already hightailing it for the front door. As we turned the corner to run along the far side of the home, the sight I saw nearly stopped me in my tracks. The flaming wall of trees all around us looked as though a giant paintbrush had been swiped along the evening sky, using the canyon as a gargantuan canvas to spread an array of oranges, reds, and yellows throughout the smoldering foliage. The fire seemed to hang above like a great tidal wave, stalling at the height of its apex, just waiting to come crashing down upon our heads and obliterate us from all existence.

As we made our way toward the front entrance of the home, I could see the roof holding firm. The shingles we had soaked were stalling the inferno for the moment. As we circled to the front of the home, I saw the grass on Gus' front lawn catching fire, curling up like the paper of a lit cigarette, and the heat was so intense that it felt as though the sun had reached out and kissed the very spot where we stood.

Filling the night sky and swirling all around us, the burning smoke singed my throat, causing me to choke and gasp for air. The tiny embers flittering from the flames made my eyes water, and I squeezed my eyelids shut in a vain attempt to eject the ash. It was no use. Blind and stumbling, I followed Gus into his home as he nearly crashed headfirst through the closed front door. Once inside, I fell to my knees and began to cough and hack, forcing the smoke and ash from my scorched throat and lungs.

Between gasps I wheezed, "Gus what are we going to do? We're going to die!"

Without a word, Gus ripped open his basement door, grabbed me by the scruff of my neck, forcing me to my feet, and nearly dragged me down the cellar stairs. The basement was black as pitch, but Gus knew every inch of the way. With one hand, he guided himself along the stair railing; with the other he held my right elbow in a death grip and pulled me down the steps until we reached the cement floor.

Once there, he loosened his grip and disappeared into the darkness. Exhausted, I hunched over and placed my hands on my knees, sucking in air, my stomach heaving. As I did, I could hear Gus working in the shadows. He shoved around boxes and crates. Suddenly there was an intense metal clang followed by the sound of a heavy door grating and scratching across the cellar floor. I walked forward a few paces toward the sound.

As I did, I heard a guttural animalistic cry so ear-piercing, I nearly jumped out of my skin. Looking down I could see Zoey, hair standing on end and hissing. In my blindness, I had pinched her tail between my shoe and the floor. Relieved, I scooped her into my arms. As I did, Gus appeared from the darkness.

"Come on, Chris" he urged. "This is the only chance we've got."

Following him, I noticed him shoving several cardboard boxes out of the way of a large steel vault door. As I entered the vault, I saw several intricately rolled architectural plans as well as banker's boxes containing the same. Gus, during his working life, had been an architect. At the pinnacle of his career, he had designed the famous ARCO twin towers in downtown Los Angeles.

"Help me shut the door, Chris!" he yelled, snapping me back to reality.

Throwing Zoey into the room, I summoned all the strength I had left in my weakened limbs to help Gus pull the massive door shut. As the clanging of metal on metal pierced the darkness, I thought this would be the end of my life. I would be sealed in this tomb amongst Gus' architectural drawings, never to be seen alive again. With my mind racing, my thoughts turned to the realization that even if we did survive, we might never be found. We could be stuck in a vault only to die from a lack of oxygen or starvation. Entombed like the still living pets of the Egyptian pharaohs.

"Get on the floor and cover your head, Chris!" Gus screamed.

His words shocked me back to reality like a splash of cold water in the face. Following his orders, I hunkered down on one side of the small vault room behind a mess of rolled drawings. We sat in our duck-and-cover positions waiting for the inevitable. It didn't take long. The fire swallowed the home in only a few minutes. The whizzing and snapping sounds of the fire caused a monstrous roar to fill the vault.

Peering through my intertwined fingers, I could see smoke slowly seeping through a tiny screened opening near the ceiling of the vault. Smoke was rapidly filling the room, sucking oxygen from our sanctuary and threatening to suffocate us both.

"Gus," I said. "The smoke is coming in."

Grasping for something to divert it, I remembered the poorly fashioned bandana that I had around my mouth and nostrils. I yanked off the rag and barreled for the screen. I bunched the shirt up and began to stuff it into the space with my fingertips. Watching me work, Gus followed suit. In a moment, we had the space plugged. We then both returned to our separate positions in the room, knees underneath us, heads covered in our hands, ready to kiss our asses goodbye.

The entire building seemed to shimmy and groan as the flames enveloped it. Total darkness engulfed the room, followed by muffled sounds of hungry out-of-control flames busily devouring everything in their path. We stayed there, stunned, silent, and terrified, for the next 20 minutes as hell passed over our heads. Interestingly, as quickly as the inferno had come, it passed. The loud rumbling and shadowy gloom of the fire so intimidating only moments before drifted into the distance. Gus and I gingerly rose to our feet.

"I think it's passed," I said.

"Me too," Gus replied.

We walked to the door of the vault. Turning the levers on it, I heard the pins drop, signaling the lock's release. We both pulled with all our might, and as the door swung open we were welcomed by a scene of complete devastation.

2

Enemy in Our Midst

We could see the sunlight peering in through the lingering smoke, a welcome beacon of hope signaling that the fire had nearly died down. Looking at Gus' home, I saw that the eaves were still on fire and his once pristine tiled lap pool was blackened with ash. We searched for an unburnt hose to quell the flames that had not yet been extinguished and save his house.

Taking in my surroundings, I felt as though I had been whisked away from Earth and transplanted to some alien landscape devoid of all life. Black scorched earth covered everything. In the distance, the canyon fire continued to rage. I saw brighter, more vibrant eruptions amid the inferno, and I knew that each one of these pulsating patches was a home bursting into flame. During the intensity of the passing blaze, I ignored every other impulse except to survive. In this moment, however, I realized I was dying of thirst, and the sweat pouring out of me lathered my skin and drenched my clothes. I fell to my knees in exhaustion.

Later, I would learn that the fire had left a trail of complete devastation. According to the Los Angeles County Historical Archive, researchers of the destruction that day said the fire had been fed by the immense unimpeded oxygen supply from the Pacific; the fire had raged down upon the mesas and arroyos.[1] By 4 p.m., the eastbound Pacific Coast Highway had carried several residents away from the

Malibu neighborhoods. Children whose parents could not make it back into town in time found shelter at Point Dume's Malibu Community Center.[2]

As dawn broke the next day, the western flank of the fire burned through Puerco Canyon Road. By 5:30 a.m., flames from Tuna Canyon raced to the Pacific Coast Highway and eastward toward Topanga Canyon. Firefighters saved businesses, including the Malibu Feed Bin, where 400 bales of hay and two drums of kerosene posed a combustible threat.[3]

According to *The Malibu Times*, by midmorning the eastern and western flanks still raged out of control; Civic Center east to Big Rock was almost entirely deserted. On Wednesday night, backfires were set along the east side of Malibu Canyon Road. But within an hour, flames raced across the road, burning two buildings at Hughes Research Labs and threatening faculty housing on the northern portion of Pepperdine University's campus.[4]

With 90 percent of Las Flores' homes gone, there was not a house left on Rambla Orienta in the La Costa neighborhood—Malibu's oldest.[5] As the fire scorched through Malibu, Governor Pete Wilson affirmed that it had attracted the largest mobilization of emergency equipment and personnel in the state's history, including the L.A. riots, up to that point. More than 7,000 firefighters, 1,000 fire companies and 450 agencies were called in for assistance.[6]

On Rambla Pacifico, where 80 percent of the homes were lost, a firestorm overwhelmed several firefighters. They narrowly escaped with their lives. Likewise, on Rambla Vista, only 20 percent of the structures were saved.[7] The Old Topanga Fire would not be fully contained until November 11, eight days after it began.[8]

Exhausted from my near-death experience, I told Gus I was going to try to see if my home had survived the fire. Miraculously, the preventative measures we had taken to fight the fire at Gus' home had actually worked. The water we had sprayed staved off the engulfing fire and allowed his house to survive. From there, we decided to part ways so we could both assess the damage.

After I got my bearings back, Gus wished me well while he and Zoey turned in for the night. After traveling a short distance toward my home, I realized there was not much I could do in the dark, as the day was spent. Needing a place to stay, I looked around and noticed my neighbors' home. As I approached, I was shocked by how untouched their home was. The searing flames that had laid many homes to waste had simply passed over theirs. The fire seemed so indiscriminate.

Knocking on the door, I received no answer. I walked around the home to see if anyone was there. As I peered through the windows, it appeared my neighbors had evacuated sometime earlier in the day. As I circled around the building, I found the back door unlocked and let myself in. The house had fallen dark when the sun dropped behind the canyon walls. I stumbled to the kitchen, rummaged for a glass, flicked on the tap at the sink, and drank until my belly was full.

After my eyes adjusted to the darkness of the residence, I made my way to the couch in the room adjacent to the kitchen. Utterly exhausted, I crashed on the couch and fell into a deep sleep. I did not rouse until the midmorning sun shone brightly on my face. Rising to my feet, I made my way to the unlocked door and stepped out to greet the morning.

The devastation from the night before was even more bewildering in the daylight. Los Flores Canyon was a barren wasteland of charred and blackened trees and gutted homes. The fire had been so complete in its destruction that if I had not known the forest was once lush, green, and vibrant with wildlife, I would have thought I was looking at the aftermath of a great nuclear disaster. Images of napalm being dropped to clear the thick jungles of Vietnam flickered in my mind.

Closing the door behind me, I stepped out onto the road in the direction of my home. Walking the short distance to the lodge, I felt my heart sink as it came into view. With the amount of destruction around me, I should not have been surprised to find my home burnt to the ground. Nonetheless, I was devastated by what I saw.

There was virtually nothing left. The eucalyptus around the home burned white hot, like an ignited can of gasoline. The fire had gutted the brick structure and left a violent black and ashen heap where the lodge had once stood. A home that had survived six previous Malibu fires was now reduced to utter rubble. It was all a total loss.

Of all things, however, I found that my BMW 735iL was still intact, seeming to have suffered only peripheral damage to the body. The car no longer resembled the automobile I had purchased, but I figured I would see if it was still usable. The fire had burned so hot that it had boiled the car's paint, peeling and curling it back in thin strips that rolled up toward the windshield. The headlamps were melted and most of the windows had combusted, leaving shattered and crystallized shards of glass all over the seats and floor.

I approached with caution, pulling on the corrupted driver's-side door handle, expecting to find it welded shut. Surprisingly, the door swung open with little effort. After sweeping out the glass bits with my hand, I sat on the lightly toasted seat. The interior of the car stank of wood ash and melted vinyl. I pulled the car key from the pocket of my slacks. I stabbed it into the ignition; the starter cranked for a while, then finally caught. Although I had the means to exit the canyon, I could not force myself to leave.

I think it was pure shock that kept me frozen in place. After seemingly having so much going in my direction, to have life yanked from underneath me in one swoop was completely devastating. I let reality wash over me for a few moments, then decided I should find a phone. When I eventually called my wife, Karan, she was glad to hear from me. She had been at her medical office most of the day before and did not know I had survived the inferno. As we talked, she said my brother, a Ventura County sheriff's deputy, had contacted L.A. County Search and Rescue, and people had scoured the countryside searching for me.

After letting Karan know I was alive, I returned to the rubble of my home. I hung around for a few hours picking through the ruins. When a couple of sheriff's deputies eventually showed up, I related my story to them. They stared at me in stunned disbelief. The deputies relayed the information to my brother to put his mind at ease, and checked my vitals. I informed them my BMW was operational and I had the ability to get out of the canyon.

I let them know I wanted to stay. Without the authority to make me go, the deputies decided to go. I thanked them and watched them drive away in their rescue vehicle, no doubt headed to another charred and hollowed-out home to search for survivors. When they were out of sight, I collapsed to my knees in the wreckage of my home, allowing tears to stream down my face.

Realizing there was nothing more I could save, I slid into my melted BMW and peeled out of the canyon. As I pulled onto the Pacific Coast Highway, I worried about the tires giving out but they, much like the BMW's engine, seemed to have withstood the firestorm with ease. Gliding down the highway, I was left to my thoughts. I realized in that moment that my life had inexplicably changed forever. My historic family home was gone, I had nowhere to stay, and nearly 50 percent of the inventory of my historical rarities business was ash. The only thing I had left to my name was an option to purchase a southern Montana town on a scrap of land in the middle of the Crow Indian Reservation. At the time, the whole situation seemed dire to me.

Later that day I would finally find Karan, and we would both be overcome by emotion and the joy of finding one another still breathing. As I explained the devastation to her, I could tell by the look in her eyes that our relationship would never be the same.

In the days following the fire, Malibu was declared a federal disaster area by President Bill Clinton. During this time, I petitioned the Red Cross and the Federal Emergency Management Agency (FEMA). Both organizations eventually provided minimal funds to help me get back on my feet. Using the money from them, I rented a temporary, fully furnished apartment for Karan and myself in Santa Monica. While living there, I started applying for a very complicated Small Business Administration (SBA) disaster loan request. The application was very lengthy and confusing. But I thought that it might be the only way I could possibly rebuild my Malibu home.

Before the fire struck, I had been planning to participate in the Western American Indian artifacts show. This large exhibition alternates between San Francisco and Los Angeles every year. I had already rented a $2,000 booth to display my artifacts. Feeling utterly depleted by my circumstances, I decided I would most likely have to excuse myself from the event.

Because I had lost over half of my collection in the fire, I felt like I had nothing to offer at the show. But many of my friends and associates in the business encouraged me to saddle up and do the show with what I had. So, just 10 days after the fire, I participated in the Santa Monica show. One of the marquee items I displayed there was an original Edward Bohlin sterling silver parade saddle.

Bohlin was born in Sweden in 1895, and ran away from home at age 15. Inspired by Buffalo Bill Cody's Wild West show, Edward worked cattle drives around Montana before opening his first saddle shop in Cody, Wyoming, where he performed rope tricks in front of his shop to draw business.[9]

Bohlin met famous Western actor Tom Mix while performing at the Pantages Theatre in Hollywood, and Mix convinced him to stay and produce silver and leather items in the Los Angeles area. Bohlin crafted more than 12,000 saddles, including many grand silver outfits for the Tournament of Roses Parade. He also dressed many silver-screen heroes and Presidents Reagan and Johnson with his grandly styled buckles, spurs, and gun belts.[10]

In a stroke of luck that broke my way, the Bohlin I had on display at the show eventually drew the attention of the king of Golden Age–era cowboys, Gene Autry. At the time, I had been selling many items to the Autry Museum of the American West in Los Angeles, including many one-of-a-kind Indian artifacts. After Autry and I became acquainted, I told him about my loss during the Malibu fire just 10 days prior. Much like the many men he portrayed in his classic cowboy movies, Autry showed his true kindness. He clapped me on the back, told me how sorry he was for my loss, then proceeded to give me a bejeweled sterling silver buckle right off his own belt. It was his personalized Bohlin belt buckle with his name engraved on it.

After he placed it in my hand, I looked at the buckle, completely speechless. Without a word, he turned and walked off. It was as if I were watching my childhood hero stroll off into the sunset as he had so many times on the silver screen. In that moment, the buckle meant more to me than anything I had bought or bartered for in all my years as a collector.

Sadly, however, even after the success of the Indian artifacts show, things in my life did not get any easier. I barely kept the Historical Rarities Inc. business afloat with the few assets I had remaining from the fire, the majority of which were rare books, photographs, and historic manuscripts. Adding to the stress of my floundering business, my relationship with Karan started to buckle under the pressure of life after the fire.

My SBA disaster loan application to rebuild the lodge was going to be a long, tedious endeavor with a massive amount of bureaucracy and red tape, but I was focused. I really didn't have any other choice. I had just lost everything in my life. In shock and extremely depressed, I moved forward by speaking with the SBA disaster loan department daily. I rapidly found out that I probably wasn't going to be able to rebuild the lodge on the Malibu property. Our water supply was being pumped out of Las Flores Creek. Our septic system was antiquated. Both the water and the septic system had been grandfathered in, meaning I didn't have to have them up to current building codes, since they had been installed before the codes even existed.

But since the structure was gone, I would be required to start from scratch. The city of Malibu required that a water main be brought up Las Flores Canyon two and a half miles for a fire hydrant and water for our property at the cost of $3 million. So, rebuilding on the property was out of the question.

Since I had signed an option to purchase Garryowen before the fire, SBA disaster rules allowed me to use the loan money outside of the disaster area. In fact, I was the only recipient of the Malibu SBA disaster funding ever to be allowed to rebuild outside of the federal disaster area. My SBA loan came from the Department of the Treasury for the amount of $220,000, with a 30-year payback period. I eventually borrowed money from First Interstate Bank in Billings to help complete the project.

After I secured the SBA funding, the initial construction began on the historic town of Garryowen and the Custer Battlefield Museum. Throughout the year I flew back and forth to Montana to confer with the architects and the construction contractors. During this period, I also made the decision to move permanently to Garryowen. This decision altered everything in my life.

Karan was justifiably upset about my purchasing Garryowen. I had not consulted her fully before acting on what I believed to be an appropriate activity associated with my business. She simply thought I had pigheadedly forged ahead without her. In my defense, the option to purchase Garryowen happened so quickly, there was very little time to think, let alone confer with her, about it.

On the day I placed the option, I had woken at 8 a.m., read the Custer newsletter in Putt's home at 10 a.m., and met with the seller, Larry Martin, at an attorney's office at 2 p.m. Afterward, I strapped myself in a plane and flew back to Malibu. All of this happened on the same day. I tied up the purchase of the town in less than three hours. Then fate dealt me a blow: nine days later, nearly everything we owned was burned to the ground.

I know it came as a shock to Karan when I made up my mind to focus my life on building the Custer Battlefield Museum and making the transition to Garryowen. I can't blame her for being upset. She had just started working in a successful dermatology business in Westwood, catering to the Hollywood and political elite. I know she felt like she was not only doing well in the L.A. scene but thriving.

Over the next year, Karan allowed me to deal with the architect designing the museum. I was flying back and forth between California and Montana finalizing plans to make our new home in Garryowen. To compound our problems, California began to rumble. While we were living in the FEMA-funded apartment, we also lived through the Northridge earthquake in the winter of 1994.

The earthquake lasted for approximately 10 to 20 seconds. In those few moments, my life and well-being were shaken once more. The initial jolt of the quake produced the highest ground acceleration ever instrumentally recorded in an urban area in the United States. It was reported that when the initial quake took place, the ground tremors were felt as far away as Las Vegas. It apparently was the fastest peak ground velocity ever recorded.[11]

Including the aftershocks, the death toll was 57 people. More than 5,000 were injured. The property damage was estimated to be between $13 billion and $40 billion, making it one of the costliest natural disasters in U.S. history.[12] Although the quake was only a few seconds in duration, it felt like hours. Everything we owned was torn asunder and tossed around the apartment. Karan and I clung to each other during the ordeal. I can still recall her clinging so tightly to me that my arms and shoulders were heavily purpled from bruising.

The quake was so great, it permanently damaged the building we were residing in and forced us to move into a new Red Cross/FEMA building. It was around this time that my mental state began to spin out of control. I became very depressed and felt as though the whole world was caving in on me. In what seemed like a matter of days, I went from a man who had everything to a man who literally had just the clothes on his back.

Accompanying these tragedies, I discovered that my home insurance provider was going to pay for nothing after the fire. My family home was insured with Lloyd's of London. I believed it was the highest-quality insurance I could carry on my uncle's home. Three months before the fire destroyed everything, I was in a disagreement with Lloyd's. It had decided to raise my premiums by a third because my home was in a hazardous "fire zone."

I felt my rates should have remained the same because my home had withstood so much for such a long time, including multiple fires. I also installed a $10,000 sprinkler system on the roof. So, during negotiations, I allowed my policy to lapse. Disaster then hit only a few months later when the fire swept through my home and life.

These circumstances exhausted me mentally, as I believe they would anyone. My marriage of four years with Karan suffered greatly for it. We eventually divorced. I do not blame her for the marriage's failure. We suffered through some very trying times, and we were not able to come through them unscathed. As at the conclusion of most relationships, circumstances are not always clear-cut. In the end, we both had our issues that the marriage could not survive.

Leaving California without Karan and flying towards Billings in the spring of 1994, I thought of my failed marriage. I thought when the plane touched down I would not only be in a new state but I would also be starting a new life. The thought did not frighten me. In fact, I saw it as a chance to start anew. When I did finally reach Montana, I had very little time to get acclimated to my new surroundings when work accelerated on rebuilding Garryowen and the new Custer Battlefield Museum.

Larry Martin informed me that the site had cleared all the proper soil sample tests to determine whether the gas tanks under the earth of the gas station were contaminating the ground. I was given what I believed to be a quality environmental impact statement and a clear go-ahead by the state of Montana to begin building. Thinking there were no problems, I began construction in earnest in the fall of 1995.

But things would not turn out to be so simple. As the construction crew dug through the grainy earth to remove the remnants of the run-down gas station, I encountered a gargantuan problem that was as daunting as the fire I had survived in Malibu. A buried, rust-riddled gas tank was contaminating the earth with toxins. The ground was so corrupt that it eventually led to the largest environmental cleanup in Montana history.

When word of the soil contamination spread around the area, the United States Postal Service threatened to cancel its letter of intent, basically leaving me without a renter on the land. This threw my SBA loan disbursements into question, because I had just lost a lifetime renter in the federal government. The whole mess happened only 16 days after I purchased Garryowen.

The state of Montana, the Environmental Protection Agency, and representatives from the federal government were threatening to shut my operation down completely and leave me with absolutely nothing. When I was given the news of the decomposing gas tank, I knew Larry Martin had misrepresented the situation and that the state-certified and licensed plumber who took the soil samples had also conspired against me in some way.

I quickly realized that to save my investment, I had to begin sleuthing to find out what had happened with the environmental impact statement. The first place I started was with Martin and the certified plumber. As I began following the paper trail, I found that the plumber was a friend of Martin's and the paperwork he filed had some glaring issues. When he retrieved the soil samples, he did not draw his specimens from the contaminated area of the gas station site but from the back of the property, where the soil was purest.

When I discovered the blatant fraud, I sued the state of Montana for not catching the error. In a review of the environmental report the plumber submitted to the state board, I found he had left blank the sections discussing where his samples were taken. This was a gross and negligent oversight by the state reviewer who reviewed the application process. Apparently after evaluating the plumber's report, the reviewer simply authored a closure letter and the property was transferred into my name.

The fact that a majority of the report had been left blank, allowing the plumber to not admit to committing fraud and further allowing him to plead ignorance by saying, "I forgot to fill out that section," was egregious and unforgivable. So, after a long battle in the courts with the state of Montana, a fight lasting from 1995 to 1998, I was eventually awarded $250,000, which went mostly toward paying attorney fees and court costs.

Along with the monetary amount, I was awarded a letter of admittance wherein the state of Montana owned up to its negligence in the matter, and the state was forced to remove every bit of contaminated granular soil from Garryowen, replacing it with clean fill. I also received a letter from the state and federal government declaring my site clean. That letter is in perpetuity so the property can be transferred to a future owner. After I won that court battle, the U.S. Postal Service decided to come back on board.

After construction of the Custer Battlefield Museum was finished, an adjoining trading post was built as well as my home and guesthouse. The museum and surrounding buildings had a nice rustic look, with the charm of an Old West–style log structure. Putt Thompson wanted to rent the trading post and to be the curator of the Custer Battlefield Museum while I continued to work at Historical Rarities Inc. I also opened a Subway sandwich shop franchise and modernized the gas station with a convenience store attached. With a U.S. post office in tow, the entire operation was underway. I felt better about my situation and I felt as though my life was heading in the right direction.

During the same year, I returned to California to bring legal action against Los Angeles County. Three Malibu residents and myself, who had lost our homes in the disastrous wildfire, sued the county and the city of Malibu. The reason for the suit was that we felt there was inadequate road access to the homes in the canyon, which directly led to the destruction of our properties.[13]

The other plaintiffs and I noted that the closure of Rambla Pacifico Road, blocked since 1984 because of a landslide, prevented firefighters from getting to homes and businesses in time to save them. Every one of us in the lower Las Flores Canyon lost our homes. In the lawsuit, we requested that the courts declare the complaint a class action, contending that 280 other individuals and businesses also suffered emotional and financial damages.[14] We contended that after the head of the fire passed, many homes and much of the Las Flores watershed caught fire and burned unnecessarily. We also felt the county knew about the condition of Rambla Pacifico for many years but failed to act, at the expense of the Malibu homeowners.[15]

A superior court judge ruled that the city was not responsible for Rambla Pacifico Road, because it was outside Malibu's city limits.[16] Even with the dismissal of the court case, I felt as though life was heading in the right direction. As construction commenced on the Custer Battlefield Museum and Garryowen, I tried to familiarize myself with the people of Montana, the Crow Indian culture, and the reservation that I was going to find myself living in.

I was eager to move on with life in Montana and become part of the greater community. When I started to familiarize myself with my new surroundings, I was surprised at what I found. Garryowen is the only town inside the perimeter of the Custer battlefield. The town and battlefield sit in the middle of the Crow reservation. This is a federal Indian reservation created by the War Powers Act.

Here's where it gets confusing. All land inside the exterior boundaries of an Indian reservation has a federal designation of "Indian Country." By its legal definition, it includes "all land within the limits of any Indian reservation, and all dependent Indian communities within the borders of the United States."[17] This legal classification includes all American Indian tribal and individual private fee patent land holdings as part of a reservation, an allotment, or a public domain allotment. All federal trust lands held for Native American tribes are also considered Indian Country.[18]

Usually, to be recognized as Indian Country, the land either must be within an Indian reservation or must be federal trust land (land technically owned by the federal government but held in trust for a tribe or tribal member). Tribal courts in these areas are distinctly different from state and federal courts, since Native Americans exist in an undefined segment of United States citizenship.

Defined as U.S. citizens since 1924, indigenous people do not have to apply for citizenship, nor do they have to give up their tribal citizenship to become a U.S. citizen. Most tribes have communal property, meaning that to have a right to the land, the Indians must be recognized members of the tribe. Thus, dual citizenship is allowed. The Dawes Act of 1887, one of several treaties, allocated land to individual Native

Americans. It stated that because they were landowners and would eventually pay taxes on the land and become "proficient members of society," they would be granted citizenship.

Indian tribal governments are considered the sovereign authority over Indians in Indian Country. This authority extends beyond the specific boundaries of a tribe to encompass any enrolled or able-to-be enrolled Indian anywhere in Indian Country. The use of tribal prosecutors as quasi-federal prosecutors provides tribally administered criminal sanctions for any crimes charged in Indian Country even if the defendant is not an Indian.

Law enforcement is thus a patchwork of intermingled laws, with intertwined jurisdictions and multiple law enforcement agencies, all trying to protect and serve within a complex, occasionally contradictory legal system that is striving generally to be all things to all people and working effectively for none. This includes any hapless non-Indian attempting to lawfully reside and do business within the confines of Indian Country.

Federal civil jurisdiction is very limited in Indian Country. Federal courts have jurisdiction over claims that arise under federal law and in cases of diversity of citizenship. Federal courts have limited jurisdiction in civil cases involving divorce, adoption, child custody, or probate.

The Major Crimes Act passed by Congress in 1885 applies in Indian Country as well. Per that act, tribal criminal jurisdiction over Indians in Indian Country is complete and exclusive unless there is a federal statute deeming it otherwise or limiting it in some way. Exclusive original jurisdiction is given to the tribal courts over nonmajor crimes committed by Indians against Indians in Indian Country, as well as victimless Indian crimes.

Jurisdiction is also granted, though not exclusively, to tribal courts over nonmajor crimes by Indians against non-Indians. In these cases, federal courts also have jurisdiction through the General Crimes Act, so jurisdiction is shared. Tribal courts have exclusive jurisdiction in civil cases against any Indian in Indian Country. This includes cases brought against an Indian by a non-Indian in Indian Country, and all cases between tribal members that arise in Indian Country.

In general, states exercise civil jurisdiction in cases involving non-Indians, and sometimes nontribal members, even when these cases arise in Indian Country. In divorce cases, states have jurisdiction if both parties are non-Indian and living in Indian Country. In matters involving adoption and child custody proceedings between parents, the division of jurisdiction is very similar. The states have jurisdiction only over cases involving the adoption and custody of Indian children not domiciled in Indian Country. In probate cases, states have jurisdiction regarding cases of nontrust estates of Indians who died while they were domiciled outside of Indian Country, and in cases dealing with any land outside of Indian Country.

Upon my arrival at Garryowen, I was not aware of any of this information, let alone the definition or meaning of "Indian Country." This, however, would soon be something I would have to grapple with. But in the meantime, I really did not think the reservation would be much different from anywhere else I had lived up to that point. So, I became very involved in local activities, and in promoting the area to increase and improve tourism.

In 2004, Montana Governor Judy Martz named me the Tourism Person of the Year. I received the award for 10 years of efforts to restore the historic town of Garryowen, where the Battle of the Little Bighorn began. I was also elected to the board of directors of Custer Country, a state-chartered nonprofit tourism organization that promotes historical sites and other attractions to states throughout America and countries across the globe.

Living right in the middle of the Crow reservation, I met many of the locals. One of the many Crow people I met and quickly befriended was Joe Medicine Crow. We found we shared a love of history.

Joseph Medicine Crow-High Bird was born in 1913 and is the step-grandson of White Man Runs Him, who had been a scout for General George Armstrong Custer at the Battle of the Little Bighorn. An enrolled member of the Crow Nation, Joe was a tribal historian and revered elder. He was also a Crow war chief, a U.S. Army veteran, and an author, and served on the board of directors at the Custer Battlefield Museum. Joe was the first member of the Crow tribe to earn a master's degree, which he received from the University of Southern California in 1939. His writings on Native American history and reservation culture are considered seminal works and are all still in print today.

Joe joined the United States Army in 1943, became a scout in the 103rd Infantry Division, and fought in World War II. He said that whenever he went into battle, he wore his war paint beneath his uniform and a sacred eagle feather beneath his helmet. While in battle, Joe completed all four tasks required to become a Crow war chief.

He counted coup (the act of touching an enemy without killing him), captured an enemy's weapon, led a successful war party, and stole his enemy's horse. Joe accomplished the first two deeds by disarming and engaging in hand-to-hand combat with a young German soldier who was hiding in a corner of a room. For the third task, Joe successfully led seven soldiers to retrieve dynamite from a lost Allied position. The same war party blasted the Germans with dynamite without losing a single man of their own in the process. The fourth and final task was completed in 1945 after Joe learned that Nazi soldiers had seized a thoroughbred farm. Joe singlehandedly snuck past the sleeping guards and found the best horse. He used a rope as a bridle and rode the horse bareback to herd 50 horses out of the corral. After completing the tasks, he became the last war chief of the Crow tribe. Joe was also the last living Plains Indian war chief until his death at the age of 102 in 2016.

Following his war exploits, Joe returned to Crow Agency, Montana, in 1948. There, he was appointed tribal historian and anthropologist. In 1999, Joe addressed the United Nations with an invocation as the guest of Ted Turner when Turner gifted $1 billion to the UN. He was so honored that Turner had asked him to address the United Nations that he gave his eagle feather war bonnet to Turner to show his gratitude. He recalled that the proceedings at the United Nations became a bit monotonous, so he began to write a poetic speech about peace. He continued by delivering the speech, which received a standing ovation.

Joe was a frequent guest speaker at Little Big Horn College, the Little Bighorn Battlefield National Monument, and the Custer Battlefield Museum. He appeared in several documentaries about the battle, and became so revered not only by his own people but to the world at large that he was interviewed for and appeared in the 2007 Ken Burns PBS series *The War*, a documentary about World War II.

Joe was recognized time and time again for his prominence in the academic and social communities. He was awarded three honorary doctorates—one from Rocky Mountain College in 1999, one from his alma mater the University of Southern California in 2003, and one from Bacone College in 2010. It was my family that nominated Joe for his honorary doctorate from USC, and I had the honor of attending that ceremony as well as joining Joe for brunch with the chancellor.

In 2007 his memoir, *Counting Coup: Becoming a Crow Chief on the Reservation and Beyond*, was chosen as a notable trade book for young people by the National Council for the Social Studies. At Garryowen in 2008, Joe was awarded the French Legion of Honor Chevalier medal and the Bronze Star Medal for his meritorious service in the U.S. Army during World War II. For his time in the military, he was also awarded the Army's Good Conduct Medal, the European-American-Middle Eastern Campaign Medal, and the World War II Victory Medal.

Joe was eventually nominated for the Presidential Medal of Freedom (the United States' highest civilian honor) in 2009. He and I were then invited to be guests of President Barack Obama, and we flew to Washington, D.C., where he received the medal on August 12, 2009, at the White House. When Joe met President Obama, he sang a Crow victory song for him while playing a ceremonial war drum. Because Joe had given his only war bonnet to Ted Turner, he wore an eagle feather war bonnet that I provided for him out of the Custer Battlefield Museum's collection.

In addition to befriending Joe Medicine Crow and helping tourism in the state of Montana and more specifically on the Crow reservation, I became active in Montana law enforcement, volunteering as a reserve sheriff's deputy. Eventually, I ran for Big Horn County sheriff in 2001. Unfortunately for me, not everything I experienced in my early years living in Indian Country was happy. I became involved in a court battle challenging a tax imposed on non-Indians by the Crow tribe. This case was eventually decided in my favor by the U.S. Supreme Court, influencing present and future case law.

I also met other people outside of the surrounding Indian tribes. One was a woman I began a relationship with. Her name was Cathy Lingard. She was the ex-wife of Lee Lingard, a Bureau of Land Management special agent and former Navy Seal. My relationship with Cathy would eventually help lead to one of the more heinous acts of injustice perpetrated by a federal agency against U.S. citizens in recent memory. Through Lee Lingard, I would find that the Bureau of Land Management had created a web of deceit and was entrenched in the deep state that was set to ensnare not only me and my business but one of the largest guitar makers in the world.

3

I Knew There Was a Woman Involved in This Somewhere

On a cool summer evening in 1996, a tall brunette in her early 30s slid her hand into mine and, with a flirtatious smile, whispered, "I'm Cathy. It's really nice to meet you." She was good-looking although not a classic beauty. Her quiet, almost shy nature drew me to her immediately, however. I caught the light hint of her jasmine perfume tickling my nostrils and found the smell intoxicating and a nice reprieve from the smoky mesquite wood smoldering in the nearby fire pit.

A week earlier, my friend Dennis Burkhartsmeier had asked me if I would like to get together with him and some friends on the Yellowstone River for a day of jet-skiing. I liked Dennis, and I realized I needed a break from all the work going on at Garryowen. He sweetened the pot by telling me there were going to be several women at the party as well. Being that I was recently divorced and feeling rather lonely, it did not take much arm-twisting to get me to agree to show up.

Following a fun afternoon on the river, we gathered at Dennis' home for a barbecue. It felt good to be in a normal situation again and to be amongst folks who wanted nothing more than to enjoy friends, food, and each other's company. After showing my face to Dennis so he knew I was there, I walked over to a cooler full of cold beverages and plunged my hand into the freezing ice water to snatch a beer swimming in it. Fishing out a Coors Light, I snapped back the pull tab and then drew a long, cool swallow.

While drinking the brew, I noticed Dennis striding towards me with Cathy in tow. After I nervously shook hands with her, Dennis left us alone and returned to his post at the grill flipping hot dogs and hamburgers. Cathy and I talked for a bit by the coolers but soon realized the place was like Grand Central Station with people every few seconds dipping their hands in the cooler to extract soda pops and beer. So, we decided to find a quieter place to talk. I snagged two more beers, and we walked away from the party's watering hole.

Luckily, Dennis had a large piece of property, and we found a secluded place to get to know one another. Sidestepping party-goers playing cornhole and horseshoes, Cathy and I made our way to an outcropping of trees near the edge of Dennis' property. After some boring get-to-know-you chitchat, Cathy and I found we were both recently divorced and were both feeling a little lonely. She soon opened up about her life, and I did likewise. We seemed to have a lot in common, and after the party we decided to see each other again. During this time, we eventually touched on the subject of her ex-husband, Lee Lingard, who turned out to be one of the most frightening men I've ever encountered.

When we had been dating no longer than four weeks, Cathy nervously told me over the phone that she wanted to meet. I agreed and we met at a small diner in Billings. As I walked into the greasy spoon, I saw Cathy sitting in a booth by herself, staring into a cup of murky coffee. Before I even sat down, I could tell she had been crying. Her mascara was dried in black tracks across her pretty face, and her lipstick was askew.

"I told Lee about us dating to taunt him," she abruptly blurted out before I settled into my seat.

A bit surprised, I said, "Oh? What did he say to that?"

"I told him I brought my daughter to Garryowen to visit you, and I told him that you were in the antiques business," she blubbered.

As I look back on it, the whole situation seemed overblown to me in the moment. Calmly, I began to flip through the pages of the diner's breakfast menu and asked her what was so bad about her ex-husband.

"He's a vindictive man, Chris," she said.

I was not quite sure what to make of her assertion, but I knew something was wrong as I peered over the top of the menu and into her watery eyes.

"He's paranoid and abusive," she continued. "He told me on the telephone that if we had continued in our marriage, he would have beat the crap out of me.[1] He just can't seem to leave me alone even though we're divorced."

I honestly felt she was afraid of him, but I also felt she might be embellishing her circumstances a little. Putting the menu down on the Formica tabletop between us, I reached out for her hand.

"Slow down, Cathy. What are you telling me?" I said.

"Lee! I told Lee about us to piss him off, and I think he's been watching you. He's got it in his head that you have something to do with our daughter."

Flabbergasted, I wasn't sure what to make of what she was telling me. I could see the fear in her eyes and knew she was telling me the truth.

"What do you mean, 'watching me?'" I said.

"He is watching you at night to spy on my overnight stays with you," she muttered. "He wants to catch you doing something illegal."

I could feel my heart beginning to race and my blood run high. It seemed like life would never cut me a break. It was just one quagmire after another.

"How can he catch me in anything illegal? I haven't done anything wrong!"

As my voice began to rise, I could see the patrons in the diner looking up from their blue-plate specials and turning their attention to our conversation.

Finding my self-control, I said under my breath, "What do you mean? Is he trying to entrap me or something? How does he have that kind of authority?"

"He works for the Bureau of Land Management as a federal law enforcement agent," she said. "He can pretty much do whatever he wants. He's a former Navy Seal, and he uses his law enforcement position to manipulate me and other family members. His physical and mental training from the Seals and the FBI Academy give him superior skills to manipulate and coerce anyone into a physically threatening situation."

"What have you got me mixed up in?" I said.

"He arrests people who sell stolen Indian artifacts. That's why I called you down here. I wanted to let you know what was going on."

With that said, she withdrew sweaty, crumpled Polaroid photographs from her pocket and flung them on the table between us. The images I saw were of a muscular, prematurely white-haired man with a long ponytail snaking down his back.

"This is him," Cathy said. "If you see someone who looks like this skulking around Garryowen, it's Lee."

I took the pictures and looked them over. I still couldn't believe what I was hearing. I dated this woman for a couple of weeks and then I was being tracked by some government spook with a badge who thought he could do whatever he wanted, including keeping surveillance on me? It seemed like I was caught in a conspiracy right out of a movie.

Cathy was scared, and the man I saw in those photos gave me cause to believe that he was capable of what Cathy was accusing him of. At that moment, I felt like I should just get up and leave. Not just Cathy or the diner, but the whole damn state of Montana. I didn't want or need a repeat of the social trauma I had just been through with Karan. Logic told me to put the whole ugly mess behind me and cut away clean, get another fresh start.

Unfortunately, I didn't get up and leave. I stayed right where I was, in that red plastic booth across from a woman whose ex-husband was supposedly obsessed with her, an overzealous BLM agent misusing his BLM position, who couldn't seem to distinguish reality from fantasy. He couldn't come to grips with the fact that his marriage was over. I was being told that he felt the need to stalk anyone who came close to his former wife. She explained to me that it was as if he owned her.

Cathy went on to tell me that Lee Lingard was trying to enhance his career in the BLM while attempting to capture suspected thieves and swindlers in the rare-antiquities market—specifically, those people who were dealing in rare Indian artifacts and archaeological resources recovered from government lands. Since my artifacts were acquired from private property, not government lands, I felt that I was being unfairly targeted because of my relationship with Cathy.

At that point, I decided I had heard enough. I thanked Cathy for telling me, and told her I had to go home and let everything marinate in my mind. As I left Billings, I wasn't sure if I would see Cathy again. I felt like I had been used as a pawn in a lover's spat. And now I was in the crosshairs of a lunatic because of it. That night I decided I would stop seeing Cathy, thinking that my doing so would be the end of the issue.

Not more than a few days after my conversation with Cathy, however, a man named Jason Pitsch entered the trading post looking to sell Custer-related artifacts. This happened from time to time, given my location and business. Pitsch was a young man sporting a pudding-bowl haircut and equipped with what seemed to be not much more than an eighth-grade education.

Pitsch's father and mother, Irvin and Charlene, owned and operated a private ranch on the Little Bighorn Battlefield. That portion of land is known as the Reno Valley area. This is where Major Marcus Reno of the 7th Cavalry was to attack in the valley and act as a diversion, or the "anvil," so to speak, while Custer maneuvered to strike the flank, or be the "hammer" of the combined attacks. Reno commanded a third battalion of three companies. These three battalions made up the main force of the advance.[2] Unfortunately for Custer and Reno, they were unable to complete their maneuver. With the destruction of the 7th Cavalry, the Reno Valley became the place where Reno's troops began their retreat. This land surrounds Garryowen.

Irvin Pitsch, along with his brother Harvey, who also had an ownership stake in the Reno Valley land, had sold most of their land to the Custer Battlefield Preservation Committee (CBPC). This organization's mission is to raise money from private donors within battlefield boundaries and to increase the size of the national monument. CBPC was founded in 1982 after receiving a blessing from the secretary of the interior. The CBPC's mission was to acquire lands surrounding the 760-acre Custer Battlefield National Monument and Reno Hospital area.[3] Because of their sale, the Pitsch family only owns a few hundred acres of the original parcel, land that is not connected to the battlefield.

Jason Pitsch began excavating a large portion of his family's land years before I came to Montana. During his excavating, he unearthed several battlefield-related artifacts. He used these finds to build a collection for a museum he called The Reno Battlefield Museum. This establishment was to be supported by the highly respected Glen Swanson Collection. Glen Swanson is a well-known sculptor and historian who had spent the previous 45 years collecting 7th Cavalry artifacts. He is also seen as an expert on the Reno skirmish line and the Battle of the Little Bighorn. The Swanson collection lent much credibility to Pitsch's proposed museum.[4]

This fact, accompanied by a BLM letter signed by BLM agent Lee Lingard—who, Cathy told me, was conducting nighttime surveillance on me—allowed Pitsch to secure a federally granted SBA loan to finance the construction of his museum. The bank required this letter to use the Pitsch artifact collection as collateral for the SBA loan. Lingard addressed the letter to the Ranchester State Bank after the institution inquired about the legality of Pitsch's collection. The letter from Lingard reads:

> This letter is in regards to our telephone conversation today. Recently I was contacted by Jason Pitsch to view and determine if his archeological [sic] artifacts were legally obtained. I feel very confident that Mr. Pitsch's artifacts are legal. The Pitsch Family owns approximately 30,000 [incorrect; it is 3,000] deeded acres

of land that surrounds the Little Big Horn Battlefield. Many of the portions of those battle sites are on the Pitsch's [sic] private land.

It is illegal to remove archeological [sic] artifacts from Federal and Indian land without a permit and I have enclosed a copy of the 1979 Archeological [sic] Resources Protection Act (ARPA) that explains the law in detail. Thank you for your time and attention regarding this matter.

Lingard signed the letter, which was printed on United States Department of the Interior letterhead. This not only allowed Pitsch to secure an SBA loan, but it also acted as a blanket certificate of authentication every time Pitsch sold any of his artifacts. Pitsch secured his loan in 1996 and began construction on the Reno museum in the same year.[5]

Not soon after the completion of construction in 1996, Pitsch's hopes for a great museum and cultural center began to crumble. Upon receiving the loan amount from the SBA, he pocketed a great deal of the money and used only a small portion to keep his museum afloat. Pitsch also lost the support of the Glen Swanson Collection, because he neglected to pay insurance for the items from the collection that were being displayed.

Pitsch soon found himself swimming in debt. In 1998, he would consent to a default judgment with the SBA totaling approximately $700,000 plus additional interest accrued during his loan period.[6]

This judgment forced Pitsch to begin selling the lion's share of artifacts he had extracted from his family's land. As I established the Custer Battlefield Museum, trading post and built up my Historical Rarities Inc. business, I, among others, began to acquire some of Pitsch's items and dealt with him on a regular basis. Each time I purchased an "authentic" item from Pitsch, it would be accompanied by the letter. I, in turn, would use the letter in my eBay auctions as authentication for the artifacts.[7]

As Pitsch tried to repay the judgment against him, he began to skirt the perimeters of the law. He started falsifying the provenance, or original order of ownership, of the artifacts he was selling—not only to me but to multiple artifact dealers across the country.[8]

I Knew There Was a Woman Involved in This Somewhere

In the year 2000, Pitsch sauntered into the Garryowen Trading Post. Clutched in his dirty hands was a pair of weathered, black, punch-dotted United States Cavalry boots.[9] Putt Thompson, who was the curator of the Custer Battlefield Museum and to whom I leased the Garryowen Trading Post, greeted him at the door.

"What do you have for me today, Jason?" Putt said.

"I have some boots that I think you're really gonna be interested in," Pitsch happily replied.

Raising his hands from his sides, Pitsch dropped the cavalry boots onto the service desk's glass counter top with a thud. Scum, mud flecks, and other filth flaked from the boots.

"What am I seeing here?" Putt asked.

"They're authentic one-of-a-kind 7th Cavalry boots found on my section of the battlefield," Pitsch answered.

"No kidding?" Putt replied incredulously, hefting up one of the muddy, rock-hard, tattered boots, giving it a once-over.

"Would I lie to you?" Pitsch asked with a scoundrel's grin creeping across his face.

Scoffing, Putt placed the boot alongside its partner and asked, "How much are you looking for, Jason?"

"How about $8,000?"

"How about all right?" Putt replied.

Putt asked Pitsch to provide a certificate of authenticity, and Pitsch left to retrieve it. After several hours passed, he returned with it and a copy of the Lingard letter. Taking the certificate and letter, Putt opened the cash register, handed a sweaty wad of bills to Pitsch, and wrote a receipt. When Pitsch left, Putt placed the boots in a secure place, then drew up the required paperwork to loan the boots to the Custer Battlefield Museum.[10]

When I returned from some business I was tending to, Putt informed me of his purchase. I was ecstatic when Putt produced the pair of boots. I saw the punch-dotted "WW" at the top shanks of the boots and immediately believed we had an incredible find. At least six 7th Cavalry troopers with the initials "WW" had died in the battle.[11]

Pitsch had told Putt the boots more than likely belonged to W.W. Cooke. William Winer Cooke, which was the officer's full name, enlisted in 1863 with the 24th New York Cavalry at Niagara Falls during the Civil War. After serving as a recruiting officer, he fought on the front lines in the IX Corps, commanded by Ambrose Burnside. He was later wounded during the Siege of Petersburg. After being released from the hospital, he served on commissary duty. Cooke then rose to first lieutenant on December 14, 1864, but did not return to front-line duty until March 1865.[12]

In 1871, Cooke became the regimental adjutant under Lieutenant Colonel George Armstrong Custer. Cooke died at the Battle of the Little Bighorn; his corpse was found close to his commanders'. Cook's true claim to fame is that he is the author of the famous "last message" dictated to him by Custer which was carried by Sergeant John Martin and delivered to Major Frederick Benteen. The letter is now held in the West Point archives. It reads:

> Benteen. Come On. Big village. Be quick. Bring packs. WW Cooke.
> P.S. Bring Packs.

In death, Cooke was scalped twice; the second scalping was of his prodigiously long flowing side whiskers.[13] Knowing all of this, Putt and I immediately began to converse about the boots.

"Did he say where they came from?" I said.

"He said they came from his folks' place," replied Putt.

"How much?" I asked.

"Eight," Putt said.

The amount seemed a little steep to me, but I knew items like these didn't come along very often. Most times people find only bullets, spent shell casings, or other cavalry accoutrements that are not altogether intact. So, to find something like this, in this shape, and to have a matching set was a big deal for the museum.

"He give you a copy of the Lingard letter?" I asked.

"Yep," said Putt. "You know even though you've had some trouble with this Lingard fella, his letter has done all right by you. You've been able to make some good sales because of it."

I didn't want to get into the paranoia Lee Lingard had caused me in the previous several months, so I just agreed with Putt's assessment. I thanked him for loaning the boots to the museum and found a place in the gallery for the pair almost immediately.

In my haste to celebrate the new acquisition, I produced a new brochure featuring the boots as "battle relics" as well as many other unique artifacts I had recently come in possession of. The brochures cost me around $15,000 to print and mail to various Custer enthusiasts, collectors, and institutions. These brochures were also distributed free to the public at 350 locations throughout Montana, North Dakota, and Wyoming. No sooner had I started with the promotion of the boots than I realized Pitsch had duped Putt and me.

A 7th Cavalry amateur historian and artist by the name of Ralph Heinz questioned Pitsch's "find" as soon as my brochure made it into the public realm. Heinz stated that he had bought this exact pair of boots in the 1980s from a man named Hayes Otoupalik. Not a replica but the exact pair. A militaria dealer from Missoula, Otoupalik acquired the boots from a man who had unearthed them in the remnants of Camp Stambaugh, Wyoming.

Camp Stambaugh had been garrisoned for only a couple of years, by troops from the 3rd Cavalry who left the post not too long before the Rosebud Battle, an engagement that took place directly before the Battle of the Little Bighorn. The pair of boots and an 1872 infantry shoe (which also had the "WW" initials punch-dotted in it) was found inside a filled-in privy. Apparently, it was a practice to throw items that were no longer in use into privies; when camps like Stambaugh were abandoned, the privies were often filled with junk. I also learned there were at least three cavalrymen in the 3rd Cavalry with the initials "WW."

Ralph Heinz went on to state that in July 1995, after purchasing the boots from Otoupalik, he traded the boots to Jason Pitsch. The transaction had taken place at the Pitsch household and was witnessed by a captain in the Kalispell, Montana, fire department, along with a member of a respected Custer battlefield association and Heinz's wife.

Heinz also produced a photograph of the transaction that included Pitsch holding the boots.[14]

Although the boots were an authentic 1870s pair, which is quite rare, they were worth only a few hundred dollars instead of the $8,000 sum Putt had shelled out for them. Because I had promoted their acquisition and display, I had egg on my face. The Custer aficionados and historical collecting community read me the riot act. Before I found out about the false provenance of the boots, the high-gloss brochures I published had already found their way into the hands of several people who were all too eager to attack and chastise me for the fraudulent footwear.[15]

After this incident, I immediately stopped my dealings with Pitsch and filed a lawsuit against him. Through the press, Pitsch said he had not misrepresented the boots when he sold them to Putt. Pitsch instead insisted he had sold them to Putt tagged as "Camp Stambaugh privy boots" and not as "Custer battle boots," even though I had a certificate of authenticity with Pitsch's signature on it stating that the boots were retrieved from the Reno retreat.

Through litigation in 2004, Pitsch admitted, in a written jailhouse confession, that he had misrepresented the provenance of the boots. He signed the letter, which was also witnessed, admitting his guilt in the matter. Unfortunately for me, I would come to find that this incident was not the only time Pitsch had misrepresented the authenticity of historic artifacts.[16]

It later came to my attention, during my various dealings with Pitsch, that he was working as a paid confidential informant for Lee Lingard and the Bureau of Land Management. Apparently, I was not the first person to catch Pitsch falsifying artifacts. Lingard used Pitsch to set up individuals suspected of dealing in stolen artifacts, counterfeit artifacts, and illegally collected archaeological resources acquired from federal lands.[17]

From 1995 to 1998, Pitsch functioned as a double agent by providing information to Lingard and his BLM counterparts, all the while slipping counterintelligence to dealers in the artifacts community.

Pitsch first entered Lingard's radar by selling Custer battlefield–found artifacts. After Lingard contacted Pitsch, and found out that the artifacts were acquired on fee simple, private family property, his concerns about Pitsch lessened. Pitsch used eBay under the handle "sittingbullscamp" for his connection to the online artifact-dealing world. Based upon his connections to dealers in the Custer- and Indian-related-artifacts community, the BLM agents believed they had the perfect snitch to help them catch counterfeiters.[18]

Even though Cathy Lingard and I were no longer a couple, I received confirmation of Pitsch's informant status from her. Pitsch was unaware I knew he was working as an informant. I also learned that Pitsch, while working with the BLM, had developed a close friendship with Lee Lingard after learning that they shared a commonality in collecting World War II Nazi material.[19]

During all the time I spent acquiring artifacts from Pitsch, the two of us were more acquaintances than anything else. He sometimes offered me interesting artifacts I would sell on eBay using the Bureau of Land Management's Lingard letter as further proof of the artifacts' origins. But as far as contact and interactions went, Pitsch and Putt had a stronger friendship and more business dealings with one another than I did. Because Putt leased space and ran the Garryowen Trading Post, he dealt with most of the people who came to his store. From time to time, the people who came to the trading post were looking to sell or purchase artifacts.

One afternoon, I was in the back office working at my desk and heard a knock at the door. I was surprised to see Pitsch standing behind it. He seemed to be quite agitated and nervous. Pressing forward, he asked if he could come in. I blocked him with my hand and said no. At this point, I was wondering why he wanted to enter my office. I figured he was scouting for Lingard and was looking to drum up something against me.

He said, "I have something important to tell you."

Pitsch came clean and proceeded to tell me that he was working for Lee Lingard and the BLM. He admitted he had been keeping tabs on Cathy and me when we were dating. Blubbering, with tears running down his face, he attempted to apologize for spying on us. He stated that Lingard and the BLM were not focusing on me and Putt but others in the artifacts business. I kept the knowledge to myself of what I had known for weeks about Pitsch. I couldn't believe this was unfolding right before my eyes. It seemed surreal.

After telling Pitsch I did not have anything to hide and I was confident the BLM would find no malfeasance on my property or in my businesses, I decided to enter a formal complaint against Lee Lingard because I feared for my safety.

On October 30, 1995, my attorney recommended writing a letter to the Office of Inspector General (OIG) at the Department of the Interior (DOI) in Washington, D.C. Some of my grievances outlined in the letter to the OIG were Lingard's threats to Cathy if she continued to date me, slanderous statements made to Cathy about me, and threats that he made to Cathy and informant Jason Pitsch, saying that I would "go down." Furthermore, Lingard had made slanderous statements saying that I was involved in drug-related and other illicit activities, that I was a convicted felon, and that I had been arrested for domestic violence, all of which is patently untrue.

On top of the misconduct, Lingard was divulging information regarding ongoing federal investigations to third parties who were not affiliated with law enforcement, and had been using government vehicles and equipment for personal use while surveilling his ex-wife at my residence.[20] Not only was this letter sent to the Office of Inspector General, but it was sent to senior Montana Republican Senator Conrad Burns' office as well. Burns was copied on all correspondence in this matter.

Pitsch's and Lingard's surveillance was the main reason I cut all ties with Cathy Lingard. It was sad at the time, but I believe our mutual attraction came more from both of us being divorced and lonely than anything else.

Following his confession, whenever Pitsch came to Garryowen, he covertly advised me of Lingard's intent to visit Garryowen and report any contraband activity. I must reiterate, no such contraband activity ever took place at Garryowen, but Pitsch had an interest in parlaying his informant status into other avenues he thought would give him a boost and elevate his status with Uncle Sam.

I never participated in any such activity and never entertained Pitsch's delusions as a double agent. But still, he persisted. From then on, Pitsch bragged about his position with the BLM constantly. I even witnessed him carrying concealed weapons like he was part of the good ol' boys club. He had no concealed weapons permit. Not only that, but the bureau's agents would have flipped if they knew he was packing while working for Lingard. He went so far as to inform me that Lingard was using the undercover name Lee Wade when conducting sting operations against artifacts dealers. I assumed he had adopted the pseudonym based on David Wade, the curator at the BLM's Billings Curation Center.

Around 1998, Pitsch was caught in a nationwide child pornography sting known as Operation Avalanche. This was the largest operation of its kind. The internet was still in its infancy, and it provided a new conduit for pedophiles. The U.S. Justice Department has made it a priority to enforce child pornography laws, and especially since the internet was born. This operation was one of the very first of its kind conducted by the FBI.

In the sting, Pitsch was caught navigating several websites containing sexually graphic images of underage children performing sex acts. For this offense, Pitsch received three years of federal probation. Following his sentencing, Pitsch violated the conditions of his probation by once again downloading child pornography.[21] He was mandated to complete sex offender therapy and to adhere to restrictions on computer use.

Pitsch's original conviction carried a standard sentence of 27 to 33 months in prison, but chief U.S. district judge Jack Shanstrom reduced the sentence to probation. Judge Shanstrom is an avid firearms collector and a Custer buff. Word circulated that he knew Pitsch because of the Custer connection. I suspect that's one reason

Shanstrom did not throw the book at Pitsch, instead giving him a slap on the wrist. It is important to note that Pitsch was likely still a BLM informant for Lingard at the time this sting took place.

As an undercover confidential informant for the BLM, Pitsch's conviction was not only damning to himself but to his BLM employers. The BLM had egg on its face and dropped him like a hot potato. It was not public knowledge that he was an undercover, confidential informant; however, the FBI's arrest of one of the BLM's esteemed confidential informants would have been juicy news.

Also around this time, I was a reserve law enforcement officer with the Big Horn County sheriff's department. I would later become a full-time deputy. As I mentioned, Putt and Pitsch had developed a good business relationship; Putt dealt with Pitsch on an almost daily basis. Because of this fact, Putt hired Pitsch full-time in the trading post, giving him free rein over the premises. Putt eventually allowed Pitsch into the trading post offices, where he had access to the computers.

On a brisk April morning in 2002, I was in my uniform getting ready to leave for my shift at the sheriff's office. I left my home, which was connected to the complex in the back of the museum property. As I was walking past the trading post's rear-facing office window, I noticed Pitsch slumped over in one of the office chairs with his eyes glued to the computer screen.[22]

As I peered in the window to ascertain what was happening, a sickening feeling came over me. On the screen were images of nude girls well under the legal age of 18. Horrified that Pitsch was on the town of Garryowen's internet service, which was in my name, I felt my stomach hitch. I immediately knew I had to report to the federal authorities what I had stumbled upon. I went inside and calmly waited for Pitsch to leave. As I saw him exit the office, he and I exchanged pleasantries. I could hardly contain the disgust that welled up in my very core.

When I returned to the office on Monday, I told my all-female office staff about this, and then contacted Putt and told him what I had seen and that I was going to turn Pitsch in to the feds. My staff members told me that if I did not report Pitsch's porn activity, they would resign immediately. Later that day I turned Pitsch in to the United States Probation Office. The probation officer was Carlos Jones, who visited me that afternoon.

After I showed him the computer that Pitsch had been on, they found other evidence of his purchasing child pornography while logged into his personal eBay account on the trading post computer. Jones immediately printed screenshots. Not too much later, Pitsch was arrested on probation violation. Pitsch's arrest set in motion a series of events that would bring the federal government directly to my doorstep.

4

Button, Button, Who's Got the Button?

Putt Thompson was not in Garryowen at the time of the child pornography incident. After Pitsch's arrest, Putt confronted me about turning Pitsch in to the authorities. When I had initially told Putt I was going to turn Pitsch in, he exploded. We ended up having a very intense argument, because Putt was outraged that he would lose his highest-grossing salesperson. Obviously, it was only about money with Putt, not the letter of the law. I was concerned about saving the legacy of Garryowen, not to mention my own ass. When I learned that Pitsch was committing these crimes on the internet service that was in my name, I was gravely concerned. When I spoke with Putt over the phone, our argument intensified.

"Putt," I said, "I need to speak with you."

"Hold on a minute," he said into the receiver.

"Putt, I need to talk to you now," I sternly commanded.

Silence on the phone.

After a few moments: "What's the issue, Chris?" he asked.

"It's Jason. I think we have a problem."

"What's this all about?" Putt asked as I stepped into a private room to continue the conversation.

"I was walking past the office window over the weekend, and I saw Jason on the computer looking at porn," I said.

"What?"

"He was looking at child pornography," I reiterated.

As if stupefied by the words that were coming out of my mouth, Putt sighed on the other end of the line.

"I'm going to turn him in, Putt," I said.

"*Turn him in to who?*" Putt shouted over the phone.

"The feds. I'm a sheriff's deputy, and I can't have a scumbag like that under my roof here in Garryowen," I told him.

"I'll lose my only full-time employee and best salesperson!" Putt shouted.

"That really doesn't matter at this point, Putt. I have to turn him in. It's the law."

"We have to destroy the computer," Putt murmured.

"What? Why?" I questioned, sitting down in one of the office chairs.

"Because the cops will think we've had something to do with it."

"Why would the cops think that?"

"Because it's the Garryowen Trading Post computer that my company owns," Putt continued. "They can trace this stuff, and they'll think we were looking at it."

"Get a hold of yourself, Putt," I told him. "I'm going to turn him in and let justice take its course. And that will be the end of it."

Putt was still furious and insisted that the computer needed to be destroyed, but I assured him I would take care of things.

Pitsch was arrested for his second offense related to child pornography in June 2003, and was later remanded into federal custody. Because this was a second offense, it constituted a parole violation. Pitsch was looking at five years in a federal prison, a sentence that would provide no opportunity for parole. I believe that when he found out I was the man who had turned him in, he sought revenge and decided to try to take me down for being caught for his own disgusting crimes.[1]

When he was taken into federal custody, I could only imagine the fear washing over Pitsch's face in what must have been a sweltering interrogation room clogged with federal agents who, under hot lights, forced their will upon him. Surrounded by feds and facing a multi-year prison sentence, Pitsch knew the noose was tightening around his neck. He had to try to save himself anyway he could. In what I'm sure was a blubbering state, Pitsch began pointing fingers and, like a man drowning, lashed out at the one person he could think of to help save his hide.

During this intense interrogation, Pitsch implicated me in the selling of illegal artifacts. As the agents turned the screws on him, Pitsch also implicated me in the selling and buying of eagle feathers. Under federal law, the buying, selling, and bartering of eagle feathers is a crime that carries a sentence of two years in prison and a $250,000 fine.[2]

His allegations were totally false. But Pitsch had sold many items to me, and furthermore had gained access to almost everything at the Garryowen Trading Post while working for Putt. He had been a BLM informant and knew enough to spin an almost credible story, unless you looked for facts. The federal agents did not look. They just proceeded as if Pitsch were speaking the gospel truth.

The feathers Pitsch was spouting off about are contained in eagle feather war bonnets in the museum. There is a long and interesting history revolving around the feathers in the Custer Battlefield Museum. War bonnets were worn by male American Plains Indians who had earned a place of great respect in their tribe. Originally, they were worn in battle but are now primarily used for ceremonial occasions. They are items of great spiritual and political importance to the Plains Indians of the American West.[3]

Native American tribes consider the presentation of an eagle feather to be one of their highest marks of respect. Indian males earn their feathers through acts of courage and honor, or the feathers are given to them for work in service to their tribe. Roman Nose, a Cheyenne warrior, won several feathers in his bonnet for acts that included riding in front of United States soldiers and being shot at but never being hit.[4]

The esteem attached to eagle feathers is so high that in many cases, only two or three honor feathers might be awarded in a warrior's lifetime. Historically, the warrior who was the first to touch an enemy in battle and escape unscathed received an eagle feather. When enough feathers were collected, they might be incorporated into a headdress or some other form of worn regalia. Headdresses were usually reserved exclusively for the tribe's chosen political and spiritual leaders.[5]

Northern Cheyenne chief Little Wolf, whose headdress is in the collection of the Custer Battlefield Museum, was known as a great military tactician and led a dramatic escape from confinement in Oklahoma back to the Northern Cheyenne homeland in 1878, which was known as the Northern Cheyenne Exodus. He was not present at the Battle of the Little Bighorn, but played a part before and directly after the battle. Due to the historical importance of headdresses, many Native Americans now consider the wearing of them without the express permission of tribal leaders to be an affront to their culture and traditions.[6]

Plains-style bonnets are still almost always made from eagle feathers, because the eagle is considered by most tribes of the Interior Plains to be the greatest and most powerful of all birds. Under current federal legislation, the eagle feather law enables American Indians to continue using eagle feathers in their traditional spiritual and cultural practices. The exemption is contained within the Migratory Bird Treaty Act of 1918. In the United States, only enrolled members of federally recognized Native American tribes may legally possess eagle feathers.[7] Possession by non-Indians is legal only if the feathers were owned before the Bald and Golden Eagle Protection Act was enacted in 1940, or if someone gifts pre-enactment feathers without any compensation or trade.

Another way Native Americans can acquire eagle feathers legally is if a member of an Indian tribe petitions for eagle feathers or eagle parts from the National Eagle Repository. This bank contains preserved carcasses and parts of eagles that have been illegally killed, were hit in traffic, died getting caught in power lines, and the like. Because the Justice Department has exempted Indian tribes from being prosecuted for possessing eagle parts, this practice is totally legal. These requests normally take a year to 18 months to be filled.

One traditional method of acquiring feathers for bonnets is to pluck the most mature tail feathers of young eagles while they're still in the nest. This can be done three times before the feathers do not grow back. As many as 36 feathers can be collected in this manner. If care is taken to not disturb the nest, this method can be repeated yearly.[8] The eagle feather laws are written with exceptions in them so Indians can continue their traditional and spiritual practices like using the feathers in bonnets or ceremonies.[9] However, an unauthorized person found with an eagle feather or its parts can be fined up to $25,000.[10]

As Pitsch spilled his guts to the federal agents, including numerous BLM operatives, the feds began to hatch their own plans to draw me into their sights and snares. One of the BLM agents involved in these plans was Bart Fitzgerald. With an almost nondescript appearance, neatly cut salt-and-pepper hair, a medium build, and a penchant for wearing sport coats, Fitzgerald is not someone the public would think of as a special federal agent. His look was more along the lines of that of a businessman or politician.

Fitzgerald's career, however, has been highlighted due to high-profile arrests and testifying as a star witness for several famous cases revolving around selling stolen and falsified artifacts. He is best known for being the man who captured and helped convict Earl Keso Shumway, a man described as the "John Dillinger of Archaeological Looting." Shumway robbed graves and broke into long-sealed Indian homes, all the while boasting that the chances of his ever being caught were one in a million.[11] The crafty thief used helicopters and lookouts strapped with two-way radios as he pillaged Indian burial grounds.

Shumway operated mostly in Utah and had a long history of theft. He attributed his archaeological knowledge to his father whom he said taught him how to pinpoint and rob the most valuable grave sites. Earl's distant cousin, Casey Shumway, was the first person prosecuted under the Archaeological Resources Protection Act (ARPA).[12] Shumway also once boasted that he used a bulldozer to excavate an Indian ruin. He also destroyed and robbed the grave of an Anasazi infant. Reports of this event state that Shumway tore the blanket swaddling off the child, then tossed the corpse away and proceeded to rob the grave of all valuable objects.[13]

Before agent Fitzgerald dropped the hammer on Shumway, the bandit had been arrested 10 years earlier on a charge of looting 34 prehistoric baskets. Shumway was finally indicted after a former business partner turned him in. His business partner's reason for turning him in to the authorities: he claimed Shumway deprived him of his share of the profits from the grave looting.[14]

Another story from Fitzgerald's career, which had more bearing on my case, was one involving Jeffry Stevens. Stevens was a history buff from Fallbrook, California, who over several decades stole American Indian artifacts, Civil War–era memorabilia, and other valuables from small museums in at least six states. Stevens was captured in Montana when he tried to steal hood ornaments from an antique car collection held at the Daniels County Museum and Pioneer Town in Billings. An alert staff member wrote down his license plate number before he could escape.

Not long after this incident, authorities including Bart Fitzgerald apprehended Stevens. They found that his preferred method of pillaging from institutions was to befriend older members of the staff at libraries and museums and then shove loot into his baggy pants or his oversized coat while the staff member's attention was elsewhere. Using this method, he was even able to steal a large rifle—he stuffed it into his pants and walked out of the institution with a slight shuffle.

After the adoration surrounding the Shumway capture and confession, Fitzgerald rose to new heights in the BLM and became a "rock star" at the outfit. He benefited both financially and in rank—so much so that he wielded great influence in the BLM's allowing his transfer from Utah to Montana, where he became a special agent in charge.

As the decade wore on and his notoriety and fame waned, it is believed Fitzgerald needed to justify his lofty position and large salary (well into six figures). I think, pushed by his superiors to make high-profile arrests, Fitzgerald struggled to keep the BLM in the spotlight. As special agent in charge of Montana, Fitzgerald was Lee Lingard's supervisor, and I believe that he was most likely in charge of the unconstitutional covert sting operation intended to entrap me. Fitzgerald was also responsible for shutting down the undercover operation after Pitsch was pinched for child pornography.

A reasonable person could assume that, armed with the lies from Pitsch and needing a big arrest to buttress his lofty position as special agent in charge, Fitzgerald hatched a plot to destroy my business and turn me into the high-profile hit he needed. Along with Special Agent Brian Cornell, Fitzgerald concentrated BLM's Montana resources on surveillance of Garryowen, the Custer Battlefield Museum, and the online dealings of my historical rarities business. After setting up the sting, Fitzgerald eventually turned the lead on the investigation over to Agent Cornell.

Also during this period, a man named Robert Nightengale, an amateur Custer and Little Bighorn historian, began hanging around Garryowen and the museum. A balding, thin man, Nightengale did not strike me as an imposing figure but soon became a menace to me. Nightengale authored a coffee table book titled *Little Big Horn* and would eventually be the subject of a television documentary entitled *Betrayal at Little Big Horn*, narrated by the star of several A&E television programs, Bill Kurtis. His book was also the focus of a documentary on the PAX channel called *Encounters with the Unexplained*.

Nightengale's *Little Big Horn* book was seen by multiple critics and historians as a "cultist" interpretation of the battle, rife with disproved conspiracy theories. The thesis Nightengale puts forward in this tome is that Custer was betrayed by several officers who deliberately disobeyed his orders with the specific intent of causing his death. In support of this thesis, Nightengale claims that Major Marcus A. Reno and Captain Frederick W. Benteen committed deliberate perjury at the Army court of inquiry after Custer's annihilation. Nightengale is also very critical of Benteen's actions during the battle, almost to the point of obsession.

Unfortunately for me, I would come to find out that obsession was a major driving force in Nightengale's life, and it soon bled over into mine. I first met Robert Nightengale in about 1995, when he was writing *Little Big Horn*. He often came to the museum to study the artifacts on display, but we often ended up talking shop about the Custer battle and other related subjects. Usually, he tried to push his paranoid delusions of conspiracy against Custer on myself and my employees. I found it odd but let it go.

Before publication of the *Little Big Horn* book, in an attempt to promote it, Nightengale approached Putt Thompson to have a book signing at the trading post. I interviewed Nightengale, and he seemed to have a genuine interest in the battlefield and the history surrounding it. Being a fellow fan of history, I allowed him to remain on my property and volunteer in the museum. In one of the more bizarre acts I have ever witnessed, which should have set my internal alarms off early on, Nightengale started sleeping in his van parked in the Custer Battlefield Museum's parking lot. I would often find him outside the door of the trading post at the crack of dawn, waiting for me to unlock the doors.

Not wanting to discourage his love of history, however, I allowed Nightengale to volunteer at the museum beginning in 2000. Allowing him onto the premises as a volunteer ended up being a terrible idea. I repeatedly found Nightengale intoxicated on the job, and his status as a volunteer gave him access to the museum six days a week. His drunken demeanor included being belligerent with the staff and museum patrons.

We soon began experiencing other issues with Nightengale as well, involving pornography and displaying suggestive sexual behavior toward other employees and museum volunteers. Specifically, Nightengale started making overt sexual advances toward female employees and toward my special-needs son.

One of the many inappropriate things Nightengale did in the workplace was purchase a small cardboard box from an adult bookstore. The box had "horny toad" printed on the outside, and inside the box was a frog with an erection. He went around and showed this to my female employees and my son, making crude comments the whole time. In addition, Nightengale made violent threats directed toward me, including making wild and aggressive actions with his arms, slamming doors, and screaming profanities at the top of his lungs.

The staff and I attempted an intervention with Nightengale at one point, to give him an opportunity to control his behavior. Several employees and I confronted him about his actions and frequent intoxication. I offered to pay for alcohol detoxification treatment, but he violently denied that he had a problem. All of this took place in about a year's time, at the end of which I dismissed him from his volunteer duties. I also ordered him to never set foot on Garryowen property again, or I would take legal action against him.

Nightengale's girlfriend Janice Smith, an American Indian who is an adopted and enrolled member of the Snoqualmie Tribe in Washington state, soon became involved in our confrontations as well. Smith's status as a Native American Indian is not recognized by the Snoqualmie Tribe or the Bureau of Indian Affairs for any benefits; she has no tribal voting rights or medical coverage, and does not share in any per diem or dividend disbursements. She has no blood quantum, but the tribe took her in and gave her a tribal ID card anyway, which technically makes her an Indian with *no* Native American blood.

It is important to this story, because when the Small Business Administration foreclosed its loan against Jason Pitsch, Janice Smith purchased his museum and land after receiving special Native American preference in securing an SBA loan due to having the Native American ID card. She and Nightengale took possession of the Reno "museum" but did not operate it as a business. At various times, they allowed travelers to park RVs there and on the adjacent property, which they did not own. However, this activity brought them into a conflict with the Custer Battlefield Preservation Committee, which owned the adjacent property.

Finding out about the mock trailer park, the CBPC initiated a quiet title auction in the Big Horn district court to clear title to the disputed land. I was at the SBA auction when it went up for sale, and I bid the property up to $65,000. The property had a minimum bid of $100,000, so it did not sell. In retrospect, not purchasing the property is one of the biggest mistakes I have made. Had I acquired it, I would not have had Robert Nightengale in my life.

Continuing my troubles with Nightengale, in 2002 I sought to be elected Big Horn County sheriff after serving as a reserve deputy and later as a full-time deputy from 1998 through 2000. During this time, Nightengale became my extreme adversary. He made numerous scandalous accusations about me. His girlfriend Janice Smith aided his efforts. I attempted to counter the libelous and slanderous statements, but they eventually traveled through *The Moccasin Telegraph*, a local newsletter read by many in the area.

Incumbent sheriff Larson Medicine Horse, a Crow Indian, fired me without cause and reported me to the state for what he said were allegations of worker's compensation fraud. He created false evidence against me because he knew I would be running in the upcoming election for sheriff. The Montana attorney general ended the investigation of me in July 2002, finding no evidence of wrongdoing. It was purely a political move by Medicine Horse during the campaign. Nightengale also circled on the periphery of the investigation and election, and continued to verbally harass me by making assertions of moral turpitude.

After the general election, which I lost by only a few hundred votes, Nightengale went with his allegations to a county newspaper called *The Briefs*, run by a man named Al Sargent. After the report with Nightengale's allegations about me was demonstrated to be false and libelous, Sargent published a retraction statement in December 2002.[15]

Five days after the election, Nightengale physically assaulted me in the Garryowen Subway shop. The assault led to his arrest by Big

Horn County deputy sheriff Deb Winburn. During the altercation, Nightengale came into the Subway shop and screamed at me that I had no business running for sheriff. Slurring his words and unsteady on his feet, he blurted out, "I'm glad you lost!" He then proceeded to cock his fist back and take a swing at my face. Missing his intended target, he hit me in the chest. I called the Big Horn County sheriff's office immediately, and he was detained shortly afterward.

Following this altercation, Nightengale pled guilty to a misdemeanor. Thereafter, I obtained a restraining order against him. One of the elements of the restraining order was that Nightengale could not defame my reputation or character, either verbally or in writing, by implication or outright statement. As a result of the litigation, Nightengale was declared a legally recognized stalker by a Montana district court judge. The order was made permanent in 2007, and that also took away his right to possess firearms for the rest of his life. All of this is important because after his scrape with the law, Nightengale would fall into the clutches of the BLM. BLM agents eventually used him as a tool against me during their investigation.

Nightengale provided the BLM federal agents with falsified reports of my supposed dealings in "illegal activity" and the sale of stolen Indian artifacts. Although he had no documentation or hard evidence of any wrongdoing, the BLM agents were all too eager to listen to his rants. With Nightengale's ramblings and Jason Pitsch's implicating me in the illegal sale of eagle feathers to enhance his status with the feds, Bart Fitzgerald and Brian Cornell green-lit a plan to take me and my businesses down.

Cornell and BLM supervisory officials knew I was the subject of a United States Fish and Wildlife Service undercover operation as well. During this operation, it was found that no illegal or scandalous activity was going on with my business or the museum; it was done as a matter of routine. Yet the BLM used this investigation as a further excuse to put its sting operation into motion. Cornell focused on the fact mentioned in the (USFWS) operation report that I often asked people if they had anything to sell or to trade when they entered the museum. In the museum world, selling, trading, and bartering of artifacts happens quite often and is completely legal. All purchases of this nature deal with one-of-a-kind items, so there is a lot of discussion between sellers about bartering.

Evidently there had been another complaint against me made to the USFWS that reportedly mentioned I was a "bad guy"; however, there was nothing illegal happening at Garryowen. Based on this totally manufactured and preposterous evidence, the BLM determined that the allegations outlined in the complaint had merit and "required further investigation."

Cornell's plan began with his or another agent's acquiring a Civil War–era 7th Cavalry uniform button from the Department of the Interior (DOI). These buttons are the same type of buttons I often sold. There is little to no difference in buttons from the Civil War era through the Indian Wars era, because the uniforms soldiers wore during the Indian conflicts were often surplus Civil War uniforms. Cornell instructed other BLM agents to microdot the DOI-supplied button.

A microdot is text or an image substantially reduced in size and placed onto a small disk to prevent detection by unintended recipients. Before the BLM used the microdotted button, Cornell sent several undercover agents to Garryowen at different times throughout 2003 and 2004. These agents portrayed themselves as artifacts dealers or tourists looking to buy and sell certain Indian and Custer-battlefield-related relics.

After seeing tens of thousands of tourists every year with the same stories, I normally did not entertain these types of proposals. I usually left the decision of a purchase up to Putt Thompson, as I did in the case of the boots he purchased from Jason Pitsch. Most of the time I told the sellers flat-out I had no interest, rejecting them on the spot.

I cannot be certain about the legitimacy of all the people who walked through my doors during those years the BLM attempted to entrap me, but I believe many of these people were undercover federal agents looking to catch me in an illegal transaction. I knew I was on their radar screen. Most of those people who came through the museum's doors were trying to sell shell casings, bullets, or rusted bits of metal from cavalrymen's uniforms.

Most of the time, I instructed my employees to tell them I was not interested no matter what. The BLM got around this by sending undercover agents to Garryowen asking to sell something for gas money. They knew I had to deal with him or her directly because the person was "stranded." Also during that time, I was approached on numerous occasions by Native Americans wanting to sell eagle parts; I also feel, even though it cannot be proven, that these Indians were most likely confidential informants working for federal agents. Either way, I never took them up on any of their offers. Every time I was offered eagle parts, I called the Bureau of Indian Affairs (BIA) police to report them; nothing ever happened in these instances.

When it came to the bullets, casings, and so on, I already had literally hundreds of these artifacts that had been dug up on private ranching Battlefield property when I rebuilt Garryowen. I am certain my unwillingness to entertain any of these traps upset Cornell and the other BLM agents. Presumably frustrated by the fact I was not gobbling the bait shoveled out by his undercover agents, Cornell doubled his efforts to entrap me.

In December of 2004, an undercover BLM agent who called himself Rudy Zapada showed up in Garryowen. I had spent most of that day in my back office dealing with eBay auctions and filing paperwork for my businesses' end-of-the-year transactions. As I read through financial statements, one of my managers, named Stuart, poked his head into my office.

"Hey, Chris," Stuart barked, startling me.

"What's up, Stuart?" I said, looking up from my paperwork.

"There's a fella out here who is trying to sell some stuff. Do you want to talk to him?"

"What kind of stuff?"

"Oh, I don't know; a buckle and a couple of buttons. Seventh Cavalry stuff by the sound of it. You interested?"

"Not really," I replied and then began rifling through my papers again.

"Okay I'll let him know," Stuart said.

In a few moments Stuart was back poking his head into my office.

"Sorry, Chris, the guy says he's desperate. Says he ran out of gas and he's stuck here."

"Where's his car?" I asked, annoyed.

"He says he was able to coast it into the museum parking lot. You want me to tell him to take a hike?"

"No, no. I'll talk with him," I said, frustrated and rising to my feet.

Ever since I rebuilt Garryowen, I have dealt with stranded travelers who just need gas money to get down the road. At the time of this particular occurrence, Garryowen had the only gas station for 20 miles west and 75 miles east, so encountering motorists down on their luck happened quite frequently. Walking out of my office, I was greeted by a short Hispanic man with a wall of thick black hair swept across his forehead in a lump. His appearance was that of a disheveled, road-weary, unshaven, middle-aged man. As I peered out the trading post's front window, the sight of the man's rusty yellow Chevy pickup made me feel bad for him immediately.

"What can I do for you?" I questioned.

"I need some gas. My truck died and I need to get down the road," he said in a thick Mexican accent.

"I've been told," I said. "What's your name?"

"Rudy Zapada."

"Where's this stuff you want to trade for gas?"

"It's out in my truck. I didn't know if you would want it, so I thought I'd come in and ask first."

"Well, Rudy let's see what I can do for you."

On the way out the door, Rudy explained to me he was not a freeloader but was hoping to sell me a couple of items he'd inherited from his uncle. After I agreed to look at them, he and I headed out into the cold Montana night. As we walked out of the door, the brisk air slapped me in the face. For a split second, I felt a sense of dread wash over me. I could not pinpoint the feeling, but I knew there was something wrong. I was not sure if I was afraid I was walking into a mugging or if Rudy had something else on his mind, but the whole situation did not sit right with me. I should have listened to my instincts and my better judgment. But I didn't.

"The stuff I have is real nice," Rudy said.

"What kind of stuff do you have?" I replied.

"It's old-time stuff. You know, from the battlefield—I don't know for sure. My uncle used to collect it, and I got this stuff when he died," Zapada said, opening the door of his jalopy.

"I'm not in the mood to purchase any more battlefield relics," I said.

Pretending not to hear me, Zapada withdrew a small, neatly folded oilcloth from his car's front seat. Pulling back the folds, he revealed period uniform buttons and a suspender buckle. He told me again that these were inherited from his uncle who was a collector and he did not know the value. For me, it was nothing new. Over the years, I had seen many items like these and had several of them in my collection. I did not want to leave the man stranded with no gas money, however, and he seemed eager to sell them instead of just taking some charity from me. At the time, I thought his wanting to sell something rather than take charity was rather honorable of him. Little did I know his whole story was a total lie.

After taking his items, I wrote Rudy a check for $50. To ensure the legitimacy of the transaction, I made a copy of the check, the receipt, and his Arizona driver's license. Looking at the trinkets in my palm, I had a feeling of unease wash over me again. I put the thought to the back of my mind and walked back inside the trading post, leaving Rudy in the parking lot. I did not know it at the time, but the items in my hand would turn out to be the most cursed objects I ever possessed. Walking back to my office with Zapada's paperwork, I noted that his Arizona driver's license matched the state license of his truck. I then went back to work in my office, assuming Zapada cashed the check in Garryowen, bought some gas, and went on his way. Only later did I discover he cashed the check in Billings, more than 60 miles away.

The next day I had one of the museum interns take an inventory of the new items. She placed the buttons and the buckle with others of the same style in a tackle box I used to organize similar small artifacts. I asked her to be certain to place the new items in a separate compartment away from the authentic buttons. Because I was not sure of the provenance of the new ones, I did not want them to get mixed in with the original period artifacts.

Weeks slipped by and the new year came and went. Then, in early 2005, I began receiving calls from a U.S. soldier's father who was insistent he get his hands on an authentic 7th Cavalry button from the battlefield. It is my impression that the public does not realize that the United States 7th Cavalry did not disband when mounted horse troops became obsolete in warfare. The regiment has lived on as an integral part of the American military. Although no longer on horseback, troopers in the 7th Cavalry were heavily involved in World War II, the occupation of Japan, the Korean War, the Vietnam War, Operation Desert Storm, Operation Iraqi Freedom, and eventually Operation Enduring Freedom.

In fact, during the second Iraq campaign, the 7th Cavalry, 3rd Squadron, was the spearhead and the screening force for the main elements of the U.S. 3rd Infantry Division. The 3rd Squadron engaged the enemy earlier and more often in the war than any other unit. Battling both the Iraqi Republican Guard and the Fedayeen Saddam, the 7th captured Baghdad and then transitioned to stabilization operations. By the time the squadron redeployed, the unit had killed 2,200 Iraqi personnel, demolished 64 tanks, 41 armored vehicles, and numerous active air defense systems; and destroyed countless civilian vehicles used by suicide bombers.

When the 7th Cavalry was formed in 1866, its official nickname became "Garryowen," after one of Custer's favorite songs, which was also adopted as its marching tune because he liked the cadence. Due to that connection, I have tried in all my years owning the town of Garryowen to make it a special place for those who have served. I have hosted individuals from the current 7th Cavalry and Special

Operations units, including those who served during the Benghazi attacks on the United States embassy in Libya in 2012. Having such an intimate connection with the regiment, I was more than willing to listen to this father's plea.

I plucked the phone from its cradle after my office assistant forwarded the call to me. Before I could get out a greeting, I was cut off by a bellowing overly excited voice.

"Hi! Is this Garryowen?" the voice blurted.

"Yes, this is Chris Kortlander. I'm the mayor and owner of the town of Garryowen and the Custer Battlefield Museum," I replied.

"I'm so glad to reach you. I'm just so happy that I found someone like you. See, my son is fighting in Iraq right now. It's his second tour, and I really wanted to get something special for him. You know, for his service. He's in the 7th Cavalry."

"I would love to help," was all I could say before I was cut short again.

"Well, I saw that you sold antiques and stuff from the Little Bighorn fight, and I really was hoping to get my hands on a 7th Cav button. You know, one of those from the battle that has some real history behind it. I think it will really make my son's day."

"Well," I said. "I think I can find something for you…"

"I'll pay whatever you want! I just would really like it for my son. You know, for his service to our country," he interrupted, reiterating his point.

In the moment, I thought it was odd a father would want to purchase something from a losing command. Wouldn't that be bad luck? That was my initial gut feeling. One I should have listened to.

"Right, for your son's service," I said, reassuring him. "I will put one of our buttons on my eBay auction site. I'll make sure you are the winning bid. Are you aware of my online business?"

"Oh, totally!" he blurted. "I know all about your business. That's where I thought of this idea after I saw you had all that great Old West stuff."

I couldn't help but feel a little annoyed by the man. He seemed overzealous almost to the point of being extremely anxious. During our conversation, the man was so enthusiastic I had the feeling he might just burst through the receiver.

"All right, all right," I continued. "I'll get a hold of a nice item and put it on the auction block for you."

"Oh wow! Man, that's just great. I really appreciate it. You know I'll pay anything that you need me to. I just want it for my son."

"Okay, don't worry. I'll get it up there. Just keep your eyes peeled."

"Okay, great!" he said emphatically.

We exchanged information about what his bidding contact name would be so I could make sure he received what he wanted. He thanked me profusely again, mentioning his son, and then hung up the phone. As I nestled the receiver back into its cradle, I instructed my office assistant to place the proper button online, gave her the man's bidding info, and told her to accept the bid from him. She walked over to the tackle box I kept in my office and extracted a 7th Cavalry button from it.

Within the following week, she placed the button for sale on eBay and the man bought it through the "best offer" option. After it was mailed to him, I thought that would be the last I'd hear of it. But within a few days, most likely the moment the button was received via the U.S. Postal Service, I received another call from him. He was just as jumpy and excited as he'd been in our first conversation. Excitedly, he told me his son loved the button and several of his 7th Cavalry buddies wanted similar ones. I went through an almost identical conversation as before and assured him I would put the items online for him to buy.

A few weeks went by, and I simply forgot about our conversation. I was swamped with more important transactions and the daily duties of running my town. It was also getting close to the busiest season of the year, and I wanted to be sure the museum and trading post were prepared for the hundreds of thousands of tourists who would be coming to town. My forgetfulness and attention to other pressing matters led to several hounding phone calls by the man.

He implored me multiple times to sell him three buttons that were authentic 7th Cavalry, and he acted quite upset when he found I had not put them on eBay. Annoyed by the constant calls, I instructed my office assistant once again to fish through the tackle box and find the requested buttons. She pulled out three buttons and listed them on eBay, with an end for the online auction later in the week.

All the sales ended with the man getting his buttons. Later in the same week the auctions ended, I was asked to take part in a radio show in Hardin on March 31, 2005. The radio producers asked me to discuss my recent award of being named Tourism Person of the Year in Montana. This was also the day I was to meet BLM agent Bart Fitzgerald in Garryowen to get a list of items that had been pilfered from museums in hopes I might recognize some of them.

I forgot that I had made an appointment with him, and did the radio show instead. As I finished the radio interview, my cellular phone nearly exploded in my pocket as it rang nonstop. Pressing the receiver to my ear, I heard the frantic voice of Putt. In a frightened, wavering voice, he said, "Chris, you have to get down here right now! The BLM is raiding Garryowen! The whole town is surrounded!" At first, I thought Putt was playing an early April Fools' joke on me.

Almost laughing, I said, "Are you BS-ing me?"

In a stone-cold tone, Putt responded, "This is for real. You've got to get here right away!"

Shocked, I felt my stomach hitch and I nearly lost my breakfast. Before I could ask Putt what was happening, I was accosted by an angry voice. A voice I would never forget.

"This is special agent Brian Cornell with the Bureau of Land Management!" the voice screamed. "You need to give us the keypad combinations to your doors or we're going to use a battering ram and break them down!"

"Please," I frantically pleaded. "Please don't do that. I'm in Hardin right now for a radio interview. Just give me 30 minutes and I will be there. Please don't destroy anything."

"You better get your ass down here now! If you're not here in 30 minutes, we're going to tear this place apart!"

"All right, all right, I'll be there," I said.

With that, he hung up. I thanked the radio hosts and I rushed for my truck. As I sped down the road, the all-too-familiar and horrible feelings crept back into my mind. My home and my property were under assault again. This time, however, it wasn't a raging inferno threatening to demolish everything I owned; it was agents of the federal government.

I could barely control my emotions as I raced toward Garryowen. My heart was beating out of my chest, and the trip seemed to pass in a blur. On the way, I dialed my lawyer, Sol Neuhardt. I hurriedly informed him of the situation, and he told me to keep him abreast of everything. As I turned off the road and into the parking lot of the Custer Battlefield Museum, the sight I saw shook me to the core.

5

The Bones of Little Girls

Like a scene coming to life out of the dystopian future described in George Orwell's *1984*, I saw a host of black-clad federal agents in hiked-up jackboots swarming Garryowen. It was total chaos. Storm troopers run amok sent by an all-powerful central government. The deep state entrenched. Some of the agents' faces were masked in riot helmets with the letters "FBI" and "BLM" scrawled across the backs of their flak jackets in large white block letters.

They had Garryowen surrounded by black Suburbans and vans. I counted 14 vehicles. One of the agents saw me drive up and recognized me. He waved me through the barricaded town. As I exited my truck, a militant federal officer gripping a steel black M-16 automatic rifle accosted me.

It is interesting to note at this point that agent Bart Fitzgerald wrote an article a few months before this raid, asking people to check for items and artifacts pilfered from local and regional museums and archives. To be a good citizen, I responded to the request by calling and asking the Billings BLM office for a list of recovered items. I did this for two reasons. First, I wanted to see if I recognized any of the pilfered artifacts, which I may have seen at trade shows and among the offerings of other dealers. Second, I wanted to make sure none of the items were from the Custer battlefield.

Fitzgerald and I set up a meeting on the day of the raid so he could give me the list. I completely forgot about the meeting and double-booked the radio show that day by mistake. The brutal reality of the situation is there was never any such list. It was all an elaborate ruse Fitzgerald used so he and his heavily armed BLM agents could catch me in Garryowen. They had planned the raid and planted the article from the very beginning.

"Kortlander's here!" the officer bellowed into the microphone attached to his Motorola radio, alerting the multitude of officers swarming the premises. Whipping his head around, he asked if I had any weapons. Nervously, I answered no. In a flash, he abruptly tore me from the truck and proceeded to commence with a head-to-toe pat-down search. Afterward, he informed me that he was going to search my truck. I thought, "Search my truck? I didn't give him consent. He can't do that without my consent." Apparently, that didn't matter to anyone.

After roughly escorting me toward the trading post and instructing me to remain perfectly still, the black-clad minion began rummaging through my vehicle. Watching his movements through the truck windshield, I could see papers and my belongings being flung about the cab. The entire process gave me the feeling that I was the most wanted criminal in the state of Montana. Perhaps even in the entire country. I got gooseflesh and my neck hair stood at attention; this was all a sickening nightmare from which I could not wake. After finding nothing of interest, the agent sprung from my truck, slammed the door, and snatched my arm, whisking me into the trading post.

After being hustled into the building, I saw Putt Thompson, Fred Oyebi, and Lucinda Small (employees of the Garryowen Trading Post) standing behind the service counter. All three had been present when the agents arrived. They had all been detained and held at gunpoint. Later, I learned Putt received the same aggressive pat-down and questioning about weapons that I did.

When my three employees were detained, they were interrogated for at least 25 minutes by agent Cornell. He questioned them in a Gestapo-type manner, ordering them to divulge any information regarding the whereabouts of the keys for the locked doors in the museum and my adjoining residence. Cornell told the three of them that if they did not produce the keys, he would instruct his men to break all the doors down. According to my staff, Cornell repeated this statement multiple times, barking the order into their faces. After the intense interrogation, he ordered them to stay at the front counter of the trading post until he released them. As I was shuffled past the employees, I saw terror etched across their faces. An agent with light brown hair and a medium build confronted me. My instinct told me this man was Special Agent Brian Cornell.

Seething, Cornell informed me that he had a federal search warrant and thrust the document in my face. With all the chaos going on around me, I told myself to take a moment to gather my thoughts. After gulping down a deep breath, I took the warrant from Cornell and reviewed it. As I did, I realized it was not for the whole complex. Reading the specifics of the warrant, I noted that my residence and other areas in Garryowen were not on the document. In short, it authorized the agents to search only the store and the Custer Battlefield Museum for two buttons, suspender buckles, and computer records and invoices, but not the rest of my property.

Cornell and a second man, Joe Waller from the Office of Inspector General, brought me to the office in the trading post at the rear of the store, shoving me along as they kept their hands on my back. As we were about to enter the office, I glanced into the adjoining hallway leading to my home above the trading post. As I did, I saw a BLM agent standing at the wide-open door to my residence. The door is an expensive steel one with an electronic push-button combination lock and an automatic door closer. The agent propped it open and I witnessed he and others freely going up the stairs.

At the time, I was not aware who had opened the door, but I later found out that James Fowler, a Custer Battlefield Museum volunteer intern, either let the agents in or was coerced into divulging the combination to them. From there, the raiding party gained access to not only my private home but to the basement, where my vault is located. All of this was done without my consent and without any legal authority through a warrant.

After I was shoved inside the office and the door was thrown shut, I said, "What the hell is this all about? Why are you raiding me?"

As Cornell nosed around my office and thumbed through my personal papers, a ghoulish smirk etched its way across his face. "I'll let you know when the time is right," he replied.

"What the hell does that mean?" I fired back. "Your search warrant lists two buttons, suspender buckles, and computer records with invoices! Not my residence or anything else on my property. You're searching areas you have no legal authority to search. I know my rights!"

Outraged at being caught over a technicality, Cornell realized he would need my permission to continue his witch hunt throughout the facility. Dropping the papers he was picking through, Cornell glared at me and pounded his fist on the desk.

"We need you to sign a consent form," he bellowed.

"For what?" I asked.

"We need you to sign a consent form to clear the whole property for security purposes!"

"Security purposes?"

"Just sign the goddamn consent form, Kortlander!" Cornell fumed.

"Look, I am here with the Office of Inspector General and am acting as backup assistance," agent Waller quickly cut in, seeing his fellow officer flying off the handle. "Agent Cornell is here with the Bureau of Land Management, and we are investigating some suspected malfeasance."

"What malfeasance?" I said.

"Look, Kortlander," Cornell venomously interjected again, sidling up alongside Waller. "You can cooperate with us and make our job easier. Or you can refuse and we'll just break all your doors down. It's up to you."

"This consent is for a security walk-through to make sure no one else is on the property," said Waller.

I sat for a few minutes in silence, contemplating my options. Sitting there with Cornell standing over me nearly foaming at the mouth, I heard the massive number of agents upstairs stomping through my home and businesses. I felt my heart drop to my shoe. I had a sick feeling that my life was over. How had I gotten to a point where federal agents armed with long rifles were in my secured residence? After sitting in awkward silence for what felt like an eternity, I finally uttered, "Let me call my lawyer."

Blowing out a stiff guffaw, Cornell spun round and stomped out of the office in a huff. Waller followed. I watched them both proceed to huddle with Bart Fitzgerald and others. After conferring for a few minutes, Waller returned to the office and once again told me to sign the consent form. It was almost comical. As if somehow in the few moments when these federal agents were pooling their thoughts, they could get me to change my mind. If I had not been under stress and afraid, I might have laughed. Instead, I emphatically responded, "I want to talk to my attorney, and that is all I'm going to do right now."

Waller made a motion to the rest of the agents standing outside the office, letting them know I would not comply with signing the consent form and I wanted to lawyer up. An angry Cornell came into the office, withdrew a cell phone from his pocket, and dropped it on the desk in front of me.

"You can use this phone, but you cannot leave this office," he growled.

"I don't know his number by heart. I need a phone book," I said.

Clearly pissed, Cornell stomped out of the office, returned with a phone book, and tossed it on the desk next to me. "Need anything else?" he asked.

Without responding, I picked up the phone as Cornell hovered over me. Sweating, shaking, and without my reading glasses, I had a hard time finding my attorney's number. Meanwhile, Cornell was growing more and more impatient with the knowledge that he and his men were violating my constitutional guarantees by violating the search warrant. He desperately needed my permission for his men to continue their search in places not covered on the warrant.

While I thumbed through the phone book, Cornell began grilling me about the corporate structure of Garryowen. I told him the Custer Battlefield Museum was a non-profit 501(c)(3) corporation with myself as president. Cornell asked about the structure of my other corporations as well. All the while he was interrogating me, Joe Waller, who had re-entered the room, frantically scribbled notes on a yellow lined pad of paper. I told them the other corporations, which included Historical Rarities Inc. (HRI), had me as the only corporate officer. I also identified Historical Land Preservation Inc., and informed them it conducted business as Garryowen Subway and Garryowen Conoco.

I further explained that Historic Land Preservation Inc. was the operating identity for the town of Garryowen. I informed them how HRI supports the activities of the nonprofit museum, so the museum can continue to exist financially. Detailing the nuances of my businesses, I told them how HRI loans the museum money earned by selling historical rarities. HRI has made many financial and artifact loans to the Custer Battlefield Museum to keep it afloat and financially solvent, and to put pieces on display in the museum that the museum could not afford, for the general public's benefit.

While informing them about my business interests, I continued to search the phone book for my attorney's number. Becoming irritated with my lack of progress, Cornell snapped, "Give me the phone book. I'll find the number for you." I did and he quickly paged through it. Finding the number, he snatched the cell from my hand and dialed the number. When it rang, he shoved the phone back into my trembling hand.

My attorney, Sol Neuhardt, answered on the second ring and I told him what was transpiring and about the consent form. Instead of discussing the implications of the consent form, Neuhardt quizzed me about anything illegal on the property. He specifically mentioned illegal drugs or any other type of contraband. I vehemently denied owning anything illegal, and Neuhardt instructed me to comply with the officers and sign the consent form.

Not wanting to make the federal officers any angrier than they already were, and not wanting to have the doors on my property destroyed or go against my attorney's instructions, I reluctantly agreed to sign. I told Cornell to give me the pen, and I signed the consent to search for the buttons and suspender buckles...or so I thought. This would turn out to be a crucial mistake.

Neuhardt was not the man I thought he was. In 2011, he was accused of having sexual relations with a client, an offense that he was also disciplined for in 2007.[1] This may not have been a criminal offense, but it was an ethical offense. He was an out-of-control attorney who thought he was above the law. In fact, in 2014, Neuhardt was suspended and later disbarred for misusing client funds.[2] The violations regarding client funds combined with his prior offenses warranted his disbarment.

After signing the consent to search, I explained I had a small quantity of medicinal marijuana, which was legal for me to possess, on the premises. About 20 minutes after I signed the "security walk-through consent form," Cornell and Waller came back to me, explaining they had made a mistake and did not have the right areas on the warrant they felt they needed to search.

Once again, agent Cornell aggressively got in my face and intimidated me into agreeing to sign a federal general search consent form. Cornell told me if I did not sign the form, it would cause the federal government to spend more money. He said this would anger the federal judge who had initially signed the warrant and would cause him to give me a harsher jail sentence. Out of total fear and in the face of Cornell's belligerent intimidation, I reluctantly signed.

As I signed, my mind was flooded with questions. Why would I get "more" jail time? What had I done wrong in the first place? No matter what, I was automatically guilty? My thoughts were a confused jumble. My life was passing in front of my eyes in slow motion. The earth and reality seemed a million miles away. I urge anyone in a similar situation to call a reputable lawyer immediately before consenting to anything.

While all this happened, I was told I could not leave the office, and an armed federal agent was assigned to stand guard over me. At one point, I asked the agent if I could go to the bathroom. After consulting with Cornell via radio, he okayed it. The federal agent followed me to the restroom and stood outside the door. When finished, I was escorted back to the office and told to sit down and shut up.

Waller and Cornell, after coming in and out of the office multiple times, explained to me they thought I was fraudulently selling historic artifacts reportedly found on the Custer battlefield. The two men insinuated that I had purchased three buttons and a suspender buckle from one of their undercover agents during the third week of December 2004, and that those items were never identified as being from the Custer battlefield when sold to me.

In that moment, I realized the man I had unwittingly helped in the dead of winter to buy gas for his broken-down Chevy was an undercover agent sent to entrap me in a sting operation. I also learned this operation was two years in the planning. When asked, I told Cornell I did not recall the story I had been given about the artifacts when I bought them. However, in the months of anguish that followed, I had an opportunity to remember the details. I did remember that following my encounter with the undercover agent, the artifacts were inadvertently commingled with identical buttons known to be from the Custer battlefield.

The planted microdotted eagle buttons I had purchased from the undercover agent were essentially identical to those issued to the 7th Cavalry and other Indian Wars military personnel. The minor discrepancy here was that these buttons were not 7th Cavalry and therefore had nothing to do with the Battle of the Little Bighorn. During our conversation, Cornell informed me that the buttons and suspender buckle I had purchased from Zapada were marked with microdots.

After telling me about the microscopic markings, Cornell accused me of knowingly selling false artifacts and getting rich from it. I told

Cornell that a mix-up happens occasionally; with the large number of items I sell, sometimes there is a mistake with orders. I told him I had completed more than 13,000 eBay auctions, so of course there would be the occasional errors in shipment. I assured Cornell I always corrected any discrepancies with an order. In addition, I told him I have always offered a lifetime full-refund guarantee for any problems encountered, which has always been published on my website. He wasn't interested in my explanation.

With a beet-red face, Cornell screamed, "I know you're lying, and I know you have done this on purpose! You're getting rich off this scheme, and you're lining your pockets with cash!"

"Don't put words in my mouth!" I yelled back. "This was not an intentional act! We're talking about a button! A button no bigger than a thumbnail; it's insane that this is being turned into a federal crime!"

Part of an element of a crime is intent. If there is no intent to defraud, there is no crime. I never had any intent to defraud anyone with any of my historical items.

Frustrated by my answers, Cornell returned to his diatribe about my supposed intention to use false documentation for historical artifacts for personal profit and gain. I denied this again, stating that apparently it had been a simple and honest mistake.

Then, as if flipping a switch, Cornell became quiet and reserved, then leaned in so close to my face that I caught a whiff of his stale breath. He then hissed, "I'm the one you spoke to on the phone about the buttons, so quit lying to me."

Cornell went on to accuse me of deaccessioning materials from the museum collection and selling them on the open market. I feel it is important for me to address this accusation. From time to time, I displayed battle-related buttons from my personal collection in the museum; these buttons were legally purchased from owners of fee lands on the Custer battlefield. By rotating this private stock through museum exhibits, I was later able to sell the pieces with an accurate statement saying they had been on display in the Custer Battlefield Museum. It was a small benefit for my Historical Rarities Inc.

business, especially after financing many of the Custer Battlefield Museum displays with my personal funds.

I wanted to cooperate with the federal agents during the raid, and I did not want to offend a federal judge, as had been threatened by Cornell. I did everything I could to help, hoping for a quick resolution of the matter. During the entire ordeal, however, I was never read my Miranda rights. This was another clear violation of the law. I was obviously detained and *not* free to leave.

Switching subjects, Cornell asked, "Is there any contraband in the building?"

"There is some medical marijuana in my home that I don't believe is contraband. I have a permit, so it is legal. It's for my spinal condition," I replied.

I have had four spinal surgeries and can anticipate more as my condition worsens. I suffer from a chronic ailment—Ehlers-Danlos syndrome (EDS)—that was eventually diagnosed during the federal investigation following the raid. EDS is a group of inherited connective tissue disorders, caused by a DNA defect that affects the synthesis of collagen (a protein in connective tissue). The collagen in connective tissue helps the tissue to resist deformation. It is the "glue" that holds the body together.

In the skin, muscles, ligaments, blood vessels, visceral organs, and spinal discs, collagen plays a very significant role by increasing elasticity. Without sufficient or healthy collagen, spinal discs flatten and collapse. Then bone rests upon bone, causing intense pain and discomfort throughout the body.

Depending on the individual mutation, the severity of the syndrome can vary from mild to life-threatening. Mine happens to be the worst kind. There is no cure or treatment. Corrective surgery may help me with some of the problems that develop in certain types of EDS. The condition dictates that extra caution is advised and that I must observe some special practices to get through daily life.

Rather than depend on doctor-prescribed opioids for pain relief, which would have muddled my brain and made it impossible to run my businesses, I sought and received state approval for the use of medical marijuana. I told Cornell I had my medical marijuana permit paperwork from the Health and Human Services Department of the state of Montana.

He responded by yelling, "*Where is the pot?*"

"It's in a secure spot in my home in a zippered pouch," I said.

"Are there any booby traps, or anything else that might hurt or injure my officers?" Cornell questioned.

"No," I said, almost shocked at the accusation.

Cornell instructed the agents to rip into my medicine chest, and they tossed out all my prescription medications on the bed and photographed them. I asked agent Cornell what would happen to the medical marijuana. Cornell told me his boss, Bart Fitzgerald, was not interested in it and would not charge me with possession of such a small amount (a 35mm film canister, not half full). Many months later, the United States attorney threatened me with 30 years in prison as a habitual addict while in possession of firearms. This was one of nine federal felonies I was threatened with following this raid. When they tore through my prescriptions, Cornell accused me of prescription shopping.

I explained to him about the nature of my degenerative spinal disease. I also told him I didn't like taking pills, but as my disease progressed, it paralyzed me and became extremely painful. Often, it was so debilitating that I needed polio crutches to get around. Cornell brushed off my explanation by responding, "Sounds like prescription shopping to me."

Cornell continued to be in my face. It was a position where he took the most comfort. He said, "Rhoda is facing prison time, and she's looking at a long stretch. If you cooperate, I'll see what I can do for her."

Rhoda Elkins was my administrative assistant at the time; among other duties, she helped me list items for the internet auctions. I told agent Cornell that Rhoda simply input information that she was given for the eBay auctions. I went on to explain that she had nothing to do with the sale in question and had no idea about my corporate finances or how I obtained items for the collections.

There were several agents coming in and out of the office as Cornell continued to browbeat me. The agents had questions about locked drawers in my back office, and I cooperated by opening them. For some reason, whenever the agents wanted to enter the office area they would yell, "Mr. Kortlander is with me. Let us know when we can enter."

Cornell began to question me about my basement walk-in vault, a very large bank vault from the 1940s with a massive, heavy door. He and his fellow federal agents had once again failed to put the basement of the main building on the search warrant. Cornell incessantly threatened me, saying, "If you don't open the vault, I will call a locksmith with an acetylene torch and destroy the vault door to gain access."

Keeping in mind I had already signed a general consent to search, I thought this would be the perfect time to revoke the consent, since I knew I already had given him carte blanche. I told him, "I revoke the consent," but Cornell told me that the paper had already been signed and it was a done deal. It is publicly not well understood that it is a felony to lie to a federal agent. But it is not a crime, nor are there consequences, when a federal law enforcement agent lies to you.

Feeling forced into submission, I approached the door and fumbled around in my mind for the combination. After coming up with it, I turned the dial and heard a click after aligning all the tumblers. I gave the wheel knob a spin and turned the adjoining large handle, opening the door. When the door swung open, I felt it was symbolic of my last defenses being wrenched open and laid bare. At this point, I had had all I could take. I was at my wit's end, and I began to tear up. I could hear some agents snickering and full-out laughing as I opened the vault in tears.

Cornell and a bevy of other agents escorted me into the vault. Among the items inside were some unidentified bones that had been found in 1996 during the excavation and construction of Garryowen. After their discovery, I sent them to Dr. Douglas Scott, then an archaeologist with the National Park Service and the author of *Archaeological Perspectives on the Battle of the Little Bighorn*, to make sure they were not human remains. This was done to satisfy Native American Graves Protection and Repatriation Act requirements. Dr. Scott returned the bones to me with a letter identifying them as small animal bones.

When they saw the bones, the jackbooted raiders immediately seized upon them. I told the agents about Dr. Scott and how he had authored two important books on archaeology and artifacts from the Custer battlefield, and was employed by the Department of the Interior. I also told them that I still had his letter, written on DOI stationery, confirming the bones were those of an animal. They immediately scoffed at me, and with an elevated voice, one of them exclaimed, "We don't know any Douglas Scott!"

Once again, my explanations did not matter. While in the vault, U.S. Fish and Wildlife Service agent Doug Gossman snatched the bones from their perch on a top shelf and waved them three inches in front of my face, screaming, "These are little girl bones! Where is she buried?" Gossman had a smirk on his face and kept repeating the statement over and over. Several agents were outside the vault, and one was inside videotaping. Cornell chuckled as he persisted with his harassment.

Gossman eventually cast aside the bones and set his sights on yet another item he thought he could humiliate me with. He drew a bead on my medicine bundles and snatched a pair of them up. "*Where did you get these?*" he screamed.

Medicine bundles are wrapped collections of sacred items, held by designated carriers, used in Indian ceremonial cultures. They can contain many types of items thought to be sacred, such as feathers, small animal carcasses, and even peyote. In some American Indian tribes, medicine bundles are believed to have supernatural powers and to be alive—these bundles are believed to have a heartbeat. Some bundles are controlled by the tribe or a main medicine man. In the Crow tribe, individuals own the bundles. Under the Native American Graves Protection and Repatriation Act (NAGPRA), it is illegal to buy or sell them. But if a bundle is owned individually, it is considered private property, and it is not illegal to possess one if it does not contain post-act eagle feathers or peyote.

I tried to explain that many items were left at the museum by individuals, some anonymously, which was the case with the medicine bundles in my vault. I further explained that when Native Americans convert to Christianity, they are instructed to shed their medicine bundles because they do not need such physical items to have direct contact with God. The Crow know that I have a secure facility. So, in the past, some have left medicine bundles with me to keep them intact and preserved for future generations. Again, the agents were not interested in my explanation.

Changing the subject, Grossman questioned me about where the eagle feather war bonnet in the museum had come from. I explained it was from the Spear family and had originally belonged to Chief Little Wolf. The Spears obtained it directly from the Little Wolf family in the 1930s. I explained, that I, as the director of the Custer Battlefield Museum, had required Brad Spears to complete the proper IRS documentation for the donation of the bonnet. Grossman responded by saying, "That's a felony, Kortlander! You're going to be doing hard time in a federal pen! I hope you like the inside of a cell!"

Receiving donated feathers acquired before the Bald and Golden Eagle Protection Act is a legal practice among Native American and Western museums in the United States, and there is plenty of federal case law to back this up.

Grossman went on to say, "You're not an attorney! The good news is that I'm not going to smash all your cases in the museum and take your bonnets. Do not move anything outside of this museum; it is part of a crime scene."

Grossman then asked about a footlocker that contained articles of Laban Little Wolf's. I explained that this specific collection had been exhibited for three years at the Gene Autry Western Heritage Museum in Los Angeles, and had been exhibited at the former Custer

Battlefield Museum (now the Little Bighorn National Monument) on Last Stand Hill as well.

Almost as soon as I finished defending myself against Grossman, two agents burst into the vault informing Cornell they had found two oversized firecrackers (M-500s) in my bedroom. One was seven inches long, the other 10 inches long. When asked where they came from, I told the agents that every Fourth of July, Indians on the reservation built these fireworks and I traditionally received one as a birthday gift. In fact, one of the firecrackers had the words "Happy Birthday, Kortlander" written on it.

The interrogation did not stop there, however. Cornell asked why I had confidential Bureau of Indian Affairs law enforcement manuals in my office. I told him I could produce a letter signed by former federal BIA chief of police Darren Cruzan authorizing me to help start a BIA/tribal reserve police program. Cruzan had given me the manuals for that purpose. When Cruzan left his position as the supervisory special agent at the Crow reservation and a new chief of police was appointed, this reserve police department never materialized.

To add injury to insult, on the morning of the raid, the BLM had contacted Big Horn County sheriff Larson Medicine Horse and advised him that the raid was about to occur. The BLM agent asked for a county deputy to be part of the raid team, and he agreed to send one, which is done as a professional courtesy when one department is within another department's jurisdiction. After assigning the deputy to the raid team, Medicine Horse immediately contacted the press to alert them of the raid and to send someone to Garryowen to cover the story.

After I left the radio station that morning, Rich Solberg, who was conducting the interview, left to attend a regular meeting of the Big Horn County commissioners. While there, he saw Larson Medicine Horse, who passed him a note alerting him to the raid at Garryowen. Medicine Horse had been my opponent, spreading malicious and false rumors in the last election. It would be correct to believe that both bureaucratic and Indian politics were fueling the federal assault on Garryowen.

Also at the time of the raid, agent Cornell and members of his investigative team told Medicine Horse that I was a grave robber. While the raid was still in progress, Medicine Horse called Deputy (and former judge) Debbie Winburn into his office. He gleefully told her that the bones of a Native American had been found in my vault. He also reiterated that I was a grave robber and that I was out digging up Indian graves to obtain artifacts for my own enrichment.

I believe that complaints from Jason Pitsch and/or Robert Nightengale spurred the raid on my businesses. The complaints, as reported in the application for the 2005 search warrant, alleged that I "was selling artifacts purported to have been recovered from the battlefield where the infamous Battle of the Little Bighorn took place." The BLM implied that possessing or selling items from the battlefield is illegal and worthy of investigation. The fact is, selling artifacts from privately owned land that happens to be part of the Little Bighorn battlefield is in no way illegal.

The battlefield is an area of land amounting to more than 15 square miles. The area of the national monument is barely one square mile, with the remainder being a jumble of tribal, private, trust, and commercial fee lands, and farms and ranches. The number of competing laws and regulations on any acre of ground is staggering.

The BLM, through agent Brian Cornell and through the search warrant application, advised the federal district court in Billings, Montana, that Cornell and the BLM believed the reports (the complaints) they had received, and that they had determined further investigation was warranted. It should be noted, however, that no violation of any federal law was alleged in the reports. There was only an allegation that I was selling artifacts. As any specific allegation of a crime—any crime—was lacking, the conclusion is that BLM law enforcement in Montana had a proclivity to simply go after me.

In the application for the search warrant, the BLM also told the same court that I advertised that I bought, sold, and appraised artifacts. Again, these are completely legal activities, but the BLM implied that something was happening that was improper or even illegal. The federal agent even reported that I "accepted walk-in sellers of artifacts," a statement that was attributed to a former business associate. Again, this is all legal activity.

Reviewing the button count between 2003 and 2005, I found that three buttons were sold and delivered to the person (a federal agent) on the phone who had pressed me to sell them on eBay. No false certifications were delivered, and no crime was committed, unless you suspect the BLM of making false statements and following illegal entrapment procedures.

The BLM obtained a search warrant asserting that I "knowingly [tried to] defraud, or devise a scheme to defraud, using wire in interstate commerce or through the mail." The problem with this portion of the search warrant is that the facts alleged did not demonstrate that any crime had been committed.

The only truth is that the BLM and its agents, including agent in charge Bart Fitzgerald and Special Agent Brian Cornell, created their own scheme to entrap me. It is interesting to note that in *Sorrels vs. United States* (287 U.S. 435, 451), a Supreme Court case unanimously reversed a conviction, citing the controlling question as "whether the defendant is a person otherwise innocent whom the government is seeking to punish for an alleged offense which is the product of the creative activity of its own officials." The government's scheme and the allegations that resulted would be things I would end up fighting for the better part of the next decade.

6

The Smoke Clears

Immediately following the raid, the ramifications of the event began to take their toll. One of the first calamities that befell me was that my business line of credit at the Little Horn State Bank was recalled. This occurred because the government convened a federal grand jury, which issued a subpoena for records from the Little Horn State Bank. Immediately following the publicity of the raid and the issuance of the subpoena, the bank sent a letter notifying me of the grand jury subpoena. The bank alerted me they would not renew the note, thus terminating my line of credit. The feds were effectively putting pressure on me. Without an arrest or even charges, they had upped the ante. I cannot begin to tell you how great the financial, as well as the emotional, stress was.

Rescinding the line of credit nearly destroyed my livelihood. I was forced to scramble and utilize noncommercial friendships to obtain the funds I needed to pay back the bank loan. The fallout, however, did not end there. During the years of my battle with the feds, several incidents occurred that were directly part of the federal government's plan to sabotage my business and destroy my sanity as I attempted to defend myself against their insidious and scurrilous accusations.

As their investigation began to rage like the fires in Malibu that had nearly claimed my life, government agents told many of the people I had done business with that I engaged in criminal activity. Some friends of mine were intimidated and encouraged to speak negatively about me in the press. Numerous federal agents spoke publicly and privately about the investigation, further impugning my character and disparaging my reputation.

Repaying the Little Horn State Bank placed a considerable and unnecessary strain on my business and personal friendships while jeopardizing my creditworthiness. I had to impose on personal friendships, placing a $500,000 second mortgage on the town of Garryowen that continues to accrue interest to this day.

During this investigation, all my complex business activities were scrutinized in an exhaustive federal audit. The federal agents seized computers and, with grand jury subpoenas, they also seized my bank records, thereby examining every aspect of my life. Through this process, however, I could solidify my defense by proving that every corporation was up to snuff on its bookkeeping, payroll taxes, and every other aspect of its business activities. Throughout the entire process, the feds were unable to find any unlawful practices.

Seeing as my previous attorneys had failed me in one way or another, I sought out one more attorney under the direction of Timer Moses. Charles "Timer" Moses was a successful, tenacious criminal defense attorney. He was widely recognized and well known across the region. One of his more notable clients was Tony Boyle, former United Mine Workers president, in the 1970s. He defended Boyle against charges that he had arranged for the murders of a union rival and his family. Boyle was eventually convicted and spent the rest of his life in prison.

I eventually befriended Moses after his retirement. He was a mentor to me, and we often met at his home. He treated me like a son. Timer pushed me in the direction of one of the greatest criminal defense attorneys in the area, Penelope (Penny) Strong. I credit Penny with being the person who kept me from giving up.

As anyone who has mistakenly been accused of a crime knows, it can be easy to agree to a guilty plea out of fear of being wrongfully found guilty and receiving a harsher sentence. On three occasions, I pleaded with Penny to enter a guilty plea for me so I wouldn't unjustly be given the harshest sentence the feds had threatened. Each time, Penny strongly counseled me not to confess to a crime that I did not commit. Both Timer and Penny encouraged me to keep fighting for what was right. I am grateful that they stood with me through my journey of being wrongfully accused.

In 2007, during the criminal audit, I received a phone call from the Herbert Hoover Presidential Library. The library president told me they were going to feature an exhibit called "History's Mysteries," named after a show on the History channel. One of the eight historical mysteries they were going to focus on was the Battle of the Little Bighorn. They requested a museum-to-museum loan between the Custer Battlefield Museum and their institution. For six months, beginning in March 2007, 10 historic Native American artifacts were loaned by me and the Custer Battlefield Museum to the Herbert Hoover Presidential Library, including John Sitting Bull's eagle feather war bonnet.

This library is one of only seven presidential libraries funded and operated by the federal government through the National Archive and Records Administration. The library arranged to have the borrowed items shipped and insured, with a declared value of about $1.5 million on the entire loan, including about a $40,000 value on the eagle feather war bonnet alone. It is interesting to note that it is a federal crime for a financial consideration to be placed upon eagle feathers or items containing eagle feathers, but this federal institution did it anyway without there being any legal ramifications.

As the war bonnet made its way to the Hoover library, I continued to fight a looming federal indictment. The cost of defending against the threat-filled federal prosecution was staggering. A draft of a proposed indictment alleged nine serious felonies and multiple misdemeanors, the combination of which would see me serving a maximum of 89 years in a federal prison.

Fighting these allegations caused me to incur tens of thousands of dollars in attorney's fees. In addition, I was advised to secure a minimum of a quarter of a million dollars for a defense fund, in anticipation of an impending federal indictment. Seeking additional financing, I decided to sell the township of Garryowen, including much of my personal property. In 2006, I contacted a nationally known auction company—Heritage Auctions, located in Dallas—for that purpose.

Gary Hendershott, a friend and dealer in historical collectibles, worked at Heritage Auctions and was head of the Western Americana department. He traveled to Garryowen to inspect the premises and review the items I wanted to sell. After the arrangements for the auction of Garryowen were finalized, much of my personal property was auctioned off. However, an auction for the facilities and premises of Garryowen, as well as other personal items, never occurred. It is my belief that the federal government, to bankrupt me, thwarted the sale of Garryowen and blocked the auction house from following through with its commitments.

In 2008, I filed a federal lawsuit against Heritage Auctions for breach of contract and fraudulent business practices, which amounted to a civil RICO (Racketeer Influenced and Corrupt Organizations Act) action. During the discovery stage of that lawsuit, it was alleged that federal agents had contacted Heritage Auctions employees and upper management. In their communications with Heritage Auctions, several federal agents made libelous and fraudulent statements concerning me and the assets I was attempting to sell.[1]

Special Agent Brian Cornell once again slithered out from under his government rock and traveled to Dallas between November 2008 and August 2009, continuing his dogged pursuit of me. His trip to Texas occurred while Heritage Auctions and I were engaged in the civil RICO action. While agent Cornell was in Dallas, he lied to Heritage Auctions CEO Steve Ivy, his employees, and attorneys, telling them I was illegally selling items donated to the Custer Battlefield Museum through their auction, and that I was consigning a rare book for sale by Heritage Auctions that was stolen property. The book was *Machiavelli Discourses*, the first English edition (printed in 1636), by Thomas Payne. This rare prize had been in my collection since I bought it in 1988 from a Los Angeles County marshal and longtime high school friend, while I was living in Malibu.[2]

It was also alleged that Cornell insinuated I was illegally trying to sell eagle feathers and other items with feathers from protected species at the auction. Later, Cornell would repeat this ludicrous assertion to a federal judge to obtain a second search warrant to seize items from the Custer Battlefield Museum in 2008. These statements were all false and fabricated, but Heritage Auctions used the information to justify its failure to follow through with the terms of our contract.[3]

As a direct result from what I believe were tortuous, libelous, and slanderous statements made by multiple federal agents, Heritage counterclaimed against me, alleging $5 million in damages. The result was a serious degradation of my case against Heritage, directly attributable to the willful misrepresentations, lies, and malicious efforts by federal agents to malign and convict me of a multiyear prison sentence.

My problems did not end there. In his attempt to convict me, agent Brian Cornell allegedly conjured up another reason to raid the museum and the historic town of Garryowen. He relied upon the testimony of several convicted artifact thieves to entrap me in another sting operation. These felons were John Hellson and James Brubaker.[4]

James Brubaker was a criminal artifact dealer, a rare-book thief, and a twice-convicted felon. He had been convicted for counterfeiting U.S. currency ($100 bills), and for the interstate transportation of stolen property. He had been sought for a string of thefts of maps and rare books from western U.S. and Canadian libraries.[5] On some occasions, Brubaker donated items containing feathers to the Custer Battlefield Museum, which is how I know these men.

Brubaker and Hellson are an interesting pair of thieves, and were also working alongside a man named Alan Wolfleg, a Canadian Blackfoot Indian and known business charlatan. Wolfleg had come into this equation because Hellson and he are related by marriage. Though his reputation is tarnished, Hellson is a recognized authority on Indian artifacts.

Hellson was also convicted in 1981 of one of the largest thefts of maps, rare books, and documents ever from various museums and libraries in the western U.S. and Canada. From 2002 until 2006, he traveled with Brubaker stealing these items from libraries and museums in North America. Hellson told investigators that he was just a passenger when he was with Brubaker, and did not know Brubaker was stealing from these institutions.[6]

Agent Cornell claimed these men had informed him that I was offering the township of Garryowen with eagle and migratory bird feathers contained in war bonnets for sale. However, Hellson publicly denied ever saying I was offering the township of Garryowen together with eagle and migratory bird feathers for sale.[7] He further stated that while he knew the town of Garryowen was for sale, at no time did I ever offer items in the museum containing eagle or migratory bird feathers for sale.

In 2006 and 2007, Brubaker and Hellson were all on the radar and in the sights of U.S. federal officials for stealing literally thousands of maps and documents and selling them on eBay. Because of this, the agents interrogated them, inquiring if they had ever done business with me. Both were willing to implicate me, albeit without a shred of confirming evidence, as a buyer and seller of eagle and migratory bird feathers. Lighter sentences—and for Hellson, no charges at all—were the result of giving government investigators what they wanted in the way of testimony targeting me.[8] Brubaker received a sentence of two and a half years in federal prison.

Brubaker's credibility as a witness was severely compromised by his own felony convictions after pleading guilty to possessing stolen property and transporting it across state lines. Furthermore, Cornell and his federal cronies could produce no documents or emails prepared by me detailing offers for the sale of Garryowen and illegal selling of eagle feathers. But by 2008, Brubaker was singing like a canary, to try to save his own hide from another conviction.[9]

The Smoke Clears

From 2005 to 2008, after three years of intimate examination, Agent Cornell determined more intimidation was needed to coerce a confession from me. So, Cornell took the fact that I was attempting to sell the town of Garryowen and everything in it, and expanded that to mean I was selling eagle and migratory bird feathers—because, according to Cornell, the museum and its contents would be involved in the sale.

This is a clear spinning of statements and a distortion of facts, as Brubaker and Hellson have denied ever making the statements attributed to them and no documentation or evidence has ever been put forth to support these assertions. But the truth was spun for Cornell's purpose of garnering a conviction at any cost. His reputation was on the line.

In September 2008, Cornell swore under oath in front of a federal judge that I knowingly offered to sell or barter migratory bird feathers and parts to interested buyers. Once again, Cornell submitted an affidavit to the federal bench, spinning the facts to obtain a second search warrant. Once again, a search warrant was issued and a second raid took place at Garryowen, and items were seized from numerous display cases in the Custer Battlefield Museum.[10]

During the period when I was attempting to sell Garryowen, I operated continually under the advice of legal counsel. I most certainly would never have done anything guaranteed to draw the immediate attention of circling federal investigators and prosecutors. The notion that I would knowingly try to sell eagle and migratory bird feathers at a global public auction was absurd.

This would have been the equivalent of offering a kilo of cocaine for sale, shown in a color catalog, through a Sotheby's auction in New York and expecting the Drug Enforcement Administration not to notice. If Cornell's application for search warrant is to be believed, there was never any need for an undercover operation. I allegedly was handing them their prosecution case on the proverbial platter.

In fact, all the items seized in 2008 had also been present and on public display in the Custer Battlefield Museum when the March

2005 raid took place. During the 2008 raid, I was out of state visiting my son when I received a phone call from an employee at the trading post telling me that Cornell was there with another search warrant. My heart sank like a ton of bricks. I could not believe Cornell was back inside the museum with another search warrant. It also made me extremely nervous that I was not at Garryowen while another team of federal agents tore through the building seizing more artifacts.

The investigation and raids of Garryowen represent more than a conspiracy to damage me. The actions of BLM special agent Brian Cornell, supervised by BLM special agent in charge Bart Fitzgerald, amounted to an abuse of resources for personal and political purposes that had little, if anything to do with their charged purpose of protecting Indian artifacts on federal lands. This is a complete overreaching by the deep state. It is my belief that Bart Fitzgerald needed success to reinvigorate his career, and saw me as that high-visibility success after spending nearly a decade in the Montana district with nothing to show for it. He was so desperate for success that he was willing to believe I must be dirty based upon rumors and reports from highly questionable sources.

In my estimation, Brian Cornell, for his part, was an aggressive agent seeking to gain a conviction. The need for a conviction became greater as the costly investigation progressed. The cost of the raid alone, with dozens of federal agents from several states, would require results. Thus, the investigation pursuing any infraction resulting in a conviction followed. The agents' pursuit of me produced wisps of smoke that only demonstrated the utter lack of a crime. The only almost sin would have been the result of an entrapment sting staged to get an innocent man to commit a crime with the buying and selling of a single button!

Brian Cornell traveled all over the country and into Canada, talking to anyone who had ever done business with me. He talked to those who had bought from me and to those who had sold to me. He also talked to everyone he could who had ever donated anything to the Custer Battlefield Museum.[11]

The assertions made by federal agents and by the United States attorney investigating me either show a gross misunderstanding of the laws of the United States as they apply to eagle feathers and the feathers of migratory birds, or reflect the malicious statements of agents intent on intimidating me and others into giving testimony and confessions that would serve only to enhance their careers. Justice was never the goal of this investigation. Those individuals whom Cornell interviewed told him they would not have sold or bought items from me if the items had not come from the Custer battlefield. His devious questioning of my clients—as if I had already been convicted of these felonies—tarnished my reputation in the collectibles business.[12]

In 2009, Jason Pitsch was released from prison but was still on probation when he began to reappear around Garryowen. He photographed and documented his invasion of the Limber Bones native burial site on property owned by the Pitsch family for *Greasy Grass* magazine, a publication produced by the Custer Battlefield Historical and Museum Association. The Native American Graves Protection and Repatriation Act of 1990 (NAGPRA) made the very activities described in Pitsch's article illegal and felonious, and punishable by fines and imprisonment of up to five years. Yet he received no punishment.

I spoke to my attorney about this, and we reported it to Pitsch's federal probation officer, Carlos Jones. Jones mentioned to me he had seen "large jars of beads" in Pitsch's home and surmised that Pitsch was obtaining beads from the Native American gravesites he had been digging in. Jones in turn brought the matter to the attention of agent Brian Cornell and the U.S. attorneys office. A federal law enforcement agent I had known for years told me in confidence that Cornell was "not going to touch that with a 10-foot pole," because Pitsch had been a paid confidential informant and had a relationship with the Bureau of Land Management.

To protect himself and his agents, Cornell dismissed the documented evidence of the crime because it possibly had occurred on lands not within the jurisdiction of the BLM, and simply decided nothing was going to be done. Of course, Cornell is the same BLM agent who determined that allegations I was selling a misidentified button—not artifacts from desecrated Indian burial sites—were sufficient reason to raid my home and businesses. At this time, Pitsch once again began selling battlefield artifacts and Indian funerary items on eBay.

It is interesting to note that for both the Pitsch land and the town of Garryowen, the ownership type is fee simple, which is private property. Both of our properties are located inside the exterior boundaries of the Crow Indian Reservation. Our legal land status is identical. The fact is, the Bureau of Land Management agents did not want to touch Pitsch's grave-robbing incident because they would have to air their dirty laundry about their prized confidential informant who had been charged and convicted federally of child pornography multiple times.

Following the federal raid on my business in 2005, I was forced to retain the services and assistance of several lawyers and law firms. Months and even years after the raid, I was repeatedly threatened by federal agents verbally and in writing with indictments, forfeiture of my town, and prison time.[13]

To apply more pressure, I was presented with a draft federal indictment and was told I must plead guilty to federal felonies or I would face the certain full force and wrath of the United States government. Through my attorney, I was repeatedly advised that the U.S. attorneys office would be indicting me during the next term of the federal grand jury if I did not agree to plead guilty immediately. Carl Rostad, chief assistant U.S. attorney, played that card with me several times during the five-year investigation. I held firm, however, and did not agree to plead guilty to any charges, and no charges were ever filed.

At various times through the nearly five years following the initial raid in 2005, I was threatened with up to nine felonies. That number was reduced in ensuing negotiations to six felonies, then to three felonies, then to a single felony, and finally to multiple misdemeanors. I felt that the entire experience was designed by the federal agents and the United States attorney to terrorize me into confessing to a crime they knew I did not commit.

As a bit of a bright spot, in 2009 I financed a trip to Washington, D.C., for myself, Joe Medicine Crow, and his family, where Joe would receive the Presidential Medal of Freedom. Before we made the trip, however, we had to jump through several hoops to get on the same page with the White House staff.

Before we made our trip to D.C., I received a phone call from the Secret Service agent in charge of our group's visit to the White House. We chatted for a bit, then the agent cut to the chase.

"No one from your group is wearing eagle feathers, are they?" he asked, concern in his voice.

"Yes, the enrolled members of the Crow delegation will be wearing eagle feather war bonnets," I answered.

"We have a problem with that. We don't want to deal with having contraband in the White House," he politely responded.

It was then that I realized they must have read the BLM's investigative report, which inaccurately called the eagle feather war bonnets in my collection "contraband." In short, I clarified to him that all the feathers were pre-act, so they were legal to possess. He explained to me that, pre-act or not, they didn't want to deal with any gray area of the law, and they certainly didn't want any controversy to arise from a Presidential Medal of Freedom ceremony.

I explained to Joe what the Secret Service agent had told me. He was not happy with what I had to say.

"Call them back," Joe said. "Tell the Secret Service to tell the president that I won't be attending the ceremony. Tell them I'll be coming to Washington, D.C., that same day, wearing my eagle feather war bonnet on the sidewalk in front of the White House. I'll be holding my own press conference during the ceremony to explain why I couldn't come to the White House wearing my war bonnet—because the Secret Service didn't want me to be there!"

I called the Secret Service agent back and relayed Joe's response to him.

"Whoa, whoa, whoa, whoa, whoa! Give me 48 hours and I'll get back to you," was all he could say. I heard back from him just two hours later, and the Crow delegation was green-lighted to wear their eagle feather war bonnets.

Joe was always quite the character. After an uneventful plane ride to D.C., we checked into the historic Willard Hotel. When we looked out from the windows of our rooms, we could see the White House just across the street.

Many presidents have visited the Willard Hotel. In fact, it served as a temporary White House for two days. After the death of Warren G. Harding, Harding's wife, Florence, was preparing to move out of the White House. In the meantime, incoming president Calvin Coolidge and his wife needed a place to stay and work until the White House was vacated.

The next day, we made the short trek to the White House. During a meet-and-greet reception for the Medal of Freedom recipients, I was sitting next to Joe. Being in his mid-90s, Joe was basically deaf. Although we were right next to each other, he shouted my name. I just about fell out of my chair.

"Chris!" he hollered, "see that black actor sitting in the corner? I want to meet him!"

My face must've been beet red at this point, because every single Presidential Medal of Freedom honoree in the room stopped drinking their mimosas and turned to look at Joe and me. Now that everyone was staring at me, I had to think on my feet. You could hear a pin drop. In an instant, I walked over to the man Joe was referring to. It was the acclaimed Academy Award–winning actor Sidney Poitier, who was sitting in a chair across the room from us.

"Mr. Poitier," I addressed him, "Dr. Medicine Crow would like to meet you."

Without skipping a beat, he replied, "Yes. I heard something about that."

Sidney Poitier rose from his seat, walked across the room, and greeted an enthusiastic and delighted Joe. Joe was so excited and honored to meet the actor. I was fortunate to be able to capture this moment in time on camera for Joe.

Once the honorees and their guests were able to meet with President Obama, everyone once again began mingling and conversing. I looked over to keep tabs on Joe and see how he was doing. I just about fainted. Joe was waving his index finger vehemently at President Obama, barely more than a foot away from his face. I was horrified. What was Joe doing, wagging his finger at the most powerful man in the world?

I keyed in on Obama's face to see the expression. He was displaying a straight poker face. Finally, I saw him smile when Joe quit talking. I expelled a sigh of relief. Without being obvious, when Joe was finished I escorted him to the corner of the room and made sure that nobody was staring at us.

I said to Joe, "What did you say to the president?"

He proudly told me that he had said, "This is no longer the White House—this is now the Black House." This was followed by Joe's signature giggle.

Joe had met the president previously, when he was still on the campaign trail. In 2008, Barack Obama visited Crow Agency, a census-designated place in the heart of the Crow reservation, just three months before the presidential election. There was a political rally for Obama at the Crow veterans park, just four miles north of Garryowen. He was given the Crow name Awe Kooda Bilaxpak Kuxshish, which translates to One Who Helps People Throughout the Land. It was at this time Joe met Obama, who was just a senator from Illinois at this point. Joe promised him that he would sing him a victory song in the White House when he was elected president.[14]

Before our trip to the White House for the Medal of Freedom ceremony, I contacted the White House director of public engagement to inquire if Joe could sing his victory song to the president. The director said that there was no way they could allow Joe to sing to the president, because he was on a "tick-tock schedule," meaning that every single second of the busy president's itinerary was accounted for. The White House could not justify a 94-year-old man's taking up 10 or 15 minutes of the president of the United States' time.

I relayed this information to Joe, who was adamant and insisted that he would be singing a victory song for the president. I went back and forth several times with the director of public engagement, trying to arrange for Joe to sing, until one day I received a phone call. The director of public engagement also happened to be an enrolled member of the Standing Rock Sioux tribe. She was the presidential liaison in charge of Indian affairs, and brought a book of depredations of Native Americans to a presidential staff meeting. This book detailed all the offenses committed against Native Americans by the United States. She dropped the book on the conference table with a noticeable thud.

"This is why Joe Medicine Crow should be allowed to sing to the president," she stated matter-of-factly. After that meeting, Joe's request to sing for the president was approved.

Immediately following the award ceremony, the White House staff ushered the Medicine Crow party to the Blue Room, adjacent to the Oval Office. All the other recipients and their entourages were gathered in the State Dining Room for a sit-down meal, basically waiting for Joe to be done with his victory song for the president.

Joe used a ceremonial drum and drumstick that I had brought along for him to use, with which he kept a steady beat while he sang in Crow and translated in English. Joe had quite the voice. You could hear his singing resonate throughout the White House. I can only imagine what the people in the other room were thinking when the Crow song was sung. This was the only time in history that an Indian war chief had sung a song to a president in the White House.

A short while later, Joe pulled me aside. He leaned in close and whispered, "I don't think we should tell President Obama."

"Tell him what?" I asked.

He responded, "That I'm a registered Republican."

"Don't you dare, Joe! Keep your mouth closed," I said.

Joe's only response was his signature giggle once again.

Once I returned to Garryowen, I had an idea. My federal criminal investigation was now closed, and the next thing I knew, a month later, I had been in the White House with the president's arm around me. Boy, talk about going from one extreme to another. What a great "Happy New Year" card this would make—not only to send to my friends, but I thought I would include the federal agents and U.S. attorneys who had threatened and persecuted me over the previous five years. I thought I should get permission from my attorney, Penny Strong. She thought it was a lovely idea and gave me the green light.

The picture on the card is from the day of the Medal of Freedom ceremony. It is a photo of me flanked by Joe Medicine Crow and President Obama. Joe, of course, was wearing the eagle feather war bonnet I had lent to him—the same war bonnet that the BLM agents who raided me had called "contraband." I inscribed the cards in gold ink. The card I sent to Special Agent Brian Cornell read:

> Agent Cornell—thinking of you on the New Year and noting that the White House enjoyed another of the war bonnets that was loaned to Presidential Medal of Freedom Recipient Joe Medicine Crow. Sincerely Yours, Chris Kortlander

7

The Investigation That Never Happened

Amid my fight with the federal government over the raids at Garryowen, I also became embroiled in another fight with implications for the United States Senate. For 32 years straight, from 1952 to 1984, Montana elected only Democratic senators. Conrad Burns is only the second Republican whom Montana has elected to the U.S. Senate. Thus, the Senate seat held by Burns was targeted by Democrats in what is coming to light as one of the worst cases of voter fraud in recent memory. Montana is home to approximately 1 million people—darn few by U.S. standards. There are no less than seven separate and distinct Indian tribes in Montana, with a combined population calculated to be 6.9 percent of the total population, or approximately 70,000 people.[1]

The 2006 United States Senate election in Montana was held on November 7. Incumbent Republican U.S. senator Conrad Burns was running for re-election for a fourth term, but was defeated by Democrat Jon Tester by a margin of 0.87 percent, or 3,562 votes out of 406,505 votes.[2]

Due to errors with polling machines, the Montana count was delayed well into November 8. The race was too close to call throughout the night, and many pundits predicted the need for a recount. On November 9, incumbent Conrad Burns conceded defeat.[3]

The race was the closest Senate election of 2006 in terms of absolute-vote difference. Under Montana law, if the margin of defeat is more than 0.25 percent but less than 0.5 percent, the losing candidate can request a recount if he or she pays for it. However, this election did not qualify for a recount because the margin was larger than 0.5 percent. The outcome of the Montana vote resulted in the swing of the control of the Senate to the Democrats.[4]

Almost immediately on election night, reports started circulating of inconsistencies in vote counting in the state, and specifically on the Crow Indian Reservation. Lest there be any misunderstanding, Indian politics, specifically Crow Indian politics, dominate county government in Big Horn County. This was the county that overwhelmingly voted for Tester and propelled him into the Senate. Returns from Indian reservation precincts shifted the balance of power to Democrats in Congress. When Jon Tester eventually claimed victory, he credited his win to the Indian vote.[5]

Nearly all Big Horn County elected offices are held by Crow tribal members. In 2006, the county sheriff responsible for transporting state ballots from county precincts to the county clerk to be counted was a member of the Crow tribe, Sheriff Lawrence Pete Big Hair.

Here are the facts regarding the former sheriff of Big Horn County, Lawrence Pete Big Hair. He was involved in two incidents while serving as a federal law enforcement officer for the Bureau of Indian Affairs on the Crow reservation. One, in 1994, involved his BIA-issued police pistol, which was used in the murder of a Crow teenager. In the other, he was named as a defendant in the rape of a mentally impaired Northern Cheyenne woman that happened when he was transporting her in a federal BIA police car on Christmas Day in 1995.

And here's the rest of the story. He couldn't even carry a gun while serving as Big Horn County sheriff, and was arrested and charged with family member assault, endangering the welfare of children, and bribery. Furthermore, he was investigated by the Montana

Department of Criminal Investigation for taking prisoners from the Big Horn County jail for private use. Politics appeared to shield him from criminal responsibility, but enough signatures were gathered for an official recall of his office. Just the person we want in charge of our ballot boxes, right?

The issue implied by the fact that nearly all Big Horn County elected offices are occupied by Crow Indians is that on the Crow reservation, the county officials do not have the authority to enforce state law over their own Crow tribal members. Montana state law (civil and criminal) does not apply to any enrolled American Indian inside the exterior boundaries of the Crow reservation. Thus, the Crow Indians on the reservation that makes up much of Big Horn County are exempt from state authority, including the authority of those tribal members who hold state-created county and state positions of nearly every sort.

Nowhere is this more glaring than in the administration of elections. The state of Montana does not have the authority to administer and supervise elections conducted on tribal property on the Crow reservation.[6] Not surprisingly, the lack of jurisdiction colors election results, as voter fraud is rampant when there are no laws or law enforcement in place to guarantee the sanctity and validity of each individual vote.

The Crow reservation in Big Horn County encompasses approximately 2.3 million acres (5,000 square miles, larger than the state of New Hampshire).[7] Most of the county's land area is composed of two Indian reservations: the Crow Indian Reservation covers 64.2 percent of its area, while the Northern Cheyenne Indian Reservation covers about another 6.4 percent.[8]

The county also has several jurisdictions, each with its own regulations and law enforcement agencies. The Crow and Northern Cheyenne Indian tribes are administered by the tribes and by the BIA. Serious federal crimes are covered by the Major Crimes Act (18 U.S.C.), and jurisdiction for those falls to the FBI. The Little Bighorn National Monument and the Bighorn Canyon National Recreation Area are regulated by the National Park Service. Only the remainder of the county, which includes Garryowen, falls under the laws of the state of Montana.

In 2006, the Montana election between Democrat Jon Tester and Republican incumbent Conrad Burns, which changed the control of the Senate from Republican to Democrat, was challenged by several citizens complaining of many serious voter fraud instances in Big Horn County. I was one of them. However, shortly after the election results were tallied, the secretary of state informed those of us reporting improprieties that he lacked the authority to obtain and maintain uniformity in the application and operation of election laws with respect to any federal, state, county, and local district election-related activities occurring within the exterior borders of the Crow reservation.

This is because state law does not apply to American Indians located inside the perimeter of the Crow reservation. Because of this conflict of jurisdictions, there is no way to guarantee the sanctity of the ballot box. As unbelievable as this sounds, American Indians cannot be arrested for voter fraud or any other state crime, as far as that goes, on the Crow reservation.[9] However, this did not prevent the secretary of state from certifying the election results—including those from the Indian reservations and Big Horn County.[10]

Crow tribal members knew that, doing business as usual, they could have an impact on statewide issues and federal candidates in 2006. This was also known to the Big Horn County Democratic Central Committee. Some Crow tribal members boast that they travel to many reservation precincts using different names or family members to vote for tribal chairmen. Not only will they travel from precinct to precinct, but they will travel around the nation to cast their votes. So, it is alleged that they turned out in similar numbers for this election, which gave them a great deal of voting power.[11]

Elective offices in Big Horn County are nonpartisan. However, voting in Big Horn County is racially polarized, especially in those elections in which tribal members and nontribal members oppose each other. During the 2006 election, in nearly every contested Big Horn

County race, a tribal member candidate endorsed by the government of the Crow tribe was positioned against a non-Indian candidate.[12]

On November 1, 2006, the government of the Crow tribe adopted Legislative Resolution No. 06-05, entitled "A Legislative Resolution of the Crow Tribal Legislature: An Endorsement of Crow Tribal Members Running for Big Horn County Offices in the November 2006 Election." The resolution expressly encouraged bloc voting based on race, stating that the tribe "hereby approves, and decrees an endorsement of the Crow Members of the Crow Nation..." for elected office in Big Horn County.[13]

An official with the state Commissioner of Political Practices did receive a telephone complaint from a Crow tribal member. The complainant stated that prior to Election Day, the government of the Crow tribe issued multiple tribal identification cards to both herself and others, with separate cards in both their Crow and American names. The complainant further stated she had been encouraged to use the multiple identification cards to vote under both her Crow and American names at different voting precincts. The complainant stated she had indeed voted twice and now felt guilty.[14]

One of the confusing elements of voter identification in Indian Country is the voter's name. Every Crow Indian has two names: an American name and a Crow language name. And names can change without much notice. But identification documents can exist for both names, and so can voter registrations.[15] Throw in an adoption or two, a marriage—common law, church, and sometimes state—and you can have a real assortment of names that can be interchanged nearly anytime it is convenient.

The question of voter impersonation on Montana Indian reservations and on the Crow reservation is a problem that culture and custom have made the stuff of jokes and rumor. It is simply another way for ordinary Indians to gain a political advantage over the "bad white man who has stolen their land and corrupted their culture." Stuffing the ballot box seems almost passé in these sophisticated times. However, why give up a tried-and-true method?

Unfortunately, in this circumstance, the fraud did not end there. Documented election improprieties also included unsecured ballot boxes at a tribally controlled polling location; this is one of the acts of fraud I reported. I had received several phone calls during the day of the election regarding the fact that ballot boxes at precincts five and seven, in the heart of the Crow reservation, were unlocked throughout the day, a clear violation of state-mandated procedure.

It was related to me during the election that after the polls closed, when it came time to process the ballots and prepare the ballot boxes to be transported to the county clerk (also a Crow tribal member), a nontribal poll watcher was ordered by a Crow Indian serving as a Big Horn County election judge to leave the precinct location with the ballots still unsecured. The poll watcher was at the precinct from 3:00 p.m. to 8:13 p.m. During this time, none of the ballot boxes were secured.[16] When that non-Indian poll watcher filed a report and sent it to state and federal officials, they collectively did nothing.

There were many allegations supported by notarized statements documenting the irregularities at polling places on the Crow reservation. One incident occurred when a non-Indian voter reported that he could vote even though he had left his wallet at home, stating that the election judges knew him personally.

Another non-Indian voter stated that he placed his ballot in a tray and handed it to the attendant. The attendant then set the tray on the table and left it there. He had to specifically request that his ballot be placed into the ballot box. As the attendant placed the ballot in the box, the voter noticed that it was unlocked.

Finally, a former deputy sheriff on jury duty witnessed the same Native American woman stand twice during jury selection to identify herself under two different names. Seeing as the jury pool had been selected from registered voters, this woman must have been registered twice as a voter in Big Horn County.

The polling place in question was at the Crow Elementary School, a location within 1,000 feet of the Crow tribal headquarters. On November 5, the Crow tribe hosted a rally there for Jon Tester (as well as for the slate of Crow-sponsored county candidates), specifically endorsing him.[17] This was the day before the election.

Following the election, several Crow Indians came to me in Garryowen with checks drawn on the bank account of the Montana Democratic Party. The report I received from the tribal members that came to me to cash their checks was that the checks had been given in exchange for vouchers handed out at the poll on Election Day to those committing to vote for Tester. The Tester checks I cashed were for $40 per vote. On the Crow reservation, this practice still continues; in 2006 it was utilized by the Tester campaign to reward people who voted for him.

The two precincts that came into question for voter fraud were the fifth and seventh. They contained 1,718 registered voters. From among those voters, 1,098 votes were cast and 926 of those were cast for Tester. Looking at the other precinct polling locations in Big Horn County with majority Indian voting populations, you can see that the total number of those voting for Tester was 1,605 more than for any other candidate or group of candidates.[18]

The vote in Indian Country, especially in the voting precincts on the Crow reservation, provided the swing margin that swayed the control of the U.S. Senate to the Democratic Party. It is important to note that Jon Tester lost the state's largest county—Yellowstone—and just about every rural county by a significant margin, yet he still won the election.[19]

The power of the Indian vote in Montana changed things nationally.[20] An analysis by Indianz.com, a news website for Native Americans, showed that counties with a significant percentage of American Indians and Alaska natives voted overwhelmingly for Tester. With only about 2,600 votes separating Tester and Republican senator Conrad Burns, the native vote played a large role in an election that saw Democrats take control of the entire U.S. Senate.[21]

A total of 10 Indians—all Democrats—won election to either the Montana House of Representatives or the Montana State Senate. In Big Horn County, voters chose Tester over Burns in nearly a 2-to-1 ratio. Tester won 64 percent of the vote in a county that was 60 percent Native American, according to the U.S. Census Bureau.[22]

The results were similar in Glacier County, home to the Blackfeet reservation. There, in a county with a 62 percent Native American population, 62 percent of voters chose Tester.[23] In Roosevelt County, home to the Fort Peck reservation, 58 percent of voters went with Tester. The county is 56 percent Native American.[24]

Even in places where Native Americans were not the majority, the election results showed the power of their vote. In Blaine County, where Native Americans made up 45 percent of the population, 51 percent of voters picked Tester over Burns.[25] Four other counties with sizable, double-digit-percentage Native American populations—Choteau, Hill, Lake, and Rosebud—saw some rather tight margins between Tester and Burns. In all but one of these counties, Tester carried the vote.[26]

In contrast, in counties where Native Americans were the extreme minority—fewer than 10 percent of the population—Burns was victorious. The lower the Native American percentage, the more votes went to Burns—as happened in Beaverhead, Carter, Custer, Garfield, and a slew of other counties.[27]

The bias of Montana's Native American population is not the issue. The wrongful exploitation and opportunistic manipulation of the politically correct federal, state, and local election procedures in a wrongful, even unlawful, manner is the issue. This abuse of process is infectious, depriving us—all of us—of the sanctity of the ballot box, even without the aid of the Russians.

To further aggravate matters, Bill Mercer, the United States attorney for the district of Montana at the time, played a large role in the voter fraud taking place in Montana in 2006. Yes, the same Bill Mercer who was appointed by President George W. Bush and figured prominently in the raids conducted at Garryowen in 2005 and 2008. After seeing and hearing about all the fraud, it was with considerable trepidation that I participated in a lawsuit after the initial raid at Garryowen to challenge the 2006 Montana election.[28] This lawsuit would take place in Mercer's court, and he would hold all the cards.

The issue of potential voter fraud in the conduct of the 2006 election was recognized by the U.S. Department of Justice. On October 30, just a week before the election, press releases announced that the DOJ nationally and in Montana was ready to protect the vote.[29] "The right to vote, and to have that vote count, is central to the existence of freedom," said Attorney General Alberto R. Gonzales. "As the Supreme Court has characterized it, the right to vote is the 'preservative of every other right.' The Department of Justice is committed to both ballot access and ballot integrity, and together these ensure that elections reflect the will of the people, which is the foundation of our great Nation."[30]

Bill Mercer did his part, issuing a press release providing the names and numbers of a designated assistant U.S. attorney (Josh Van de Wetering), FBI special agents, and the DOJ Civil Rights Division's Voting Section in Washington, D.C.

When I attempted to pursue the question of FBI or DOJ investigations, Van de Wetering simply told me that the decision to investigate was out of his hands and made in Washington. And guess where Mercer was? In Washington, Mercer had worked himself into the number-three position in the DOJ under Attorney General Alberto R. Gonzales. One of the results was that while he retained the position of United States attorney for Montana, he worked in Washington, D.C. Not long after it was filed, the federal suit challenging the election was dismissed (on November 5, 2007), and Mercer was at the center of it.[31]

Mercer characterized the election improprieties cited as merely "garden variety," further stating that the alleged acts were not prohibited by state law (possibly because the state had no jurisdiction on the federal Indian reservation), nor did they make the 2006 election fundamentally unfair.[32]

In September 2006, Mercer was nominated by President George W. Bush to the national position of associate attorney general, and served as acting associate attorney general until June 22, 2007. Just days before his confirmation hearing for the Washington, D.C., post was to take place, he resigned, returning to his lowly United States attorney position in Montana.[33]

The judge appointed to review the voter fraud lawsuit said, "Unfortunately, not every mistake made during an election serves as the predicate for a Voting Rights Act violation." He went on to explain that "the failure to secure a ballot box or two, dismissal of a poll watcher after the polls had closed, and an anonymous complaint regarding repeated registration and voting do not amount to a standard practice or procedure."

The judge in this case was the presidentially appointed Richard Cebull, the senior judge of the United States District Court for the District of Montana. This is the same judge who, in an investigation by the judicial council of the Ninth U.S. Circuit Court of Appeals, revealed he had sent hundreds of "racist, sexist, and politically inflammatory" e-mail messages over four years.[34]

It was found on February 20, 2012, that Cebull had used his official courthouse email address and federally issued computer to forward his friends and associates an email containing a racially charged bestiality joke about President Barack Obama. He prefaced the joke by saying, "Normally I don't send or forward a lot of these, but even by my standards, it was a bit touching. I want all my friends to feel what I felt when I read this. Hope it touches your heart like it did mine." The joke he told was, "A little boy said to his mother, 'Mommy, how come I'm black and you're white?' His mother replied, 'Don't even go there Barack! From what I can remember about that party, you're lucky you don't bark!'"[35]

This event made national headlines and nightly news for a week solid. Bill O'Reilly even called for Cebull's resignation on *The O'Reilly Factor*. The joke enraged members of Congress, including the chairpersons of the Congressional Black Caucus, Congressional Hispanic Caucus, and Congressional Asian Pacific American Caucus. The heads of these groups came together to issue a joint release rebuking the judge. He is also the same judge whose court authorized and sustained the federal raids targeting Garryowen in 2005 and 2008. I find it coincidental that both Mercer and Cebull just so happened to take a stance against me in this matter as well.

Interestingly, after Senator Conrad Burns' retirement, I met with him at his home in Billings to speak with him about the Garryowen raids and Bill Mercer. Senator Burns and I had an in-depth, two-hour conversation. He told me that the biggest political mistake he made was nominating Bill Mercer for the position of United States attorney for the district of Montana. He also disclosed to me that he had never met or spoken with Mercer before giving his nomination to the president.

When I heard that Burns had never met with Mercer, I didn't say a word. Instead, I cocked my head and had a questioning look on my face.

Burns then went on to say that Mercer's father had been a close friend of his for years and a political supporter. With Bill Mercer's background being an assistant United States attorney, Burns thought that he was making the right decision, even without an interview.

Senator Burns tried to be proactive during the first few years after the 2005 raid. However, he got nowhere with Mercer's office. I remember getting a phone call one day from Senator Burns' chief of staff saying that Mercer had gotten to a point where he wouldn't even return Burns' phone calls.

In another disgusting display, Montana governor Brian Schweitzer, speaking at a trial lawyers' convention in 2008, bragged about the scheme used by Jon Tester (with Schweitzer's assistance) to unseat the Republican incumbent in 2006. The abuse and misuse of the voting process is bigger than Big Horn County, involving the office of the Democratic governor of the state of Montana.[36] Election abuse is apparently considered to be a joking matter, according to Schweitzer.[37]

By 2008, however, enough questions had been raised about election fraud that law enforcement officials across the country were taking a proactive stance about it. I guess government officials think we will just believe that, unlike violent crime, voter fraud is limited only to the cases that are reported and prosecuted, which is a senseless position.[38]

On October 30, 2006, just days before the election, Bill Mercer announced in a press release, published in the *Billings Gazette*, that Josh Van de Wetering, assistant United States attorney for Montana, would lead that office's efforts to curb election fraud. The press release ends with this quote from Mercer: "Election fraud and voting rights abuses dilute honest votes cast. They also corrupt our representative form of government. These crimes will be dealt with promptly and aggressively. Anyone who has information suggesting electoral corruption or voting rights abuses should make that information available immediately to my office." The FBI had special agents available in each of its field offices and resident agencies to receive reports of election fraud and other election mishandlings. A report hotline phone number was provided in the press release.

President Donald Trump has now created a voter-fraud commission that will review the voting history, party ID, and addresses of every voter in the U.S. dating back to 2006.[39] Hopefully the voter-fraud case that I was a part of, and railroaded in, will come under intense scrutiny, and the commission will uncover the harsh truths that have been a part of Montana politics for decades now.

8

The Nine Firings

In 2004, George W. Bush was elected to a second term as president. As the clock started to wind down on what became a lame duck presidency, politics continued to infest Washington's mindset. Bill Mercer, once a lowly assistant United States attorney for Montana, was elevated to the politically appointed position of United States attorney in that district by nomination of the president and confirmation from the Senate in 2001.

Mercer quickly moved up through the elite ranks, under Attorney General (AG) of the United States John Ashcroft and then in 2005 under AG Alberto Gonzales. Under Gonzales' tenure, the U.S. attorney general's office was embroiled in controversies regarding warrantless surveillance of U.S. citizens and the legal authorization of so-called enhanced interrogation techniques, later generally acknowledged by many as constituting torture, in the U.S. government's post-9/11 War on Terror.

Gonzales also presided over the firings of several U.S. attorneys who had refused back-channel White House directives to prosecute political enemies, allegedly causing the office of the attorney general to become improperly politicized. These firings became one of the bigger scandals of the Bush administration. They also involved Bill Mercer, who was the United States attorney for the district of Montana and instrumental in overseeing the raids at Garryowen and not investigating voter fraud in his own backyard on the Crow reservation. Following calls for AG Gonzales' removal, Gonzales resigned from the office on August 27, 2007; his resignation became effective September 17 of that same year.[1]

By law, U.S. attorneys are appointed for a term of four years, and each U.S. attorney serves at the pleasure of the president and is subject to removal by the president for any reason, so long as it is not illegal or improper. When Gonzales became attorney general in 2005, he ordered a performance review of all U.S. attorneys. On December 7, 2006, seven United States attorneys were notified by the DOJ that they were being dismissed, after the Bush administration sought their resignation.[2] The number later increased to nine attorneys.

The eighth attorney, Bud Cummins, who was informed of his dismissal in June 2006, announced his resignation on December 15, 2006; it became effective December 20, 2006. This happened upon his being notified of the appointment of Tim Griffin as interim U.S. attorney for the eastern district of Arkansas. Another attorney, Todd Graves of Missouri, was eventually dismissed as well, raising the number of attorneys fired to nine in 2006. In the subsequent congressional hearings and press reports, it was disclosed that additional U.S. attorneys were dismissed without explanation and at least 26 U.S. attorneys had at various times been considered for dismissal.[3]

Although U.S. attorneys can be dismissed at the discretion of the president, critics claimed the dismissals were motivated either by the desire to install attorneys more loyal to the Republican party ("loyal Bushies," in the words of Kyle Sampson, Gonzales' former chief of staff) or as retribution for actions or inactions damaging to the Republican Party. However, note that at least six of the nine received positive performance reviews at the DOJ prior to their dismissal.

In a press conference given on March 13, Gonzales suggested "incomplete information was communicated or may have been communicated to the Congress," and he accepted full responsibility. Nonetheless, Gonzales avowed that his knowledge of the process to fire U.S. attorneys and select new ones was limited to how they may have been classified as "strong performers, not-as-strong performers, and weak performers."

Gonzales also asserted that was all he knew of the process, saying, "[I] was not involved in seeing any memos, was not involved in any discussions about what was going on. That's basically what I knew as the attorney general."

However, DOJ records released on March 23 appear to contradict some of those assertions, indicating that according to his November 27, 2006, schedule, "he attended an hour-long meeting at which, aides said, he approved a detailed plan for executing the purge." Despite insisting he was not involved in the deliberations leading up to the firing of the attorneys, released emails also suggest he had indeed been notified and had given ultimate approval. Bill Mercer had a hand in all of this even as he continued his witch hunt to prosecute me.

Of the nine federal prosecutors who were dismissed, five represented states with significant Indian country areas and a majority as well as Mercer were leaders on the Native American Issues Subcommittee (NAIS) at the DOJ. Former U.S. attorney Tom Heffelfinger of Minnesota, the chair of the subcommittee, was also targeted for firing.[4] Heffelfinger was targeted because he was "overly focused" on Indian issues. Besides serving as U.S. attorney in Minnesota, home to nearly a dozen tribes, he was chair of the NAIS. In that role, Heffelfinger spent a significant amount of time on issues like crime, jurisdiction, domestic violence, and gaming.[5] What's astonishing in all of this is that Mercer had huge improprieties related to voter fraud in his own backyard on Indian reservations, yet he faced no repercussions from Gonzales' office.

I believe that it is more than a coincidence that all the United States attorneys involved with the firings had Native American influence and involvement—and most had reservations in their home districts. Five of the eight terminated U.S. attorneys were active members of the NAIS. Many of them were also seen as strong advocates for legal justice on reservations.[6]

Two of Gonzales' aides—Monica Goodling and Kyle Sampson—were singled out by investigators as being political appointees with too little experience. Goodling had previously told Congress that Heffelfinger was targeted for removal because he spent "too much time" on Indian issues.

When he was the number-three man at the DOJ, Bill Mercer sat on the Native American and Indigenous Studies Association (NAISA) board and defended the Bush administration's $7 billon trust settlement offer. The Bush administration in March 2007 had suggested it was willing to spend $7 billion over 10 years to resolve a wide range of major Indian issues.[7] During this time, Mercer was in line for Senate approval while retaining his position as the U.S. attorney for Montana.

In his prepared testimony to Congress on April 19, 2007, Gonzales insisted he left the decisions on the firings to his staff. However, ABC News obtained an internal department email showing that Gonzales urged the ouster of Carol Lam, one of the fired attorneys, only six months before she was asked to resign. During additional testimony on April 19, 2007, Gonzales stated at least 71 times he could not recall events related to the controversy. Imagine that: an attorney general of the United States, the top dog at the DOJ, could "not recall" information 71 times under oath, all in a single day's congressional testimony hearing. A poor memory seems to be a common affliction among those subject to investigation, especially those holding a high position in our country. It does appear suspect, even wrong.

The Office of Inspector General (OIG) and the Office of Professional Responsibility (OPR) commenced an investigation into the removal of the nine U.S. attorneys.[8] Their report was issued in September 2008. The report cited serious issues of accountability removing a few of the U.S. attorneys, but there was no finding that the nine attorneys were removed for illegal or improper reasons.

As *The Wall Street Journal* reported, "the Justice Department informed Congress on Wednesday that a special investigator in the case found no evidence of wrongdoing. The investigator's final word is that no Administration official gave 'false statements' to Congress or to the DOJ Inspector General, which carried out their own investigation." The report also found no evidence that Gonzales made false or misleading statements to Congress, thus clearing him of accusations of perjury.

The OIG report did find, however, that some statements made by Gonzales at a March 13, 2007, press conference about his involvement were inaccurate. The report did not conclude that Gonzales deliberately provided false information. He acknowledged from the outset his misstatements, accepted responsibility, and attempted to set the record straight well before congressional testimony on April 19, 2007. Gonzales testified 18 months before the OIG report said that statements he made at the March 13, 2007, press conference were misstatements and were overboard.

In August 2009, White House documents released showed that Deputy Chief of Staff Karl Rove raised concerns directly with Gonzales that Senator Pete Domenici of New Mexico or an intermediary may have contacted the DOJ as early as 2005 to complain. In contrast, Gonzales told the Senate Judiciary Committee in 2007, referring to the removal of U.S. District Attorney for New Mexico David Iglesias, "I don't recall...Senator Domenici ever requesting that Mr. Iglesias be removed." In July 2010, DOJ prosecutors closed the two-year investigation without filing charges after determining that the firings were not criminal, saying, "Evidence did not demonstrate that any prosecutable criminal offense was committed with regard to the removal of David Iglesias. The investigative team also determined the evidence did not warrant expanding the scope of the investigation beyond the removal of Iglesias."

Gonzales asked the OPR to examine the records and supported the involvement of the inspector general. He directed full cooperation with all investigations by DOJ employees and agreed to release thousands of pages of internal DOJ documents. The inspector general found no intentional or criminal wrongdoing by Gonzales.

Concerning Bill Mercer after his appointment, as acting principal deputy associate attorney general, U.S. district chief judge Donald

W. Molloy of Missoula on October 20, 2005, wrote to Gonzales that "Mercer was violating federal law because he no longer resides in Montana and was living with his family in the Washington area." He also complained that Mercer spent only three days a month in Montana.

Molloy further criticized Mercer for his double duty, saying he was neglecting his work in Montana. During a federal court session, Molloy asked Mercer, "Do you ever concern yourself with justice?" In an open letter, Molloy urged Gonzales to replace Mercer.

Molloy argued that Mercer's absence had led to a "lack of leadership" in the U.S. attorney's office in Montana that was "creating untoward difficulties for the court, and it appears for the prosecutors assigned to various tasks in Montana." Gonzales turned down Molloy's request.

At the time, Mercer defended his record, saying, "I spend a lot of time on planes. It's remarkable how many different things one can do. There's a lot of responsibility here, but I'm not abdicating any of it."

Gonzales responded to Molloy, saying according to the *Washington Post* that Mercer "is in compliance with the residency requirement [under federal law because he] is domiciled there, returns there on a regular basis, and will live there full-time as soon as his temporary assignment is completed."

On the exact same day back in Washington, D.C., new legislation was added to the USA Patriot Act at the request of Mercer, who had been assigned the task of shepherding the provision through Congress, according to congressional aides and new statements from one of Mercer's colleagues. He had a provision inserted into the reauthorization of the USA Patriot Act changing federal law so federal prosecutors could live outside their districts to serve in other jobs, the *Washington Post* reported.[9]

Mercer made his request to Brett Tolman, who was counsel to Senator Arlen Specter, then chairman of the Senate Judiciary Committee, and the provision was inserted into the Patriot Act, retroactive to a time that would cover Mercer's term. Considering these revelations,

Senator Jon Tester called on Mercer to resign, while Senator Dianne Feinstein of California announced she would introduce legislation to reverse the new provision.

This was the second provision receiving unfavorable notice over a year after the Patriot Act's passage; the other was a provision allowing the administration to indefinitely appoint interim U.S. attorneys, a key part of the controversy surrounding the dismissal of the U.S. attorneys.

Seven United States attorneys were dismissed by the DOJ on December 7, 2006. Senior members of the White House and the DOJ participated, including Mercer, in compiling the list of those dismissed. The USA Patriot Act Improvement and Reauthorization Act of 2005, which was signed into law on March 9, 2006, extinguished the former 120-day term limit of interim United States attorneys appointed to fill vacated offices.

This in effect gave the U.S. attorney general greater appointing authority than the president, since the interim U.S. attorneys did not need Senate confirmation, and the presidential nominees did. (An interim U.S. attorney's term expires upon the confirmation and swearing in of a presidentially appointed U.S. attorney, if one is put forward.) At least six of the nine had positive internal Justice Department performance reports.

A March 4, 2008, article in the *Washington Post* stated that Mercer was part of retaliatory steps against a high-level career executive in the DOJ who had blown the whistle on gross mismanagement. The *Post* also stated that Mercer was "a pivotal figure in the controversy over the dismissal of the federal prosecutors."

The use of a document dump by the Gonzales DOJ was one of the tactics used to thwart the oversight role of Congress brought on by the controversy. As one facet of the dismissal-of-U.S.-attorneys controversy, in 2007 relevant committees of both houses of Congress, controlled by the Democratic Party, requested and then subpoenaed backstory information from the DOJ on how the process had resulted in these dismissals and how they had taken place. The DOJ was reluctant to respond in a friendly manner to these requests, which it regarded as hostile; it responded with significant quantities of unsorted and extraneous information.

Mercer's appointment by Gonzales to the number-three position in the DOJ was not met with universal approval. Mercer had previously served a temporary term, starting in June 2005, as principal associate deputy general, the top deputy to the deputy U.S. attorney general. During that assignment, Mercer split his time between his U.S. attorney duties in Montana and his Washington job.[10]

The events surrounding the firing of the United States attorneys in 2006 are considered one of the major scandals of the Bush administration. The timeline of events starts in 2001 with the nomination of several U.S. attorneys and coincides with the 9/11 attack precipitating the Patriot Act. These events continued, with politics seeming to be supreme, until July 21, 2010, when DOJ prosecutors under President Obama closed the administration's two-year investigation without filing charges against Gonzales. They concluded that "there was insufficient evidence to establish that persons knowingly made material false statements to [the Office of Inspector General] or Congress or corruptly endeavored to obstruct justice."

When I was still under federal investigation, I was traveling back to Montana from Washington, D.C. Boarding my plane home, I sat down in my first-class seat only to find that for this long, nearly cross-country flight, my seatmate was none other than Bill Mercer. I told the flight attendant I needed to be reseated. I was grateful when she found a seat in coach so I wouldn't have to sit next to the man who had been a thorn in my side for quite some time.

After two invasive, well-publicized, and humiliating BLM-with-FBI raids (sponsored and approved by the Mercer DOJ), I was never charged with any crime by Mercer, although the predatory actions of his office cost me my health and a large part of my business, to the tune of a million dollars or more. That's not to mention my business and community reputation and additional hundreds of thousands of dollars of savings and wealth being stolen as a result thereof. In all, I lost a decade of my life to his allegations.

Bill Mercer resigned as Montana's U.S. attorney in 2009, and later found employment as a partner in a prestigious Montana law firm. Now the only question remaining is, where do I go to get my reputation back?

Photo Gallery

This billboard is the campaign Kortlander has funded on Interstate 90 in Montana to help combat the BLM's tyrannical tactics.

Gene Autry and Chris Kortlander

Kortlander's Malibu home before the fire.

Kortlander's Malibu home after the fire.

Garryowen before Kortlander built the town.

Burying the hatchet ceremony, June 25, 1926.

The Tomb of the United States Unknown Soldier

The Tomb of the United States Unknown Soldier with Peace Memorial built in 2001

Photo Gallery

Military groups from around the world visit the Custer Battlefield Museum to learn about the mistakes Custer made so his mistakes won't be repeated in battlefields today.

Chris Kortlander in his sheriff's deputy uniform

The words "dead man" and a swastika were spray-painted on the side of the museum during Kortlander's run for sheriff.

The boots with false provenance that Putt bought from Jason Pitsch. They were displayed in the museum and featured in the Custer Battlefield Museum brochure.

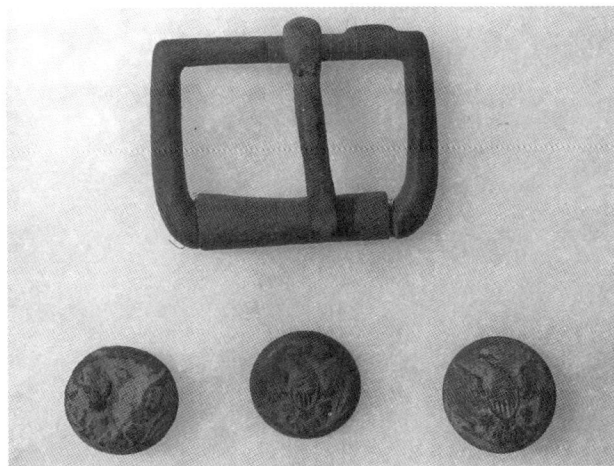

A suspender buckle and eagle buttons, much like the ones for which the author was raided.

Special Agent Brian Cornell

Special Agent Bart Fitzgerald

Special Agent Bart Fitzgerald with another federal agent standing outside of the Custer Battlefield Museum during the raid.

Photo Gallery

One of the federal agents patrolling the front entrance to the Garryowen Trading Post during the raid.

Sorting through items seized during the raid.

Leaving the Billings branch of the Bureau of Land Management with some of the items taken from Kortlander during the raid; notice the address of the building is the same as the return address for the leaked document.

Leaving the Billings branch of the Bureau of Land Management with some of the items taken from Kortlander during the raid.

Serving Brian Cornell with a federal lawsuit.

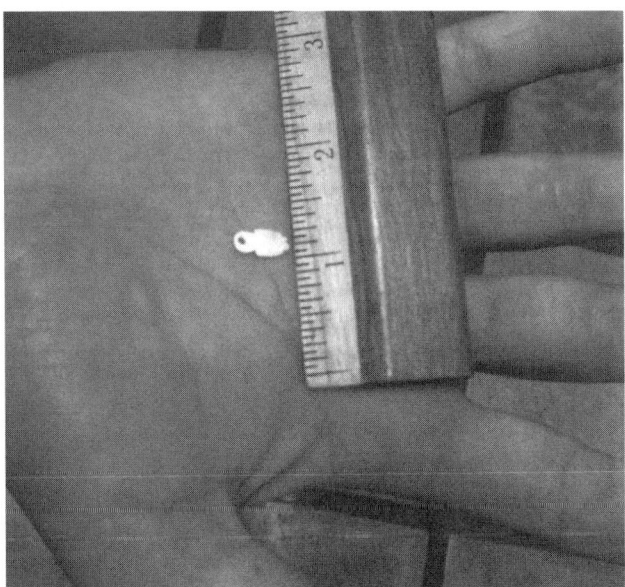

The miniscule bird bead that cost Dr. Redd his life.

Operation Cerberus Action Challenge Coin, front

Operation Cerberus Action Challenge Coin, rear

Joe Medicine Crow meeting Sidney Poitier.

Joe Medicine Crow singing the victory song to Barack Obama.

Joe Medicine Crow wagging his finger at President Obama; Joe inscribed the photo with what he said to Obama. "This is [no] longer the White House—this is now the Black House."

The New Year's card Kortlander sent to Agent Brian Cornell inscribed with, "Agent Cornell, Thinking of you on the New Year and noting that the White House enjoyed another of the war bonnets that was loaned to Presidential Medal of Freedom recipient Joe Medicine Crow. Sincerely yours, Chris Kortlander".

Photo Gallery

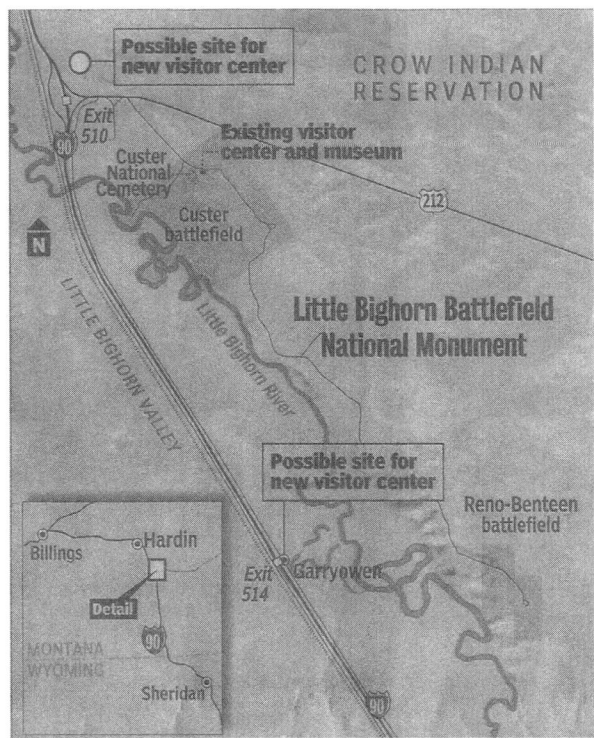

This map from the National Park Service in 2006 shows federal government plans to build the new visitor center for the Little Bighorn National Monument at Garryowen, even though Kortlander still owns the property.

The Elizabeth Bacon Custer Manuscript Collection

Kortlander with plans for the Elizabeth Custer Library and Museum.

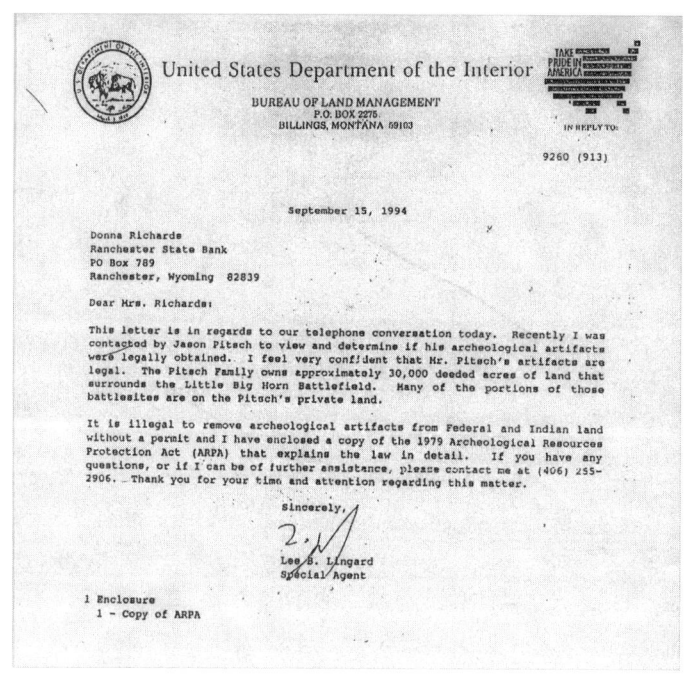

The Lingard Letter

9

Lost Freedom

The harsh, unforgiving wind sweeps over the snow-encrusted countryside in the dead of winter. Breaking the silence of the frozen tundra, a white pickup truck with an attached camper shell barrels down U.S. Route 395, just outside the Malheur National Wildlife Refuge in Oregon. As the vehicle accelerates down the highway, it hits a bend in the road and takes the slight curve at a high rate of speed; it is propelled as if by a slingshot into a long straightaway.

While it hauls down the open road, the crack of multiple gunshots rings out, a foreign sound in the frigid forested landscape. Bullets, fired by state and federal law enforcement officers, penetrate the vehicle with a jarring popping crunch, bursting into the truck's body and frame with deadly accuracy. Alarmed by the shots and an upcoming roadblock, the driver of the vehicle, rancher and foster home operator Robert LaVoy Finicum, yanks the wheel of the automobile hard to the left to avoid a policeman swiftly moving toward the truck.

As Finicum swerves to avoid the oncoming officer, he plows the large truck into a thick snowbank. An intense explosion of snow sprays over the top of the vehicle, covering the windshield in a powdery white shower. Without hesitation, Finicum opens the driver's side door. As he does, two more shots ring out. The bullets slam into the side panel of the truck, spraying flecks of shrapnel into one of the passengers sitting in the cab. Stunned by the searing pain, the passenger slumps over on the bench seat, cut and bleeding.

Exiting the cab, Finicum draws the attention of law enforcement officers. All the officers, including federal agents and local and Oregon state patrolmen, have their rifles drawn and at the ready. They quickly move away from their perches behind the makeshift roadblock they created to stop Finicum and his companions.

Finicum's feet sink deeply into the freshly fallen snow. The drift appears deeper than he expected. Trudging through the harsh terrain, Finicum raises his hands above his head, spreading them outward like a bird's wings in a "don't shoot" gesture. Two Oregon state policemen armed with handguns stand to his right, while an Oregon state patrol officer equipped with a Taser X2 approaches from his left. "Keep your hands up!" yells the patrolman as he attempts to close the distance between himself and Finicum. He comes within 15 feet, the maximum distance where he can effectively employ the Taser.

Finicum continues to move backward with his arms extended, sinking ever deeper into the seemingly bottomless drift. The snow encases and soaks his pant legs, filling the tops of his shin-high cowboy boots. In an instant, Finicum appears to reach into his cowskin coat. As he does, a bullet slams into his chest. The bullet turns his body and propels him backward, sending him stumbling through the snow, but he maintains his feet. Digging his heels in, Finicum spreads his arms like wings once again. He reaches once more into his coat pocket.

Appearing from the forest behind Finicum like an apparition, another state trooper, clad in black, focuses his rifle on him. Before Finicum can make another movement, the officer opens fire, blasting Finicum in the back with two expertly placed rifle rounds. The bullets drive Finicum from his feet to the snow-covered floor of the forest. While Finicum lies lifeless, the federal agents and troopers swarm in around him. He dies almost instantly.[1]

After Finicum's death, officials stated that he was reaching for a gun in his pocket when he was shot by a state trooper. The FBI statement also noted that a loaded handgun was found in Finicum's pocket.

It was later identified as a 9mm Ruger SR9. Reportedly, Finicum had received the handgun as a gift from his stepson. After an autopsy was performed on his body, officials withheld the findings from the press for nearly three months.[2]

As a precursor to those events, on the morning of January 26, Finicum was driving one of two vehicles containing several individuals, who were all headed for nearby Grant County, Oregon, where Ryan Payne, a main leader of the occupation of the Malheur Wildlife Refuge, was scheduled to speak at a public meeting. Both vehicles encountered a traffic stop set up by state and federal authorities on a stretch of U.S. Route 395, situated away from populated areas.

At the traffic stop, both cars initially halted, and the occupants of one of the cars surrendered peacefully. They were taken into custody from there. Another man who exited Finicum's car also surrendered peacefully. Finicum, however, did not surrender. He and a passenger recording the entire incident with a cell phone drove away at a high rate of speed and eventually met the blockade and the officers who killed Finicum.

Robert "LaVoy" Finicum was a 54-year-old father of 11 children. He and his wife, Jeanette, lived in Arizona and were foster parents, which was a main source of income for them. A second source of income for the couple was Finicum's work as a rancher. During his ranching operations, he had met and had several confrontations with BLM agents.[3] After these confrontations, Finicum stopped paying grazing fees instituted by the BLM and started to see the bureau as an intrusive, controlling organization unfairly manipulating huge portions of land, especially in the western United States. Because of his disdain for the BLM and federal agencies over regulation of grazing lands, Finicum began reaching out to people and groups sharing his common feelings of displacement.[4]

One of the men Finicum met was Ammon Bundy. Ammon is a tall, heavyset, middle-aged man with a graying beard and a penchant for wearing a Stetson cowboy hat. Ammon is the son of Nevada-based rancher Cliven Bundy, a man whose 20-year dispute with the BLM came to a head and grabbed national headlines a few years ago.

At 69 years of age, Cliven has been a rancher most of his life. He closely resembles his son Ammon in appearance. Aside from the graying beard, his face remains clean-shaven. He is a deeply religious man, and his Mormon faith guides many of the decisions in his life. Cliven gained notoriety when he and several armed protesters confronted BLM agents in 2014, in what became known as the "Bundy Standoff."[5] There is a long history of conflicting interests between citizens and federal agencies over the use of federal lands. More specifically, between ranchers and environmentalists. Ranchers have a long history of using federal lands to graze livestock, which was unregulated until the enactment of the Taylor Grazing Act of 1934.

The reason the government gives for controlling the disputed Cliven ranchland is that overgrazing of the Nevada grassland can damage or destroy habitats for the livestock themselves and for wildlife.[6] Environmental restrictions like the National Environmental Policy Act of 1969 and the Endangered Species Act of 1973 were intended to protect wildlife and the environment. Both have been expanded in their scope over time, becoming overbearingly restrictive and placing a burden on ranchers often to the point of putting them out of business. In the case of Cliven Bundy, the government had determined that his cattle were damaging the habitat of the desert tortoise, an endangered species, which triggered the restriction. According to the Bird and Exotic Clinic of Seattle:

> Desert tortoises live about 50 to 80 years, growing slowly, and generally have low reproductive rates. They spend most of their time in burrows, rock shelters, and pallets to regulate body temperature and reduce water loss. They are most active after seasonal rains and are mostly inactive the rest of the year. This inactivity helps reduce water loss during hot periods, whereas winter hibernation facilitates survival during freezing temperatures and low food availability. Desert tortoises can tolerate water, salt, and energy imbalances daily, which increases their life span."[7]

According to current studies, however, the desert tortoise's population has increased to such a size that it can no longer be contained by the refuge constructed for them, so the government is closing it. The endangered tortoises were used to provide an excuse for the BLM to violate ranchers' claims to easements, all but running the Bundy ranch out of southern Nevada. It seems, however, that the desert tortoises are doing fine. In fact, the tortoise has lived in harmony with cattle in Gold Butte, located in Clark County, Nevada, for over a hundred years. Tortoises have thrived for about as long as Cliven Bundy's family has lived on the land as ranchers. In fact, the real threat to the tortoise is urbanization, not cattle.[8] The BLM has also proven that it has a situational concern for the desert tortoise, as it has had no problem waiving its rules concerning the development of wind and solar power on these ranchlands.[9]

Regardless of these facts, Cliven was ordered to greatly reduce the number of his cattle on federal rangeland on which he had grazing rights. Cliven, in turn, refused to pay grazing fees. In retaliation, the government began removing the Bundys' "trespass" cattle, resulting in the 2014 Bundy standoff. The standoff was not Cliven's first dispute with the federal government over ranchland. His first confrontation started in 1993, when, in protest of grazing rule changes, he refused to renew his permit for cattle grazing on BLM-administered lands in Bunkerville, Nevada.[10]

The BLM tried to argue that the rules had changed, even though this happened, Cliven claims, long after he had secured his rights and paid his dues to Clark County. The BLM went on to state that its rules superseded whatever agreement Cliven had prior, and demanded that he reduce his thousand-some-odd head of cattle down to a tiny herd of 150. This heavy-handed tactic has bankrupted the other ranchers in the area, but Cliven has fought the tactic and remains today.[11]

Bundy and his family paid grazing fees to the BLM from 1954 to 1993. Cliven then attempted to pay Clark County grazing fees in 1994 when the BLM altered their deal through a mandate to protect the desert tortoise.[12] The BLM was originally established in 1946, but Cliven claims that he has, "preemptive, adjudicated livestock water rights filed with the state of Nevada...[that were] established in 1877."[13] And the website FamilySearch proves that Cliven's maternal grandparents John and Christena Jensen, whom Cliven claims his grazing rights through, were living in Nevada as early as 1901.[14] This predates the Taylor Grazing Act of 1934 that established federal grazing districts.

Although the Bundys have been living and farming in Nevada for over a century, the BLM changed the details of the setup. The bureau did this without consulting Cliven—or any other rancher—and then began systematically driving out the cattle and their owners. Cliven refused to pay the BLM, especially after it demanded he reduce his herd's head count to a level that would not sustain his ranch. Cliven also owns the water and forage rights to this land. He paid for those rights. He built fences, established waterways, and constructed roads with his own money, with the approval of the state of Nevada and the BLM. When the BLM started using his fees to run him off the land and started harassing him, he ceased payment.[15]

To punish him for the nonpayment, the BLM charged that Cliven continued to graze his cattle on public lands without a permit. In 1998, Cliven was prohibited by the United States District Court for the District of Nevada from grazing his cattle on an area of land later called the Bunkerville Allotment. In July 2013, U.S. district judge Lloyd D. George claimed Cliven was trespassing on the federally administered land and ordered him to refrain from grazing his cattle on the allotment.

On March 27, 2014, 145,604 acres of federal land in Clark County were temporarily closed for the "capture, impound, and removal of trespass cattle." BLM officials and law enforcement rangers began a roundup of such livestock on April 5. On April 12, a group of protesters, some of them armed, advanced on the "cattle-gathering operation." Sheriff Doug Gillespie negotiated with Cliven and newly confirmed BLM director Neil Kornze, who elected to release the cattle and de-escalate the situation. Cliven was then allowed to continue grazing his cattle on the land. Although Cliven was successful in retaining the ability to continue grazing his cattle on the federally owned land, the clash between the Bundys and the BLM was only heating up.[16]

The death of Robert LaVoy Finicum was the culmination of events that began on January 2, 2016, and essentially ended 41 days later on February 11, 2016. These events are commonly known as "The Occupation of the Malheur National Wildlife Refuge." The occupation took place in Harney County, Oregon; the headquarters of the Malheur National Wildlife Refuge were forcefully occupied by Ammon Bundy, his brother Ryan, and 23 other men, including Finicum. This group, led by Ammon, called itself Citizens for Constitutional Freedom and engaged in an armed standoff with county, state, and federal law enforcement agencies. One of the main government bodies at the core of this dispute was, of course, the BLM.

On January 26, five of the occupiers were arrested on U.S. Route 395 about 48 miles north of the occupation. Among those arrested were Ammon and Ryan Bundy. Ryan suffered a minor gunshot wound to his arm during his arrest. The last four occupiers surrendered on February 11, ending the ordeal. A total of 26 people, including the Bundy brothers, were charged with a single count of felony conspiracy and several other minor charges relating to the use of firearms and abuse of government property.

The occupation took place following a peaceful march in protest of the prison sentences for ranchers Dwight Hammond and his son, Steven Hammond. The Hammonds had been convicted of arson on federal land and sentenced to five years' imprisonment. The Hammonds, as ranchers in Harney County, had long had disputes with the federal government over the use of federally owned land before their arrest. It should also be noted that the Hammonds, on whose behalf the militants were ostensibly acting, disavowed the occupation of the Malheur refuge.[17]

Cattle ranching in Harney County, where the Hammonds were arrested, predates the 1908 establishment of the Malheur National Wildlife Refuge. Some cattle trails, including those used by the

Hammond family, date back to the 1870s. Disputes between local cattle ranchers (not just the Hammonds) and the federal government over management of the Malheur National Wildlife Refuge have raged for decades.

Dwight Lincoln Hammond Jr., 73, and Steven Dwight Hammond, 46, were both involved in a 20-year-long dispute of their own with federal officials. In 1999, Steven Hammond started a fire with the intent of burning off juniper trees and sagebrush, but the fire raged out of control and crossed onto BLM land. The agency told Hammond he needed a burn permit to start such a fire, and if the fires continued, there would be legal consequences. Both Dwight and Steven later set two fires, one in 2001 and one in 2006, which led to convictions of arson for the men.[18]

It is alleged that the 2001 "Hardie-Hammond Fire," as it is known, started when hunters in the area witnessed the Hammonds illegally slaughter a herd of deer. The Hammonds allegedly then set this fire to conceal evidence of the illegal killing.[19] The Hammonds counterclaimed that they started the fire to stop invasive plants from growing on their grazing fields, which is actually common practice for many ranchers, not only in Oregon but across the rest of country.

The 2006 "Krumbo Butte Fire," in which the Hammonds were also involved, started out as a wildfire, but the Hammonds set several back-burns, or controlled fires to eliminate the fuel in the path of the wildfire. The BLM later deemed this practice illegal. The fires ignited by the Hammonds were intended to protect their winter feed for their livestock. According to the indictment, however, the fires threatened to trap four BLM firefighters, one of whom later confronted Dwight Hammond at the scene of the blaze after he moved his crews to avoid the threat. It is also alleged by federal prosecutors, although without proof, that two days following the back-burn, Steven Hammond threatened to frame a BLM employee with arson if he didn't stop the investigation.[20]

In 2012, the Hammonds went to trial in federal district court on multiple charges stemming from the fires. At the end of jury deliberations, a partial verdict was rendered that found the Hammonds not guilty on two of the charges, but convicted them on two counts of arson on federal land. Striking a plea bargain to have the four remaining charges dismissed and for sentences on the two convictions to run concurrently, the Hammonds waived their right to appeal.[21] This was with their knowledge that the trial would proceed to sentencing, where the prosecution intended to seek imposition of the mandatory five-year minimum sentence.

At the sentencing, the federal prosecutors, supported by the BLM, requested a five-year sentence for the Hammonds. U.S. district judge Michael Robert Hogan independently decided that sentences of that length "would shock the conscience" and violate the constitutional prohibition on cruel and unusual punishment. On his last day on the bench before retiring, Hogan sentenced Dwight Hammond to three months' imprisonment and Steven Hammond to a year and a day's imprisonment. These sentences were served fully by both men.

In what was described by one source as a rare action, the government successfully appealed the sentence to the United States Court of Appeals for the Ninth Circuit. The Ninth Circuit threw out Judge Hogan's sentence and upheld the federal prosecutor's original request of five-year sentences, writing, "Given the seriousness of arson, a five-year sentence is not grossly disproportionate to the offense." The court then vacated the original sentence and remanded the men for resentencing. The Hammonds filed petitions for certiorari with the U.S. Supreme Court, which the court denied in March 2015. In October 2015, chief judge Ann Aiken resentenced the pair to five years in prison (with credit for time served), ordering that they return to prison on January 4, 2016.[22]

Both Hammonds reported to the Federal Correctional Institution, Terminal Island, in California on January 4, as ordered by the court. A few days earlier, the Hammonds also paid the federal government the remaining balance on a $400,000 court order for restitution related to the arson fires.

The Hammonds, whether they intentionally set fires to cover up a deer kill or to protect their grazing lands as they alleged, accepted their fate and served the sentences that were given to them. But the federal government, especially the BLM, did not accept that. This agency instead acts as an all-powerful bureau bent on seeking out and delivering the harshest punishments possible to individuals who have committed even minor and inconsequential crimes or, such as in my case, are perceived to have committed a crime, often without any proof.

Many believe the motivation of the group led by Ammon Bundy to occupy the Malheur Wildlife Refuge headquarters was to protest the control and taking of the use of federal lands by the federal government. It is believed it was also to see the refuge lands transferred into private ownership or controlled by Harney County. It is also said that they were protesting the Hammonds' bizarre and harsh sentencing. This has led to a large portion of the public's identifying with the men, giving credence to their complaints.[23]

Through these conflicts, much has also been made of the Bundys' Mormon religion and the influence it had on their decision to occupy the refuge headquarters. This focus is due in part to the Bundy family's feeling that much of their protesting and their tactic of occupation have been divinely inspired. This, in turn, has led many in the mainstream media to liken the Bundys standoffs and occupations to the 1993 Waco Texas siege that saw infamous cult leader David Koresh and his Branch Davidians resist agents of the Bureau of Alcohol, Tobacco and Firearms (ATF) as they attempted to raid the Mount Carmel Center Ranch with brute force.

During this raid, an intense gun battle erupted, resulting in the deaths of four government agents and six Branch Davidians. Upon the ATF's failure to infiltrate the compound, the FBI took over and initiated a siege of the compound. After a 51 day standoff, the FBI launched an assault that included a tear gas attack and an attempt to force the Branch Davidians out of the secure compound. During the attack, a fire engulfed the Mount Carmel Center compound, killing 76 people, including leader David Koresh.

The occupation of the refuge has also drawn strong comparisons with the 1992 Ruby Ridge incident. Ruby Ridge was the site of a deadly confrontation and siege in northern Idaho between Randy Weaver, his family, his friend Kevin Harris, and agents of the United States Marshals Service (USMS) and the FBI. The events resulted in the death of Weaver's son Sammy, his wife Vicki, and Deputy U.S. Marshal William Francis Degan.

Due to these sweeping comparisons and because the memory of these events is still fresh in many Americans' minds, the words "religious fanaticism" are often bandied about regarding the Bundys. It is true they are unabashedly Mormon and are unafraid to share their beliefs with others. But their faith does not take away from the fact that they have a legitimate gripe with the federal government.

There have also been numerous questions as to the feelings and attitudes of Cliven Bundy toward minorities, especially the African American community, because of remarks he made about a week following the end of the Nevada standoff in 2014. The following quote is from a discussion he was having about a civil disturbance he had witnessed during the 1965 Watts riots in Los Angeles. Cliven recalled seeing a public housing project in North Las Vegas where some of the older residents and the children sat on the porch:

> They didn't have nothing to do...they were basically on government subsidy, so now what do they do? They abort their young children, they put their young men in jail, because they never learned how to pick cotton. And I've often wondered, are they better off as slaves, picking cotton and having a family life and doing things, or are they better off under government subsidy? They didn't get no more freedom. They got less freedom.

It is important to note that Cliven made references to the country's current affairs when it came to his stance on illegal immigration. He is quoted as having said:

> [The Mexicans] come over here against our Constitution and cross our borders, but they're here, and they're people.... Don't tell me they don't work, and don't tell me they don't pay taxes. And don't tell me they don't have better family structures than most of us white people.

A year later Cliven called the reaction to his statements a "misunderstanding," saying he was not racist. He expressed support for blacks who had "raised themselves up to a point where they are equal with the rest of us."

Many have continued to denounce him as racist because of these remarks, although others have challenged that accusation. Whether you agree with the Bundy family's tactics and stances or not, there is no denying that much of this added information and focus has been used as fodder to undercut the point being made by incidents like the occupation of the wildlife refuge and the initial standoff with the Bundys.

These incidents are shining light on the fact that the BLM's abusive law enforcement techniques and governmental overregulation have not only taken a toll on the businesses and livelihoods of many individuals, but have also begun to encroach on the very freedoms of these people. Are the Bundys' tactics of armed occupation a version of militant extremism? Perhaps. Was LaVoy Finicum evading arrest and reaching for a gun to do battle with police surrounding him? Perhaps. Is Cliven Bundy a racist? Perhaps.

These and other questions, and issues such as the Hammonds' extended prison sentences, can be debated by a myriad of talking heads on television for hours and days at a time, but the underlying point remains. And that is, many of the people involved in these incidents feel as though they are underrepresented and are being marginalized by the very government that should be there to protect their most basic of constitutional rights. These people have begun to turn the spotlight on several governmental organizations, including the BLM, that need to be scrutinized and taken to task for their abusive use and displays of power. Because of this abuse, a growing number of citizens in this country want the government out of their lives and to stop being punished for simply living.

The Malheur occupation was the fourth in an ongoing series of armed incursions on public lands since the Bundy Standoff. An armed show of force and an off-road vehicle ride were staged in San Juan

County, Utah, in May 2014, followed by another armed show of force in Josephine County, Oregon, in April 2015 and an occupation of U.S. Forest Service land in Montana in August 2015. At least 20 of the citizens who occupied the Malheur refuge were reported to have participated in the earlier Utah, Oregon, and Montana demonstrations.

Perhaps the feds are turning the country into a communist collective? After all, they seem to believe that they know how to use our land better than we do privately. In fact, the federal government owns a staggering 640 million acres of land. The sum of all that acreage adds up to about 28 percent of the nation's total surface of about 2.3 billion acres. Nearly 80 percent of that land is in the 11 westernmost states in the country. All this land is overseen by the federal government's Bureau of Land Management, which has essentially become an armed law enforcement organization in support of the regulations it wrote, administered, and effectively sits as judge and jury upon. The question becomes, does the BLM act on behalf of the public or in its own interest?

After the attacks of September 11, 2001, President George W. Bush signed into law the USA Patriot Act on October 26, 2001. The title of the act is actually a 10-letter "backronym" that stands for "Uniting and Strengthening America by Providing Appropriate Tools Required to Intercept and Obstruct Terrorism." It was originally meant to expand the power of the federal government to better protect the country against terrorists and suspected terrorist activity. This law allowed the expansion of federal powers, and it also meant the government would give numerous bureaus under its control (the BLM, the FBI, and so on) expanded law enforcement powers.

Essentially, this allowed the BLM to police the people and businesses under its oversight, which of course includes the 640 million acres of government-owned land. As the years have gone by, the BLM's expanded law enforcement powers have been less and less about terrorism protection and have been more and more about justification of the bureau's existence as a monolithic and bureaucratic organization. Big arrests seem to be used to justify the larger and ever-increasing salaries for BLM agents. I believe that this, in large part, was the reason for the multiple raids on my businesses. I also believe this was an enormous reason for the hostility and increasing confrontations between people like the Bundys and the BLM.

These laws and regulations have emboldened and empowered the BLM and the agents it employs. The agency has become more confrontational and unruly in its attempt to punish people for doing something it sees as illegal, whether the act is substantiated or not. Most ranchers and individuals I have spoken with who have had confrontations with the BLM have acknowledged that for the most part, they once had a decent relationship with BLM agents.

For a period, ranchers, artifact collectors, and the supervising BLM agents coexisted together. It has been only recently, in the past decade or so, that the tide seems to have turned. Federal agents have become increasingly confrontational, too regulatory, and flat-out abusive in their handling of citizens and their businesses. Much of this can be attributed to the increasing amount of corruption that has seeped into the BLM and consumed the organization like a plague. Due to the expanded law enforcement powers of the bureau, there has been an emphasis on increasing the number of high-profile arrests.

These arrests by bureau agents are motivated by an increase in pay and stature in the organization. Simply put, the higher the profile of an arrest an agent makes or the greater number of arrests that an agent is involved in, the more justification there is for an increase in salary and standing. Sadly, so much of this simply serves to justify the current state of the BLM's bloated bureaucratic existence. Many of the people who are benefitting from these abuses are collecting salaries in the six-figure range but have little to no education to back up their large salaries.

These people are the beneficiaries of a level of corruption and cronyism that rivals Boss Tweed and Tammany Hall. The BLM not only has attacked citizen ranchers and artifact collectors, but has abused large international businesses like the Gibson Guitar Company and highly upstanding citizens such as doctors and other medical professionals. Not only are these groups subjected to the BLM's overt scrutiny, but information has come to light linking many of these incidents, revealing an attempt by the BLM to focus on procuring arrests and convictions in high-profile cases against high-profile individuals to grab headlines.

In 2012, I received a document through the U.S. Postal Service from an individual with intimate knowledge of the inner workings of the BLM as well as many other governmental organizations. The individual, in detail, laid bare the inner workings of the BLM and the corruption at the very heart of the organization. This document clarified the connections between my raid, the raid on the Gibson Guitar Corporation—one of the oldest manufacturers of guitars in the world—and an artifact raid in Blanding, Utah, that led to the death of Dr. James Redd.

In this document, the author also implored me to file a Freedom of Information Act (FOIA) request with the federal government. I did request access to the voluminous reports of investigation concerning misconduct issues by agents of the BLM, the United States Fish and Wildlife Service (USFWS), and the Office of Law Enforcement (OLE). My multiple requests were all denied. Subsequently, I learned that this explosive document was making its way throughout the BLM law enforcement agencies as well as into the Congressional Record.

My goal here is that by bringing this information to light, I will help make my fellow Americans aware of how federal law enforcement agencies are operating and, in some cases, overreaching and abusing their authority. I hope to be able to make the public aware that, though most people may believe they will never cross paths with the BLM, the same BLM is a potential threat to them, their businesses, their livelihoods, and their very constitutional rights because of corrupt and overzealous federal agents who believe they have the right to trample the inalienable rights of all American citizens.

10

A White Bird

On June 11, 2009, Dr. James Redd, a 60-year-old physician, was found dead in the small town of Blanding, Utah. His lifeless body was discovered on his property by members of his family. It was an apparent suicide. Friends and family of Dr. Redd gathered outside of his home to express their grief at the loss of this respected physician. By all accounts, Dr. Redd was a well-liked member of the Blanding community, with a special place in the hearts of many people. He had been a family practice physician for more than 30 years and had helped to serve the Native American population living in the area as well. He was a father of five children and a grandfather of eight.

A tall, medium-built man with hints of white streaked through his hair, Dr. Redd had warm gray eyes and a welcoming smile; his smile has been described as one of his more enduring and kindest traits. This man, whose giving personality made him one of the most admired people in a small community in southeastern Utah, was lost, or should I say taken, far too soon from his family and a community who loved him.

Dr. Redd's story with its tragic ending begins in 1996 when the Redd family—Dr. Redd, his wife, Jeanette, and their five children—were four-wheeling on land owned by family friend Erv Guymon. Guymon, an elderly rancher, had informed Jeanette Redd he had land in Cottonwood Canyon, north of Bluff, Utah, with some "mounds," or Anasazi ruins, on them. Guymon told her that she was welcome to gather whatever artifacts she wanted either by digging or screening in the dirt. Screening is the process of removing loose topsoil using a mesh screener or soil sifter. Screening topsoil removes most of the debris so items can be found. Most important, this method of exposing artifacts is completely legal on private land.

Jeanette Redd, a beautiful, slender woman with dark chestnut hair and blessed with a true independent spirit, was the inspiration behind the Redd family's collecting of artifacts. Her favorite historic items came from the Anasazi. The Anasazi people, also known as the Ancient Ones, are thought to be ancestors of the modern Pueblo Indians who inhabited the Four Corners region of southern Utah, southwestern Colorado, northwestern New Mexico, and northern Arizona. They inhabited these areas from around A.D. 200 to A.D. 1300, when these people mysteriously disappeared, leaving behind only the remnants of their ancient culture. Evidence of their incredible culture is found at cliff dwellings like Mesa Verde in southern Colorado, Chaco Canyon in northern New Mexico, and Hovenweep National Monument in southeastern Utah.

With their disappearance, the Anasazi left behind a significant number of artifacts in these cliff dwellings as well as in the surrounding areas. Jeanette simply kept the items she collected as part of her small collection to be viewed and enjoyed.

On Saturday, January 6, 1996, while traveling down the dusty dirt backcountry roads on the Guymon property, the Redd family passed Erv Guymon traveling in his old beat-up Ford truck. He approvingly waved to them, and the Redds continued to the Anasazi mounds located on his land. Anasazi burial mounds and similar ruins are not what a person typically thinks of as an ancient ruin. These burial and ceremonial structures are typically flat-topped pyramids or platform mounds, flat-topped or rounded cones, elongated ridges, and sometimes a variety of other forms. To the untrained eye they look like a pile of dirt or a small hill that a child could easily climb to the top of.

Arriving at the mound ruins by midday, the Redd family opened the gate fencing in the property. Unloading their four-wheelers, the Redds started preparing the food they intended to have for lunch. While lunch was being prepared, some of the family members kicked around the sun-scorched land searching for arrowheads. They also did some screening of the nearby dirt mounds. These mounds had already been churned up by previous curiosity seekers.

Again, this type of site is not a cliff house or the equivalent of an ancient ruin often portrayed in Hollywood films. It is basically a slightly raised area of dirt, elevated just above the flat terrain of the Western plains. In this instance, the Anasazi mound had been dug into and turned over multiple times since Mormon pioneers settled the area in 1880.

Enjoying the outdoors and the vast landscape, the Redds continued screening and four-wheeling on the land. While they did so, a sheriff's deputy named Naranjo passed by doing a routine check. Pulling up in a puff of dust, Naranjo exited his black-and-white cruiser and approached the Redd family.

With hands shielding his eyes from the sun, officer Naranjo asked, "What are you folks doing?"

"We're screening," they replied nearly in unison, barely looking up.

Then the group stopped screening and walked over to Naranjo. Naranjo inquired further, "Do you know whose land this is?"

Dr. Redd, stepping in for his family, replied, "Yes, it's Erv Guymon's land."

"Do you have permission to be here?" Naranjo asked, turning his attention toward Dr. Redd.

"Yes, we do," said the doctor.

"All right, thank you," said Naranjo, climbing back into his cruiser. He barreled down the road, kicking up dust as he went. The Redds took Naranjo's questioning as nothing out of the ordinary and knew they had permission to continue their activities.

What the Redd family did not know at the time was that about three months earlier, on a Sunday afternoon, a man by the name of

Perkowski had observed three people in a full-sized green van digging at the same mound. After this incident, there was a dispute as to whether the site was on Utah school trust land or private land owned by Erv Guymon. Acting on Perkowski's information, BLM agent Jim Ragsdale looked at the site on November 2, 1995. After observing the dig site, Ragsdale reported in his field notes, "[I] saw what appeared to be human bones on the west side of the hole."

The BLM later received intelligence that the Redd family had been seen at the site two months after bones were identified by agent Ragsdale. Then, just a few months after the Redds were seen digging at the site, the state of Utah filed third-degree felony charges against Dr. James Redd and his wife Jeanette for "desecration of a dead human body." The Redds, although they had permission to be on the land, were also charged with trespassing and felony desecration of a grave.[1]

Even though the BLM and the state of Utah knew Dr. Redd and his wife did not disinter a body because the bones had already been observed by Agent Ragsdale before the Redds arrived at the site, they were still charged. Perhaps this was because of Dr. Redd's prominent standing in the Blanding community and the fact that a high-profile arrest would make media headlines. Interestingly, a dispute currently exists as to who exactly owns the small scrap of land. There is even a question as to the history of its ownership. The accredited BLM map at the time of the Redd family's outing indicates that the small section of land was indeed privately owned by Erv Guymon.

The area in question has no fence or demarcation notifying individuals that it is anything other than private land. Guymon believed it to be his land when he allowed the Redd family to screen there. Furthermore, school trust lands require ranchers who graze their cattle on those lands to have a permit. The state of Utah never required Guymon to produce a permit, and to this day still does not require one.

In a letter dated January 10, 1996—just four days after Dr. Redd and his family were seen on the site—Kenny Winch, the Utah state archaeologist at the time, wrote:

I understand that Jim (Dr. Redd) stated they thought they were digging a site on private land, which is pretty close, just across the section line to the east. In any case, everyone close to the investigation expects that there will be some sort of pressure to forget about it because of the prominence of the alleged perpetrators. I think it is an appropriate opportunity to send a strong message that the Trust Lands Administration will not tolerate the willful and illegal destruction of the trust's archaeological assets. I recommend we take this case very seriously and support the sheriff in the criminal investigation, and that we commit whatever resources necessary to pursue the strongest civil action penalties possible.

In this letter, Wintch stated that Dr. Redd believed his family was on private land. Later in the letter he stated that it was an opportunity to send a message that the Trust Lands Administration would not tolerate the "willful" and "illegal destruction" of school trust land archaeological sites. It is obvious that Dr. Redd and his family thought they were on Guymon's land and that Guymon thought the same. Yet in this letter, Wintch didn't seem to care about any of this. He merely wanted to prosecute "the strongest civil action penalties possible" regardless of intent or knowledge, because of the "prominence" of the individuals involved.

So, on July 22, 1996, the Utah state attorney general's office sent a letter to Dr. Redd and his wife Jeanette. In that letter, John Andrews writes of the ruin and the incident stating, "The ruin in question has been designated in the National Register of Historic Places as site 42SA23040." The significance of this statement is that the site Dr. Redd and his family were seen on was never designated in the National Register of Historic Places.

The assistant attorney general in that letter referred to the land as a numbered site designated 42SA23040. To have a number assigned to a site, it must be a significant site; if the site is on private land, the landowner must apply for a site number. The applied-for site must pass certain criteria to receive "historic designation" and an accompanying number. Through meticulous research, it was determined that this site number was assigned January 11, 1996, five days after the Redd family's dig. It can be assumed that this designation was applied for, and awarded, to make the situation look as bad as possible for Dr. Redd.

In the year following, the felony charges against the Redds were first dismissed by Judge Lyle Anderson, who was a Redd family friend. The state of Utah then appealed the decision to the appellate court, which upheld Judge Anderson's initial ruling. Not satisfied with the ruling, the state eventually claimed it had new evidence and refiled charges. There was absolutely no new evidence, but the case was still sent to the Utah Supreme Court. That court did not rule on the issue of new evidence but instead said the case should have been bound over for trial on the original charges.

The case again went back to San Juan County and was placed before Judge Mary Manly, who ruled that the state violated a "Brickey ruling." This is a ruling applying to the state of Utah that says, "The refiling of a dismissed charge is limited by due process." Therefore, as the state refiled charges without new evidence, Judge Manly found the charges were not prosecutable and dismissed them.

After this ruling, the state of Utah, likely encouraged by agents of the BLM, charged the Redds with trespassing and proceeded to sue them for $250,000 in damages to repair the site. With the uproar that was swirling around a small plot of land like a tempest, it is interesting to note that archaeologist Kenny Wintch admitted that after an intense survey of the land in question, it appeared the Redds were off private land by a meager 30 feet.

The Redds' "bluff case," as it was later dubbed, lasted from 1996 to 2003. The BLM was heavily involved in the attempted prosecution. Due to the intense scrutiny of this case, legislators in Utah eventually changed the laws to include unearthing bone fragments as a criminal violation if not reported properly. Forrest Cuch, the director of Indian Affairs for Utah from 1997 to 2011, was also very outspoken against the Redds. Throughout the duration of the case, Cuch was quoted as saying, "There is clearly an attempt to interpret this law in a loose fashion, and we would certainly recommend this decision be appealed to the highest level and the Redds prosecuted to the fullest extent."[2] Cuch was later fired by Utah governor Gary Herbert, in 2011.

After seven years of dealing with this issue in the courts and in the media, Jeanette Redd agreed to a settlement with the Utah Trust Lands Administration for $10,000. She was also given six months' probation. Dr. Redd's charges were completely dismissed. With this final ruling many people, including the Redds, thought the incident was settled. Then three years later, in 2006, a secret informant employed by the BLM knocked on the Redds' door armed with a plan to entrap the family in a supposed black-market ring for stolen Indian artifacts.

It is felt by Redd family members, many politicians, and several lawmakers that the BLM, Forrest Cuch, and other federal agents were so upset that the Redd family, specifically Dr. Redd, escaped severe punishment over the "bluff case" that a plan was hatched to destroy the man and his family. The plot the BLM devised went by the code name "Operation Cerberus Action," and those involved went to great lengths—utilizing questionable and even unlawful tactics—to charge Dr. Redd with a felony.

One of the men who concocted and led Operation Cerberus Action was special agent Dan Love of the BLM. Just by looking at him, you might not expect it, but Love throws his federally sanctioned weight around as though he were Goliath. In many circumstances, Love has been referred to as a mobster or a bully who uses unethical, almost Gestapo-style tactics. Not only was Love the head of Operation Cerberus Action, but he was the special agent in charge of the unsuccessful Cliven Bundy raid in Clark County, Nevada, in 2014.

During this sting operation, the federal government hired a secret informant named Ted Gardiner. This informant conducted surveillance and later set up Dr. Redd, his wife Jeanette, and many others in Utah and surrounding states over supposedly stolen Indian artifacts. Gardiner was an odd fellow by most standards. He was a tall, gangly man with a rail-thin frame and a weather-beaten face. He did not have the look of a prototypical federal informant. Perhaps that is why so many placed their trust in him.

Before he ever spent time working as an informant for the federal government, Gardiner owned a successful chain of grocery stores. However, in 1996, he suffered a severe panic attack during a business lunch. This attack led him to see a doctor, who prescribed an anti-anxiety drug for his issues. Following his taking of the drug, Gardiner began to experience a host of issues, and his life spiraled out of control.

Gardiner's marriage crumbled, and he became an alcoholic, went bankrupt, and lost his chain of supermarkets. With the loss of income, Gardiner, who had also been an amateur collector and a self-styled expert in Indian artifacts, began selling much of his collection online. He acquired a great deal of expertise on the Anasazi throughout his 52 years of life by studying their culture and making numerous hiking expeditions in Utah's vast Indian ruins. These hiking trips led him to feel as though he was spiritually connected to these ancient people.

Gardiner's business dealings online with undocumented artifacts brought him under the scrutiny of the federal government. Instead of prosecuting him for making dubious claims about the authenticity of his artifacts, the federal government decided to "flip" him and make him a mole.

In 2006, the federal government came calling and found Gardiner huddled in the corner of a small mountain cabin, burning his furniture to stay warm. He initially refused the agents' offer to become an informant. But later, after sobering up and listening to their pitch again on the phone, he agreed to meet with two agents from an FBI art crimes task force. The FBI's pitch was to have Gardiner help them capture people they perceived to be thieves and dealers in stolen Indian artifacts. Gardiner, invigorated by the special attention he was receiving from the FBI, went on to concoct a story of a nefarious black-market ring in Utah that dealt in illegal Indian artifacts and whose participants were some of the most prominent citizens in the state.

According to Tim Furhman, the FBI's special agent in charge for Utah, this illegal trafficking was a multimillion-dollar industry.[3]

With this information in hand, federal agents initially paid Gardiner $10,000 for his work. They soon recruited him to act as an informant, an occupation that would eventually net him well over $200,000 during two years of entrapping people believed to be involved in the nefarious black market. The FBI and BLM knew Gardiner had an encyclopedic knowledge of the Indian artifact market and had the expertise and quick wit to be able to convince buyers and dealers of anything.

After the deal was struck, the FBI agents brought in the BLM, whose jurisdiction the Anasazi artifacts fell under. That is when Dan Love's involvement in the undercover operation began. Love promised Gardiner $7,500 a month and equipped him with an audiovisual camera, disguised as a button on his shirt. He was sent to Dr. Redd's house. His mission was a simple one: entrap the Redds in Native American artifact dealing by any means necessary.

Beginning in late 2006, equipped with his concealed camera, Gardiner set out on his assignment. Gardiner was code-named SU 6129 by Dan Love and his federal agent handlers. During a two-and-a-half-year undercover investigation, Gardiner repeatedly tried to entrap Dr. Redd and his wife Jeanette in numerous undercover videos. The videos allowed the feds to charge Dr. Redd with one felony count of possessing an artifact, and Jeanette Redd was charged with seven felonies.

The Redd's charge read as follows:

> On or about March 27, 2008, in the Central Division of the District of Utah, JEANNE H. REDD and JAMES D. REDD, defendants herein, did receive, conceal, and retain property belonging to an Indian tribal organization, with a value of more than $1,000 to wit: an effigy bird pendant, knowing such property to have been embezzled, stolen, or converted, and did aid and abet therein, all in violation of 18 U.S.C. 1163 and 2.

The "effigy bird pendant" mentioned in the allegations was smaller than half the size of a dime and resembled a small bead. Dr. Redd had picked this item up off the earthen floor and brought it home. At no time did he try to sell or trade it to Gardiner or anyone else. He simply presented it to Gardiner to look at. All his interactions with Gardiner were strictly ethical, and he never once tried to trade to Gardiner any artifact whatsoever. In fact, Dr. Redd never tried to trade or purchase any artifact from anyone ever. Artifacts were not his "thing."

Part of the video evidence Gardiner recorded on his hidden camera is available to be viewed by the public online through a *Los Angeles Times* article on the raid titled "A Sting in the Desert." The video is raw and unedited. The piece of footage involving the "bird pendant" shows Gardiner being welcomed into the Redds' home. Soon after his entrance, a talk arises between Jeanette Redd and him about the "effigy pendant." Jeanette begins by telling Gardiner that while she and her husband were hiking by the Baby Rock mounds in Arizona, Dr. Redd stumbled upon the pea-sized artifact. The item is then produced on a tray with a few others, and a casual conversation between Gardiner and Jeanette begins concerning the insignificant bead.

"Oh, that's sweet," Gardiner says, fingering the pendant.

"It's got to be a bird...and we found those...and that's the arrowhead I found," Jeanette excitedly responds, pointing out the small spearhead-shaped item lying on the tray.

"That's a nice bull creek," Gardiner says, referring to the type of arrowhead Jeanette had found.

"It sure is a pretty red," Jeanette gleefully interjects.

"Good job."

"It was fun, but we were only gone about an hour."

The two sit in silence for a few moments as Jeanette peruses the large items Gardiner brought. Every one of the items Gardiner provided were given to him by federal government agents with the hope of entrapping the Redds. As Jeanette picks through Gardiner's government-provided bounty, Dr. Redd enters the room and points to the "effigy pendant."

"Hey, what do you think? What do you think of that little dude there? Huh? Huh?" Dr. Redd says with a dose of sarcasm in his voice.

"That is nice!" Gardiner responds with equal sarcasm.

All three enjoy a good belly laugh due to the insignificant size of the pendant when compared to Gardiner's items.

"He knows just the thing to say," chuckles Dr. Redd as he hovers over the numerous artifacts laid out on the table.

"You are talking about the little white pendant, right?" says Gardiner in an even more sarcastic tone.

The group of friends all laugh uproariously again; they truly seem to be enjoying each other's company.

"Pretty good, eh?" Dr. Redd manages to say through gasps of laughter.

"Yeah, and the bull creek's not bad either," replies Gardiner, once again referencing the small reddish arrowhead. The group enjoys another round of laughter as Gardiner begins to examine the pendant more thoroughly.

Talking directly to Gardiner as he examines the artifact, Dr. Redd says, "Oh, you would have to bring that up. I guess those Anasazi were not quite as bad as I thought they were. That's tricky, isn't it? So, it's a stylized bird?"

"I think so," Gardiner said.

"Jeanette knew it right off."

"Jim, where did you find this little white bird pendant?" says Gardiner.

Jeanette interjects, "Baby Rock. Baby Rock, Arizona."

"Yeah," replies Dr. Redd.

"Okay," says Gardiner.

"Have you been to Baby Rock?" Jeanette asks the informant.

"It sounds familiar."

"It's on the way to Kayenta, back behind Baby Rocks," Dr. Redd explains.

"Oh, okay. Yeah, I know where it is," Gardiner responds.

"There used to be a service station there, but there's not anymore."

"Okay," Gardiner retorts.

"Get up on those mesas," Dr. Redd implores Gardiner.

This "effigy" artifact's existence would lead to the death of Dr. Redd and destroy many other lives in the process. For the U.S. attorney to charge Dr. Redd with a felony, the BLM agents had to supply evidence that the "stolen" Indian artifact in question was worth over $1,000. The feds did no research on this subject, nor did they get a legitimate appraisal. They simply plucked the $1,000 price tag out of the air and attributed that value to the small pendant. With this "evidence" in hand, the federal agents prepared to raid Dr. Redd's home.

Dan Love and the other federal agents involved in Operation Cerberus Action lied about the value of the "artifact," saying it was worth over $1,000 when it was in fact worth only $75, in order to charge Dr. Redd and his wife Jeanette with a felony. By law, if the value of the item in question was less than $1,000, it would entail a misdemeanor charge. If the agents were going to charge Dr. Redd with anything, it should have been at best a misdemeanor but that just would not work for them. They had to charge him with a felony to take away his medical license and destroy him.

So, on the night of June 9, 2009, a tribal elder from the Southwestern Pueblo Indians blessed more than 100 U.S. Bureau of Land Management law enforcement officers and archaeologists, who would mount a dawn raid on the Utah towns of Blanding, Moab, and Monticello. The residents of these towns would receive indictments for looting graves and trading in relics taken from tribal, BLM, and Forest Service land.[4]

The following morning, Love and more than 100 armed federal officers descended on the Redd residence in Blanding, Utah, storming through the home with guns at the ready. Love later boasted to Dr. Redd's daughter Jericca that he had 80 agents at Dr. Redd's house at one time, and throughout the day, he said, there were a total of 140 agents traipsing through the house. Love also told Jericca he had handpicked the agents who went to Dr. Redd's house. Those agents searched Dr. Redd's house for more than 11 hours. The other defendants involved in Operation Cerberus Action arrested that day had at the most 10 to 12 agents at their homes. No other homes were searched for more than a few hours, and none of the defendants were interrogated for more than half an hour.

As the feds entered the front door and handcuffed Jeanette Redd, they asked over and over, "*Where's the white bird? Where's the white bird?*" Jeanette was, in a sense, relieved, because she knew they did not have a white bird. She felt they had the wrong house. She did not expect that this many armed agents would storm the house because they wanted the tiny effigy bird pendant.

Jeanette was immediately put in handcuffs, and one of the agents kept repeating to her, "Do you know how much trouble you are in? Your life is over as you know it. This is the worst day of your life. This is like a death in your family." Another agent followed the harassment by saying to her three times, "Are you suicidal?"

On the morning of the raid, Dr. Redd arrived at the house at 6:45 am. He had been to the local nursing home to check on some of his patients. Pulling up to his house, he witnessed swarms of federal agents buzzing around with numerous government vehicles leading up to and in front of the house. One of the FBI agents drew his gun, pointed it at Dr. Redd, ripped him out of his jeep, handcuffed him, then sat him down in the garage, shutting the door. This would be the start of a three-and-a-half-hour interrogation concerning the pendant artifact in question. In the garage, both BLM and FBI agents interrogated Dr. Redd, calling him a liar to his face multiple times. They also went on to harass the man by asking him what shovel he liked to dig up bodies with. He was then informed that he would never practice medicine again.

During the intense interrogation, Dr. Redd had to go to the bathroom, so at least two agents marched him down the stairs to the bathroom. One agent stood six inches from his right knee and another agent stood six inches from his left knee as he used the bathroom. When he was done, they would not remove his handcuffs for him to even clean himself. They then stuffed him in a paddy wagon and drove him off to the BLM office in Monticello, where they shackled him to others arrested in the separate raids. All were driven to Moab to stand before the federal judge to hear their charges and for Dr. Redd to enter a plea of not guilty.

According to Dan Love, he placed seven snipers on the roof of the Redds' home the day of the raid. He said they were waiting for Dr. Redd's son Javalan to drive down to the house. According to Love, the reason they did this was because Javalan had called the house when the feds were there and said, "Don't touch my animals. I'm coming down to get them." Love said they (the federal agents at the home) took this as a threat to their lives and therefore were waiting for him.

Incredibly, the feds did not even take the effigy bird pendant the day of the raid. The very item they were raiding the house for was on a tray in plain sight right under their noses, yet it was left behind. That night, after being released from custody, Dr. Redd returned to his home in Blanding. He left his family a recorded message that lasted about 40 minutes. In it he describes how he loves his family, and speaks to each family member individually. While recording his last message to his family, Dr. Redd also apologizes to his office manager because he didn't get all the dictation done on his patients he had seen the day before. So just before ending his life, it is telling that one of his main concerns was he was that he had not completed the dictation for all his patient's medical records.

Dr. Redd also speaks at length about his love of and testimony for the Restored Gospel of Jesus Christ and the importance of keeping the commandments. He also mentions the government and that with him gone, "there will be one less charge to contend with." The one charge Dr. Redd refers to is the bogus felony charge for the effigy bird pendant.

Approximately 24 hours after agent Dan Love and the feds raided Dr. Redd's home, he asphyxiated himself in his jeep. Dr. James Redd is gone because of a felony charge that the federal government knowingly falsified. Interestingly, the feds went back to the Redds' house on July 7, 2009, to take more artifacts, and that is when the effigy bird pendant was confiscated.

Less than a week after Dr. Redd's tragic death, the U.S. attorneys office published a press release. In it, U.S. attorney for Utah Brett Tolman is quoted as saying, "None of the charges in the indictments is for mere possession of a protected artifact. The charges in the indictment are for trafficking in archaeological artifacts, which includes the sale, purchase, or exchange of protected artifacts." This is a total lie, and the feds know it. Dr. Redd never sold, purchased, or exchanged any artifact. Later, the Redd family had the effigy pendant evaluated by a professional appraiser. The value of the item was determined to be about $75. So, Dan Love and the federal agents involved in the raid inflated the value of the item by over 1,250 percent to exceed the felony threshold.

At a Senate Judiciary Committee meeting on June 17, 2009 (the day of Dr. Redd's funeral), Senator Orrin Hatch questioned Attorney General Eric Holder about the artifact raids, focusing exclusively on the over-the-top treatment and heavy-handedness of BLM and FBI agents in Dr. Redd's arrest and suicide. At that time, Senator Hatch had no idea the only charge against Dr. Redd was for the possession of the small pendant, which should have never led to a felony charge.

A few months after Dr. Redd's death, in a meeting at the Old Tymer Restaurant in Blanding, Utah, Dan Love and another BLM agent met with Jericca Redd to discuss an obscure email of Jeanette Redd's. During this meeting, Love asked Jericca how the family was doing. She politely tried to say not well. Love proudly stated, "I know why your mom hates me: I'm the reason your dad is gone." He continued, "[Don't] give in to the hate like the town of Blanding has done."

About a month after Dr. Redd's death, Love, BLM Special Agent Brent Range, and an FBI agent were back at the Redd home. While there, Love noticed a picture of the Prophet Joseph Smith on the kitchen table and told Jeanette and Jericca, "It's good you have his picture there; keep praying to him." Those familiar with the Mormon faith know that Joseph Smith is not worshipped but revered.

During this meeting, Love received a phone call and, after hanging up, commented to Jericca that he had just spoken to the "secret informant" Ted Gardiner and complained that Gardiner continued to ask for more money. Love and Gardiner, two of the main people responsible for the untimely death of Dr. Redd, were discussing the exchange of money for their actions against Dr. Redd resulting in his death and then letting Dr. Redd's daughter know about it. As the agents were leaving, while standing in the garage, Love gave Dr. Redd's three-year-old grandson, Sebastian, a child's BLM badge and said he could call him "Uncle Dan." Sebastian idolized his Poppy, and the guy responsible for his death was telling him he could call him "Uncle Dan." This is one of the most disgusting things Love has done.

In another incident, Love and Brent Range were at the apartment of Jamaica Redd Lyman (one of Dr. Redd's daughters) in Provo, Utah, talking to Jeanette Redd and the couple's three daughters. Jericca asked Love why he thought Dr. Redd did what he did. Love's response was, "I think he took one for the team." Love also told each of them what he had learned from reading all of Dr. Redd's private journals, and explained the private thoughts and concerns Dr. Redd had for each of his children and his wife. Love also let them know that he felt Dr. Redd had extremely poor penmanship. What Love did not know or understand was that Dr. Redd used shorthand and medical abbreviations in much of his writing.

On the day of the raid, Gardiner was paid $224,000 for his work as an informant. He continued to be paid for his work in the subsequent months. Nine months after Dr. Redd was gone, Gardiner said to a friend of his that he "felt guilty for killing two people." One of the individuals Gardiner referred to was Dr. Redd; the other was a man who also killed himself because of Operation Cerberus Action. A few days after Gardiner made these statements, his roommate reported him to the police for brandishing a firearm and acting suicidal. When police arrived at Gardiner's home, they witnessed him kneeling with his head on a bed and a gun in his hand.[5] Officers reported that he pointed the weapon at his own head and then at the officers. One of the officers, who had his gun drawn, told Gardiner to drop his weapon.

"You're gonna have to do what you have to do," Gardiner replied to the officer.

Then Gardiner swung the gun in the officer's direction and fired a shot, just missing the officer as all the policemen backed out of the bedroom. The situation ended with Gardiner putting a bullet in his head a short time later. Why would an undercover informant who was supposedly doing his job properly feel guilty for the actions of those he had caught in illegal activity?

Could it be that Gardiner and the feds knew there was no black-market ring and that Dr. Redd was not a dealer, trafficker, or collector and never had been? Gardiner knew he had played a major part in Dr. Redd's death. It appears that, after nine months of torment, Gardiner could not take it anymore and put a bullet in his head. During the two years Gardiner had spent filming and informing on the Redds, Dr. Redd gave him medical advice on an ankle injury he had sustained while hiking. Dr. Redd also encouraged him several times to quit smoking and gave him several tips to improve his health. The Redd family welcomed all his visits and treated him as a friend.

In the wake of Operation Cerberus Action, Love went on to be named the BLM's Special Agent of the Year for his work in 2009. The BLM's year-end review journal reads, "Agent Love was selected for the award because of his outstanding work conducting investigations in the protection of renewable and non-renewable resources.... Special Agent Love's exemplary effort on this investigation has brought great credit upon him and the BLM." Sometime after the completion of Operation Cerberus Action, Love was promoted to head of BLM law enforcement in Utah and Nevada. And in 2016, he became head of security for BLM facilities nationwide.

The Redd family, after dealing with the various charges against Jeanette Redd, filed a wrongful death lawsuit against Agent Dan Love and the BLM. The lawsuit accuses the FBI and BLM agents of being "excessive [and] overreaching with their abusive treatment." It also states that the trumped-up charges and abuse pushed Dr. Redd to suicide. The suit claims agents manhandled Dr. Redd and interrogated him for hours in his home's garage.

The BLM claims the excessive number of agents used in the operation was due to the seven felony charges they had against Jeanette. The federal agents added that they needed the large number of agents because Dr. Redd was a hunter and might have had a gun. Many of the other defendants arrested were also hunters, yet none of them had more than 10 to 12 agents raid their homes. The BLM also claims the excessive number of agents was needed because of the number of artifacts in the Redd home. The reality is that all the artifacts could have been packed into the back seat and trunk of a midsized vehicle.

In June 2010, Dan Love and BLM agent Dan Barnes gave a talk at a meeting of the Dixie Archaeology Society in St. George, Utah. Despite the fact that prosecutions of numerous defendants in the case were still pending, the two agents gave a formal presentation on Operation Cerberus Action. In the middle of the presentation, Love postulated that "stealing artifacts" was a way of life for the people involved, and was a family affair in one case, showing a picture of the Redd family outdoors (confiscated during the ransacking of the family home), claiming they were out "pot hunting."[6]

Not only was this behavior contrary to the professional standards of law enforcement, but Love showed complete disregard for the Redd family's privacy. Less than one hour after Jay Redd, Dr. Redd's son, found this information on a blog, the blog was abruptly changed. The names of Dan Love and Dan Barnes were removed and the information about Love showing the photos of the Redd family to the group was also taken down.[7]

On October 21, 2010, Barnes made an unwarranted and unannounced visit to Jay Redd's dental office. Barnes went there to discuss statements that had been made by Jay to members of the Blanding community concerning the death of his father. Love, following Barnes' visit to Jay's office, emailed Jeanette Redd's attorney stating that BLM agents had tried to contact Jay at home but the attempt failed. Love went on to write, according to Barnes, that Jay was visibly upset during the office meeting. He also accused Jay of being "very close to the line" in some of his statements about investigators assigned to the case.

In the email, Love implies that Barnes was making contact to visibly reinforce that statements made by Jay Redd could and, in some cases, would warrant investigative activity against him. Love finishes the email by implying that the matter is deemed closed unless Jay continues with his statements and pattern of behavior. It is interesting to note that Barnes was one of the agents handpicked by Love to interrogate Dr. Redd in his garage on the day of the raid. Barnes was also one of the two agents the Redds named in their wrongful death lawsuit.

New information was also discovered regarding a "challenge coin" being made to commemorate Operation Cerberus Action. A challenge coin is a small coin or medallion (usually military), bearing an organization's insignia or emblem and carried by the organization's members. Traditionally, these coins have been given to prove membership and to enhance morale. They are also collected by service members. In practice, challenge coins are normally presented by unit commanders in recognition of special achievement by a member of the unit. They are also exchanged in recognition of visits to an organization.[8] After Ted Gardiner committed suicide during the gun battle with police, it was discovered he had a Cerberus challenge coin in his pocket.

In the years following the death of Dr. Redd, it seems like those responsible for killing him have just continued with their lives as if nothing out of the ordinary happened, while those who knew him suffer daily. It's as if those involved in the death of Dr. Redd believe that the ends justified the means and that those who died were just collateral damage. Unfortunately, the community of Blanding will never be the same.

The results of the two-and-a-half-year undercover operation were three dead human beings, some probation for a few of the defendants, and a government that took whatever artifacts it desired whether legally obtained or not. From the Redd home, among other items, agents took

80-year-old Pima baskets just because they wanted to. They also took a collection of artifacts from Central America that had nothing to do with the raid. And destroyed a handmade bow and arrow.

A multitude of people in the Blanding community as well as in the greater state of Utah have shown an outpouring of sorrow and frustration over the death of Dr. Redd and the actions of the federal government. Members of this extended community include Phil Lowe, CEO of the San Juan Health Service District and the San Juan Hospital in Monticello, Utah; Dr. Paul R. Reay, chief of medical staff at San Juan Hospital; and many patients whom Dr. Redd touched through his work. Because of the loss of Dr. Redd, it was determined that the San Juan Hospital suffered an estimated $1.5 million loss. This amount was just in the year after Dr. Redd's untimely death.

Dr. Redd was especially favored by Native Americans in the area. They have suffered a great loss. These men and women saw him with fervent dedication, often at significant personal financial sacrifice (relinquishing completely financially subsidized care in favor of seeing Dr. Redd). The character of this outstanding man, dedicated to his job serving the people and communities of San Juan County, can never be replicated. He is gone because of a conspiracy and a vendetta by several agents in the federal government and most specifically the BLM.

11

Government Tan

In 1898, Orville Gibson patented archtop guitars employing the same type of arched tops used on mandolins. In 1902 he, along with several other partners, formed the Gibson Mandolin-Guitar Manufacturing Company in Kalamazoo, Michigan. By the 1930s, the company was also making flat-top acoustic guitars, as well as one of the first commercially available hollow-body electric guitars. The company later went by Gibson Guitar Corp., and in 2013, the company was renamed Gibson Brands, Inc.

After an era of mismanagement, the company came within three months of going out of business when it was bought by Henry E. Juszkiewicz, David H. Berryman, and Gary A. Zebrowski in January 1986. Under their leadership, the company staved off bankruptcy and expanded by opening new production plants in Memphis, Tennessee, and Bozeman, Montana. The Memphis facility is used for semihollow and custom shop instruments, while the Bozeman facility is dedicated to acoustic instruments.

Unfortunately for the company, in 2009, more than a dozen federal agents from the U.S. Fish and Wildlife Service, dressed like a paramilitary unit, invaded the main Gibson factory in Nashville, Tennessee. In a show of shock and awe, federal agents kicked down the doors. The assault unit, strapped with automatic weapons, stormed the Gibson warehouse, intent upon delivering its brand of justice. While raiding this iconic American business, federal agents seized numerous guitars and a substantial amount of ebony fingerboard blanks made with wood from Madagascar. This wood was purported to have been illegally imported for the manufacture and creation of fretboards for Gibson's much-heralded electric guitars. The fretboard, or fingerboard, of a guitar is the piece attached to the neck of the guitar, under the strings.

In a sting operation, like the one that led to the death of Dr. James Redd, the DOJ covertly intercepted Gibson's company emails in 2008 and 2009. These emails contained several conversations among Gibson employees discussing a so-called gray market in which ebony wood available from a German wood dealer—who obtained it from a supplier in Madagascar—could be purchased cheaply.

The DOJ asserted that the Madagascar ebony was contraband. It quotes those emails that seem to show Gibson taking steps to maintain a supply chain connected to illegal timber harvests. With these emails in hand, the federal government accused Gibson of buying illegally harvested hardwoods from protected forests.[1] Twisting the law to its will, the USFWS claimed this was a direct violation of the Lacey Act.

The Lacey Act was introduced into Congress by Representative John F. Lacey, an Iowa Republican, on May 25, 1900. The law initially banned trafficking in illegal wildlife, but in 2008 was amended to include plants and plant products such as timber and paper. This landmark legislation was the world's first ban on trade in illegally sourced wood products.[2] The law remains in effect today, but numerous amendments have been made to it.

Two months before the Gibson raid, lobbyists had slipped some arcane supply-chain-reporting provisions into an extension of the Lacey Act, changing the technical definition of "fingerboard blanks," which are legal to import. The federal government once again focused on a business, this time Gibson, and let loose its bureaucratic rage with full force.

In the sweltering summer morning hours on August 24, 2011, agents for the federal government executed four search warrants on

Gibson's facilities in Nashville and Memphis. The feds seized pallets of wood, much of Gibson's computers containing its digital databases, and many finely crafted guitars. Due to the disruption of the raid, the fabled guitar company had to cease its manufacturing operations and send its workers home. As the factory workers exited the warehouse, not knowing if or when they would return, federal agents toting assault rifles pillaged the Gibson warehouses.

During this raid, the USFWS agents seized wood imports from India mislabeled on the U.S. customs declaration. Henry Juszkiewicz, chairman and CEO of Gibson, released a statement concerning the raid:

> The wood the Government seized on August 24 is from a Forest Stewardship Council certified supplier and is FSC Controlled, meaning that the wood complies with the standards of the Forest Stewardship Council, which is an industry-recognized and independent, not-for-profit organization established to promote responsible management of the world's forests. FSC Controlled Wood standards require, among other things, that the wood not be illegally harvested and not be harvested in violation of traditional and civil rights. Gibson has a long history of supporting sustainable and responsible sources of wood and has worked diligently with entities such as the Rainforest Alliance and Greenpeace to secure FSC certified supplies. The wood seized on August 24 satisfied FSC standards.

Juszkiewicz is the son of Polish immigrants and was born in Argentina. He moved to Rochester, New York, with his family at the age of five. After working hard to earn his education and rising through the ranks of multiple industrial firms, Juszkiewicz acquired Gibson with help from partners in 1986. As of one of the country's most cherished companies, Gibson makes guitars used the world over—most notably by lead guitarists such as Jimmy Page of Led Zeppelin, Pete Townshend of The Who, and Slash of Guns N' Roses.

With Juszkiewicz's partial ownership of a company with such a sterling reputation, the accusations made by the government have not only tarnished his character but that of the Gibson brand. Juszkiewicz spent decades bringing a company teetering on the brink of bankruptcy to the pinnacle of the music profession. The thought that he or any of his employees would destroy that rebuilt trust is ludicrous. Juszkiewicz and the company have stated that the government is "bullying Gibson without filing charges," threatening the jobs of Gibson's employees in the process.

After the company was gutted by the raids, Juszkiewicz spoke to several media outlets, including *The Daily News* of Memphis, in which he commented, "[The raid] does not directly address conservation issues, but is about obeying all laws of the countries from which wood products are procured." He went on to say, "Everything is sealed. They won't tell us anything. Gibson was inappropriately targeted, [and the raids were] outrageous and overreaching as to deserve further congressional investigation."

Following the raid and Juszkiewicz's statements, the United States government filed a civil proceeding in June of the same year. The case was settled on August 6, 2012. Gibson admitted to violating the Lacey Act and agreed to pay a fine of $300,000 in addition to a $50,000 community payment. Gibson also forfeited the wood seized in the raids, valued at roughly the same amount as the settlement. Although the company settled, it maintained its innocence, with Juszkiewicz saying, "We felt compelled to settle, as the costs of proving our case at trial would have cost millions of dollars and taken a very long time to resolve."

This is perhaps one of the more telling statements about the federal government's procedures in cases of this nature. It draws out the judicial process over time, in some cases years, and at a high expense, depleting the resources of the individuals and companies it attacks using taxpayers' money to make their assault.

Statistics reveal that 95 percent of federal cases never go to trial. DOJ prosecutors have engineered the system to make it too risky for people or businesses to go to trial, often railroading them into a guilty plea although they are innocent. The government has effectively built a conviction machine, not a system of justice. Even if the charges against these people prove to be groundless—or based on obscure laws no one seems to understand—the process is the punishment. This is the reason the Redds agreed to a plea deal in their initial case with the government in 1996 even though they knew they had committed no crime. And that could have easily been my fate if I had not decided to fight with every ounce of my being and resources, leaving my bank accounts depleted.

Because of the Gibson verdict, many in the music community feel that because musicians lack documentation of vintage instruments made of traditional, nonsustainable materials, they may be at risk of an obscure violation of the law without even knowing it. However, officials from the DOJ and the USFWS have stated that musicians who unknowingly possess instruments made of illegal wood would not be treated as criminals. It remains to be seen.

The Gibson case was further complicated by the DOJ's interpretation of a law the Indian government never asked the American government to enforce. In an affidavit, Agent John Rayfield of the USFWS said U.S. customs agents in 2011 detained a shipment of sawn ebony logs from India. The paperwork accompanying the shipment identified it fraudulently as Indian ebony fingerboards for guitars, and it did not say it was going to Gibson. In July, agents observed Indian ebony and rosewood being delivered to a storage facility for Gibson. The agents asked in an affidavit for permission to seize Gibson's business computers.

The most problematic factor with the raid and with the government's accusations is that Gibson apparently was not violating any American law, but was being raided for violating the laws of India and Madagascar, which in turn was a surprise to authorities in India and Madagascar. The warrant that Gibson officials were shown was sealed, so management for the iconic guitar maker was never able to see exactly what crime it was being accused of committing. The government's entire case relied on the DOJ's interpretation of a law in India stating that if Gibson is going to buy wood from India, it must be in full compliance with Indian law. Meaning, if the same wood from the same tree was finished by Indian workers, the material would be legal. And to reiterate, the Indian government is not enforcing this law, but it is the U.S. government's interpretation of a law in India. This equates to bureaucratic nonsense.

CEO Juszkiewicz continues to fight this battle through numerous media outlets. He has been quoted as saying, "Our business has been injured to millions of dollars. And we don't even have a court we can go to and say, 'Look, here's our position.' The federal bureaucracy is just out of hand; it seems to me there's almost class warfare of companies versus people, rich versus poor, Republicans versus Democrats… and there's just a lack of somebody that stands up and says, 'I'm about everyone. I'm really about America and doing what's good for the country and not fighting these little battles.'"[3]

Gibson vigorously denied the allegations during the entire process. The management at the company maintained that its purchases from Madagascar complied with U.S. and Malagasy law. Attorneys for Gibson presented documents to support this claim and to show that wood legally obtained from India had been seized in the raid. The company also stopped importing wood from Madagascar in 2009.

It was long suspected that the Gibson raid was a political hit, carried out because CEO Juszkiewicz made campaign donations to Republicans. The financial disruption to the company was considerable. Whether it was because America's two main political parties were attacking one another is really neither here nor there; what is important about this incident is there seems to be an all-out war on businesses, targeting their politics. It seems government officials want to interpret the smallest minutiae in any set of laws as a reason to raid a company to acquire a conviction. The government seems to want to punish people with huge fines, or to simply damage corporations' business models.

Juszkiewicz perhaps stated it most succinctly when he was quoted as saying, "When you have a system predicated on jurisdictional interests rather than on specific, identifiable, understandable, definable violations of law, there is a great opportunity for tyranny. As a result, just about any businessperson, especially in highly regulated industries, can be construed by a prosecutor to have committed three or four arguable felonies a day. If for some reason the authorities are eyeing you and they look closely enough at your daily activities, they can find something. That makes us all very vulnerable."

Many people are afraid the law will force the owners of musical instrument businesses to account for every wooden part of their guitars when re-entering the U.S. Top dealers of vintage guitars, banjos, and other rare stringed instruments are afraid, because almost every guitar made prior to 1970 was manufactured using Brazilian rosewood. They are not contributing to the destruction of Brazilian forests today, but they can fall under scrutiny with this law. The government tried to create exemptions to cover vintage instruments, but the entire system is rife with delays, causing many in the musical instruments business to cut large percentages of their stock.

All of this is out of fear of a bureaucratic government's sending a Gestapo-style force to raid their businesses and destroy their livelihoods. The Gibson raids terrorized the guitar builders because the Lacey Act is retroactive. Many guitar and other manufacturers are worried they might be forced to prove the provenance of wood they acquired decades ago. The intent of this law is to reduce illegal logging and to make sure companies, like Gibson, are sourcing wood in a responsible way. But the way the Lacey Act and many other federal statutes and regulations are being implemented is flat-out abusive. Three years after the Gibson raids, seeing years and millions of dollars in legal fees in its future, the company settled with the federal government.

The DOJ ended up not bringing criminal charges against Gibson related to its purchase and importation of ebony and other exotic woods from Madagascar and India. In return, Gibson admitted it failed to ensure that the exotic wood it had been purchasing from its supplier was legally harvested and exported.

After Gibson agreed to pay the $300,000 penalty and make a "community service payment" of $50,000 to the National Fish and Wildlife Foundation—to be used on research projects or tree conservation activities— Juszkiewicz said, "This allows us to get back to the business of making guitars. An important part of the settlement is that we are getting back the materials seized in a second armed raid on our factories, and we have formal acknowledgement that we can continue to source rosewood and ebony fingerboards from India, as we have done for many decades."

Further, Gibson noted that the years-long investigation cost taxpayers millions of dollars and put a "job-creating U.S. manufacturer at risk and at a competitive disadvantage." This shows the increasing trend on the part of government to treat U.S. businesses in the same way drug dealers are treated—as criminals.

It seems the law allows inequity. There is no fairness in our legal proceedings or due process anymore. Now, throughout our land, the federal agency writes the law (the regulations), enforces the law (every agency now has its own federal police force), and sits in the judgement of innocence or guilt (administrative procedures). The government continues a path of criminalizing capitalism, making legislative reform by Congress necessary to control this abusive, tyrannical, bureaucratic monolith. Our government has given its many agencies law enforcement powers with militaristic resources and capabilities which they use to intimidate and arrest citizens whenever they desire.

As part of the settlement, the federal government acknowledged that Gibson cooperated with the investigation. The settlement also states, "[The government and Gibson] acknowledge and agree that certain questions and inconsistencies now exist regarding the tariff classification of ebony and rosewood fingerboard blanks."

Gibson therefore continues to import exotic woods from India. Essentially, nothing changed from the events following either of the raids accept that Gibson no longer imports any wood from Madagascar. It was punished with millions in lost revenue and hundreds of thousands of dollars in penalties. Accordingly, the government will not undertake enforcement actions related to Gibson's future orders, purchases, or imports of ebony and rosewood fingerboard blanks from India, unless and until the government of India provides specific clarification that ebony and rosewood fingerboard blanks are expressly prohibited by laws related to Indian foreign trade policy.

In mocking response to the punishment levied against the company, and to celebrate the end of its tussle with the eager enforcers of the U.S. customs department, Gibson created a Government Series of guitars.[4] In 2014, Gibson introduced the Government Series II Les Paul, constructed from the U.S.-government-seized wood returned to the company at the end of the ordeal. The guitar's finish contains tonewood, and the body is painted in a custom color the company has named "Government Tan"—suitably drab, a nod to the joyless reality of living under the heavy thumb of a stifling bureaucracy.

12

Federal Revelation

Sitting in my living room in late 2011, I switched on the television and was greeted by images of President Obama addressing a joint session of Congress regarding jobs and employment. As the roving camera panned throughout the crowd, the lens focused on then Republican congressman and speaker of the house John Boehner. Sitting directly to his right was Gibson CEO Henry Juszkiewicz. At the time, I did not know who he was or why he would be at the proceedings until I later learned why Boehner had invited him.

In the days following the address, I discovered that Juszkiewicz had been personally invited by Boehner as a symbol of abusive big government. Little did I know that Juszkiewicz's story and my own had a connection. In early 2012, while trudging out to my mailbox after working at the trading post for the better part of the day, I withdrew my mail and began sifting through it.

After discarding assorted bits of junk mail, I found a red, white, and blue USPS priority envelope with a return address of 5001 Southgate Drive in Billings. Taking it inside, I tossed it on my coffee table. From there, I headed into the kitchen to begin preparing my evening meal. I paused a moment to peer out my bay window at what had been Sitting Bull's camp on the day of the epic battle. While cooking, I stared at the package.

Something did not sit right with me. I knew that return address from somewhere. It drove me crazy. After taking a closer look at the postmark, I noticed that it was from Rolling Prairie, Indiana. I thought about how odd it was for the package to have a return address far from the postmark. Not only that, but I *knew* the address from somewhere. The package was like an ominous talisman, and I was unable to draw my gaze away from it.

With my dinner plated, I walked to the couch, plopped down, and opened the parcel. Within it, I found a 56-page document authored by an individual with intimate working knowledge of the USFWS and the BLM. The document detailed malfeasance purposefully perpetrated on my business, Gibson, and the Redd family (Cerberus Action, Four Corners raid in Utah, three suicides). The document's author intimated that all three were connected. It described the inner workings of the USFWS and the BLM with reasons they gave to justify their overblown existences, as well as the sheer corruption amongst their ranks. It was at this time that I realized why I knew the return address—it is the address for the Bureau of Land Management headquarters in Billings.

The author of the document implored me to file a Freedom of Information Act (FOIA) request with the Department of Interior (DOI) and the Office of Inspector General (OIG) for reports of investigation concerning misconduct issues within the ranks of the USFWS and Office of Law Enforcement (OLE). The author of the document alleged that the "allegations of misconduct are of a continuous and multigenerational period outlining both the corruption and the lack of ethics within the OLE, in part because nepotism and cronyism are so rampant."

The author noted that an internal review of the USFWS had discovered weaknesses in the core areas of leadership and oversight, contributing to a general mistrust of senior management. The report went on to find a lack of effective communication between USFWS and OLE headquarters and the field, which had created a perception that there was a wall between management and field personnel. Throughout the assessment, concerns were raised about the organization's failing culture of ethics and integrity. Findings in the report exposed glaring weaknesses in internal affairs policy, and in reviews of internal affairs cases, problems arose over investigative independence.

As I read through the document, I was disgusted to find an intricate detailing of high-level corruption and obstruction of enforcement. The document named multiple agents involved in a series of crimes, including stealing evidence pertaining to federal and state investigations, providing false testimony to grand juries to ensure convictions, obstruction of justice, and possession of stolen firearms. The document also provided details about agents pilfering confiscated firearms, some of which were full automatics (which is illegal), pawning them, and profiting from their sale.

The document stated that these were minor infractions in the face of the tens of millions of dollars that the USFWS and the OLE misappropriates year after year. Special agents are aware that lawmakers are merely focusing on travel, conferences, and training expenditures. But OLE special agents are siphoning public funds undetected through nepotism, grade inflation, promotions, government take-home vehicles, and government-funded moves to a retirement destination of their choosing.

Many employees of the OLE are highly inexperienced leaders who have never benefited from developmental roles in a variety of multidisciplinary field assignments or personality assessments. Because of this, the OLE lacks comprehensive supervisory and leadership programs to evaluate the personality and ethical defects of the ranks of the OLE special agents. The OLE fosters an environment based on exclusion and disengagement, which punishes special agents who speak out against these practices.

Also within this document's pages, the author laid out the corruption within other organizations, such as the USFWS, the BLM and the U.S. Forest Service. The author stated that the USFWS is the only federal agency that has two separate law enforcement divisions with separate and redundant budgets and supervisors. Every federal land management agency (the BLM, National Park Service, and Forest Service) have special agents and uniformed law enforcement officers who are unified under a single command structure and a single law enforcement policy. That is not the case with the USFWS law enforcement program.

The document continued by pointing out that OLE special agents and U.S. Fish and Wildlife Service law enforcement officers have two entirely separate command structures, law enforcement policies, and strategic plans. Both command structures operate separately and don't complement one another. This results in cost inefficiencies when both command structures require personnel at the Federal Law Enforcement Training Center in Brunswick, Georgia, or at headquarters in Arlington, Virginia. The differences in a bifurcated law enforcement program result in conflicting enforcement practices being directed at the public and in protection of the resource. The acquisition of different types of firearms, ammunition, and defensive equipment and the installation of different types of emergency police and safety equipment in government-assigned vehicles and vessels can have devastating consequences.

Many of the corrupt directors in these organizations have taken multiple trips (weeks on end) throughout the United States and Hawaii on the government dole to gain subsequent employment in the private sector. I was outraged as I read this information. The overwhelming scope of wrongdoing by the OLE and its culture of excess in violation of government policies was and continues to be abhorrent. The document named the agents who were employed by these government agencies at the time, and their administrative roles, but I have redacted their names in this section for fear of retribution.

Most of this information was eye-opening to me, but one of the document's more poignant portions was the revelation of the "Circle of Seven" command structure within the various regional offices of these vast government agencies. With the implementation of direct-line authority, the OLE unified its command structure, centralizing most of its administrative functions at the headquarters level. The regions continue to operate by the seven regional authorities, often jokingly referred to as the "Seven Kingdoms" with autonomy (that is, without headquarters oversight).

Apparently, the Circle of Seven is composed of the following seven regions: Region One: Portland, Oregon; Region Two: Albuquerque, New Mexico; Region Three: Fort Snelling, Montana; Region Four: Atlanta, Georgia; Region Five: Hadley, Massachusetts; Region Six: Denver, Colorado; and Region Seven: Anchorage, Alaska. Since 2011, with a newly created regional office in Sacramento, California (Region Eight), the Circle of Seven actually can be referred to as the Circle of Eight.

The Circle of Seven/Eight, in conjunction with the chief, deputy chief, and the division chief of each region, are the entities responsible for establishing written law enforcement policy and for recruiting new special agents. Records disclose that the Circle of Seven/Eight promoted themselves and their cronies despite their apparent lack of credentials and lack of ethics.

The annual salary of the department heads of the "circle" is $150,000, and when you add the benefits of medical and retirement plans, moving payments, and a car allowance, compensation exceeds $200,000 per year. They are greedy chiselers who game the system and walk away with a golden parachute. The Circle of Seven/Eight contrive domestic and international government travel (using official United Sates passports) to go on personal vacations, safaris, or hunting trips with friends and family, using government cell phones, vehicles, planes, and credit cards—that is, all on the dole.

The Circle of Seven/Eight and the seven assistant special agents in charge (ASAC) form the inner sanctum of this group. They are followed by the resident agents in charge (RAC). The incomes of these highly paid managers are greater than 95 percent of the incomes of state governors, federal judges, and even three-star generals. Many of the managers merely have merely a GED, and an even higher percentage of special agents have never conducted a felony investigation, testified before a federal grand jury, or made an arrest.

According to the document, the Circle of Seven has a history of patronage, favoritism, and nepotism that spans decades and generations. These administrators compromise their ethics and use their positions to inflate their grades, assign themselves government vehicles to commute to work, and also travel and move at government expense whenever and wherever they want.

All of this provides an atmosphere of exclusion and disengagement amongst the workforce. Moreover, special agents within the clique are bestowed preferential treatment throughout their careers in the OLE with respect to monetary awards, promotions, transfers to choice geographic duty stations, and domestic and international travel and training assignments at the government's expense. Those within this "good ol' boy" network are emboldened and act in a manner of entitlement.

Those in the Circle of Seven/Eight also hire their relatives and friends as special agents through the service's college internship program, known as the Student Career Experience Program (SCEP), which is administered through USAJOBS. Those in the Circle of Seven/Eight are gaming the system by preselecting their relatives and friends by alerting them to the potential job vacancies in advance and withholding said information from the public and the Veterans Administration.

They further rig the system by posting the job announcements for a limited time and for undesirable duty stations in urban areas such as Detroit, Michigan, when in fact the applicant will be immediately transferred to a more desirable duty station once the applicant completes training. If you as an OLE special agent have been hired through the good ol' boy network, you are supposed to pay the gift forward to the next generation. It is difficult to quantify the full extent of nepotism, because numerous second- and third-generation OLE employees have different last names, as they use their married name or maiden name, or are nieces, nephews, cousins, friends, and the like.

As I read on, I found the document's allegations did not end there. In a thorough description, the author told how many of the government vehicles and facilities were used to conduct extramarital affairs by more than one agent and in some instances with underage high school girls. The writer accused agents, whom he identified by name, of using the government vehicles and paid government time to go "tomcatting" and to scout around local high schools and other areas where young girls could be found.

The author also insinuated that agents were caught cheating on OLE examinations but were never prosecuted, and were allowed to graduate. Agents also violated federal law, as they didn't claim income on yearly executive branch confidential financial disclosure reports. The author said agents also violated federal law by going on international hunting trips to kill bears, then violated international law by importing their trophy kills back to the States.

There is apparently a total lack of inventory control in the OLE, and many items are merely used for personal use. Many special agents don't do any migratory bird fieldwork, yet they continue to buy hunting equipment, for their personal use.

These simple-minded agents are also notoriously hard on government equipment; when they are not sinking a government boat or wrecking a government vehicle, they are constantly losing their equipment. Some of these agents also befriend the individuals they are pursuing, and they use their newly minted relationships to smuggle contraband items like antiques, trophy kills, and rare and exotic animals into the country. The OLE vehicle fleet also exceeds 250 vehicles. The majority of them are inefficient gas-guzzling three-quarter-ton SUVs. In the purchasing of these vehicles, there is absolutely no regard for taxpayer money, it is nothing more than simple excess and total waste.

These special agents create policies to protect themselves. These policies have allowed them to use their work vehicles to run personal errands; they allow themselves to live and commute with said vehicle, in some instances more than 40 miles; they are reimbursed for highway road tolls; and, even more egregiously, they receive Law Enforcement Availability Pay (LEAP) while commuting. These agents also, at government expense, get the retirement destination of their choosing, embezzle wildlife inspection fees, and continue to employ agents who cannot possibly pass the OLE medical or physical exercise tests.

The author of the document did not want to leave out the misdeeds of federal Fish and Wildlife special agent Kelvin Smith. On government time and using government equipment (vehicles and weapons), Smith trained Ramzi Yousef and several other men who were the perpetrators of the 1993 World Trade Center terrorist attack.

Yousef and his co-conspirators built a 1,500-pound car bomb. Their intent was that the explosion would topple Tower One, which would then fall into Tower Two and kill all occupants in both buildings. The attack ended with over 1,000 nonfatal injuries and six fatalities. The terrorists were sentenced to life imprisonment in 1994. Special Agent Smith was also arrested and charged. After his conviction, Smith was merely incarcerated for one year and a day. Smith's sentence was barely a slap on the wrist compared to the 89 years I was threatened with over a button.

Disgusted by what I was reading, rage began to swell in the pit of my stomach. I had to walk away from the document for a few moments and vent. I made my way into the kitchen, poured myself a glass of cool water, and drank it down. After composing myself, I turned the television off and began to delve into the document again. After picking up where I had so abruptly left off, I wondered why I had gone back to the document, because the information I digested from that point on served only to make me nauseated.

Along with the blatant revelation of cronyism and nepotism running rampant throughout some of our nation's largest organizations, the author also detailed numerous petty crimes and felonies perpetrated by these agents. He accused them of being knowingly involved in illegal trophy hunting, using government money, vehicles, and firearms to hunt animals.

He also intimated that these agents went to great lengths to smuggle the carcasses of these endangered species in direct violation of the Lacey Act. This one accusation alone angered me to no end. The fact that the USFWS and the BLM's own agents were violating the Lacey Act and publicly flaunting it,[1] and then had the gall to turn around and accuse me of similar violations all the while waving the possibility of an 89-year prison term in my face made me want to firmly plant my fist in the plaster of my living room wall.

Restraining my rage, I read on. The author stated that in 2009, the Office of Personnel Management (OPM) held a symposium known as "The Government-Wide Veteran's Recruitment and Employment Strategic Plan." This was America's first strategic plan to increase the hiring of veterans throughout the federal civil service. The initiative was a major component of President Obama's Veterans Employment Initiative. It was an attempt to "aggressively dismantle barriers to entry and success for veterans and transitioning service members pursuing careers in the federal civil service."

Apparently, the Circle of Seven/Eight department heads have found a way to manipulate this mandate and to deny our deserving veterans employment opportunities. The Seven/Eight take a hardline stance against hiring five- and ten-point veterans by offering them positions in large and expensive metropolitan cities, such as Chicago, Dallas, Miami, Torrance, California, and Valley Stream, New York. Because these stations are extremely expensive, the qualified veterans weigh the costs of relocation and housing and often turn down the job. Then, the Circle of Seven/Eight administrators offer a nepotism applicant a duty station of his or her choosing. This tactic effectively meets the requirement of the Veterans Employment Initiative and fills the needed spot with a family member or a buddy.

The worst agent named in the document is Chief Director William C. Woody. He is the son of Jack B. Woody, the former USFWS chief of endangered species/national sea turtle coordinator (Region Two). Jack B. Woody was a highly respected and well-connected manager on both a regional and national level. William C. Woody, on the other hand, was on a rather unspectacular law enforcement career path. But through his father's professional connections, he gained entry to the

Utah Department of Natural Resources and later to the BLM, in the Office of Law Enforcement and Security.

Woody comes off as self-promoting and disingenuous, rather than making sure that American taxpayers' dollars are invested wisely. Woody's actions reinforce negative stereotypes many Americans hold of federal employees as overpaid, underworked spendthrifts and poor stewards of taxpayer dollars. Woody apparently uses his position to hire his BLM cronies who have communications or administration degrees as OLE vacancies occur.

One of the items the author highlighted about Woody and his management of the BLM that stood out to me was his use of OLE resources to wrongly pursue high-profile targets. He is known for generating press releases and slick, glossy publications chronicling the enforcement operations of the BLM and the OLE. A reasonable person could believe that his personal aim is to gain power and to eventually put money in his pocket.

This stung, especially because I felt that my raids were wrongly pursued, and this document only reinforced that notion. This important document made it crystal clear that prosecutions within the OLE had taken a precipitous decline, so Woody has given his troops marching orders to be overly aggressive and assertive, and to seek the limelight and ensure convictions by any means necessary.

It seems that the OLE fails to recognize that the single most serious problem within the organization is a pervasive culture of exclusivity, that it is exempt from the rules that govern other employees of the federal government. There also seems to be an even larger group of individuals wholly lacking in acceptance of or adherence to government ethical standards of management; through passive neglect at best, or purposeful ignorance at worst, they are blind to easily discernible misconduct. The Circle of Seven/Eight and the administrators of these groups have a total lack of moral judgment and an inability to follow the rule of law.

According to the document, it seems that most of these agents are hired on a *quid quo pro* basis. That is, individuals are hired with the promise that someday down the road those individuals will hire one of their family members. A long history of investigative experience or ethics just doesn't seem to be one of the criteria for selection. Education, experience, leadership, and ethics are absent at the OLE. The document suggests that the OLE should be applying criminal sanctions to only the most significant and egregious violators; however, under Woody and the Circle of Seven/Eight, every high-profile investigation is pursued to garner the spotlight.

In facing Congress about the Deepwater Horizon oil well blowout in the Gulf of Mexico, Interior Secretary Ken Salazar said most of the agency's employees were honest and capable, but there remained "a few bad apples." He said anyone found guilty of negligence or corruption would be rooted out. Similarly, Defense Secretary Robert Gates in the Walter Reed Hospital debacle asked for the resignations of some dozen high-ranking generals and admirals for their misdeeds. I would hope that the same would hold for the OLE.

Consuming the information contained within the pages of this document was not only eye-opening but gut-wrenching. Before the raids and my experience with corrupt federal agents of the BLM, all my life, I trusted most government officials to be good and upstanding people who were trying to follow the letter of the law. But this document, coupled with the decade of abuse I received, led me to completely mistrust nearly all federal government employees. And the greatest shock I received while reading through this scathing treatise of the Office of Law Enforcement and associated government agencies was when I saw my name mentioned in concert with the Gibson raid and the death of Dr. James Redd.

13

Threats, Intimidation, and Bullying

As distressed as I was reading through the leaked document, the most illuminating portions related to me directly. The document's author insinuated that Chief Director William C. Woody's actions in the three investigations (Custer Battlefield Museum Inc., Operation Cerberus Action, and the investigation of Henry Juszkiewicz doing business as Gibson Guitar Company) are all interconnected and part of an overreaching effort by agents in the federal government to secure high-profile convictions.

In 2014, I was asked by an elected official to submit written testimony to the House of Representatives subcommittee that investigates this type of harassment and intimidation by federal law enforcement, but nothing has come of it. It was to the congressional hearing on July 24, 2014, titled "Threats, Intimidation, and Bullying by Federal Land Managing Agencies" that I submitted the leaked document.

Following, I have quoted directly from the 56-page document and the information provided connecting all three raids.

Investigation of Christopher Kortlander dba the Custer Battlefield Museum, Inc.

Brian Cornell began his federal law enforcement career as a patrol Park Ranger with the National Park Service at Lake Mead

National Recreation Area. In 1993, Cornell transferred to the Bureau of Land Management in Las Vegas where he served as a law enforcement ranger working at the Red Rock Canyon National Conservation Area.

In 2000, Woody selected Cornell as a Special Agent with the Bureau of Land Management in Billings, MT. Following the terror attacks of September 11, 2001, Cornell was detailed for six months as a Federal Air Marshal assigned to Seattle, WA.

Despite not having any criminal investigative experience, let alone an understanding of the esoteric nuances of the Archaeological Resource Protection Act of 1979 (ARPA), nor any expertise in managing confidential informant(s), in 2003, Woody made Cornell the case agent in an investigation involving Christopher Kortlander (Garryowen, MT) who was alleged to be illegally trafficking in artifacts.

In 2005, Cornell obtained a search warrant after a year plus investigation (involving multiple undercover buys) indicating Kortlander might be selling property under false claims of historic value. Twenty-four federal agents (armed with automatic weapons) executed a raid of Kortlander's home and business. Several items were seized. No criminal charges were filed against Kortlander and no arrests were made.

Kortlander [waged] his own battle with authorities to reclaim a trove of war bonnets, medicine bags and other items seized during government raids on his privately-operated Custer Museum.

The raids came during a five-year investigation into Kortlander's alleged dealings in fraudulent artifacts and eagle feathers in violation of federal law. No charges were ever filed. The government formerly dropped its investigation in 2009, and the items seized during the raids including 7th Cavalry memorabilia, other American Indian artifacts, and thousands of pages of documents have since been returned.

Yet the dispute between Kortlander and the government rages on. Sealed court filings obtained by The Associated Press show the government still holds 22 items, partly on the word of a convicted felon who claimed Kortlander acquired them illegally. Many contain eagle or migratory bird feathers, which government attorneys said in court documents renders the items "contraband" under the Bald Eagle Protection Act and Migratory Bird Treaty Act.

U.S. District Judge Richard Cebull, who [oversaw] the case, cast doubt on the credibility of the government's witnesses, but also said Kortlander must be cross-examined to prove the war bonnets and other items were lawfully acquired. Kortlander argues the government's efforts to hold onto the seized items stem from a stubborn refusal to admit the raids against him were based on false assumptions and should never have occurred. Since the raids, Kortlander waged an aggressive legal counter-attack, including motions for the return of the remaining items seized during the raids in 2005 and 2008.

Several related cases already resolved yielded mixed results. Following an earlier lawsuit by Kortlander, federal courts ordered the government to release thousands of pages of materials related to the investigation. This release included a decision from the U.S. 9th Circuit Court of Appeals that insinuated Kortlander was not restricted in his use of the investigative materials, overturning an earlier ruling from Judge Cebull. Cebull struck down another lawsuit in which Kortlander claimed government law enforcement agents maliciously pursued him to advance their own careers.

In dismissing the claim, Cebull said the government had "rock-solid" probable cause to seek a search warrant in the 2008 raid. But the affidavit from Cornell for the 2008 search of the Custer Battlefield Museum reveals the government's case relied in part on statements from a Montana appraiser, James Brubaker, who said he sold eagle parts and feathers to Kortlander. Brubaker has since served a federal prison sentence for possession and interstate transportation of stolen property. Authorities said he travelled the country stealing rare and valuable books and maps from public libraries then sold them on eBay.

Kortlander further learned Cornell the affiant on the affidavit for the search warrant had been previously reprimanded by the Department of the Interior. The reprimand came from the Inspector General for Program Integrity on May 26, 2005, regarding a matter wherein Cornell was an affiant for a 2003 search warrant of Dr. Dan Boechler. The Inspector General wrote in part, "It is my belief that Agent Cornell's testimony was materially false."

Kortlander contends he never fraudulently or illegally sold battlefield or Indian artifacts. The feathered artifacts classified by the government as contraband include items donated or loaned to the museum and personal family heirlooms. A former associate who said he was one of the government's informants in the case disputed Kortlander's claim to innocence. The informant, Jason Pitsch, has his own credibility issues: He is currently detained in a Yellowstone County, Mont., jail on federal child pornography charges.

Kortlander claims that the investigation, subsequent raids, and forfeitures were motivated by his dating of Cathy Lingard, the ex-wife of Lee Lingard, a BLM undercover Special Agent and a former Navy Seal. Feeling threatened by her ex-husband, she obtained a restraining order against Lee Lingard. Lee Lingard is currently employed by the Department of Housing and Urban Development. Lee Lingard was later transferred off the investigation after Kortlander complained of harassment to the BLM Office of Inspector General.

On September 14, 2011, Kortlander sued the government for $188,000,000. The defendant(s) are the United States of America, the Department of the Interior, and the BLM that was the lead agency in all matters related to the claim. The USFWS worked with the BLM and the extent of its role is uncertain to the plaintiffs, however the involvement of the USFWS will be determined during discovery.

In August 2008, Woody rewarded Cornell's bad behavior by promoting him to the position of Special Agent in Charge of: Montana, North Dakota, and South Dakota. A short time later, Cornell left the agency and took a demotion to begin working, in June 16, 2009, as a Special Agent for Reclamation's Great Plains Region.

Operation Cerberus Action

William Woody initially hired Special Agent Dan Love sometime in 2005. Even though Love was an inexperienced field agent Woody hand-picked and assigned Love as the lead case agent on the joint undercover investigation (code-named Cerberus Action) conducted by the BLM and the FBI. Even though Larry Shackelford was the Special Agent in Charge for the State of Utah (Utah State Office), Woody supervised Love from Washington, D.C.

Love is an aggressive agent, seeking to gain a conviction. The need for a conviction became greater as the costly investigation progressed. The undercover expenditures alone would require results. Thus, the investigation pursuing any infraction that would result in a conviction was pursued.

Using Ted Gardiner as a confidential source, in 2007 and 2008, the BLM and the FBI purchased over 250 artifacts totaling more than $335,000. Gardiner was a well-connected dealer who permitted the installation of various video and audio recorders in his place of business. Recordings provided information on possible illegal sales involving items including Anasazi pottery and other artifacts associated with Native American Indians (allegedly in violation of ARPA).

On June 10, 2009, the case became public when 24 indictments were unsealed. Woody was present when the indictments were announced in Salt Lake City by Secretary of the Interior Ken Salazar; Assistant Secretary Echo Hawk; Deputy Attorney General David W. Ogden of the U.S. Department of Justice: Brett L. Tolman, U.S. Attorney in Utah: and Timothy J. Fuhrman, Special Agent in Charge of the FBI's Salt Lake City Field Office. Woody failed to tell the assembled officials and the press he was aware that Shackelford was having an affair with Gardiner's girlfriend.

Woody further neglected to tell the press that unlike Special Agent Rudy Mauldin's 1980's ARPA investigation involving Earl Shumway, Mauldin caught the pothunters in the act of grave robbing. AUSA Wayne Dance prosecuted Shumway using direct evidence which tied Shumway to the grave digging of archeological [sic] artifacts on federally managed lands.

Rather, Love's investigation focused merely on the braggadocios of the defendants and the sale of artifacts whose archeological [sic] provenance could not be established. Woody also failed to disclose that the BLM was aware of Gardiner's history of mental issues, substance abuse problems and emotional issues arising from a recent divorce and newly failed relationship with another woman. In 2009 Woody, ever the showman, scam artist and entertainer, named Love BLM Special Agent of the Year, before even one individual was convicted. Woody subsequently promoted Love to the position of Assistant Special Agent in Charge for the Utah State Office.

The costly 5-year artifacts case netted no prison time and three suicides. Defendant Dr. James Redd (Blanding, UT - age 60) killed himself on June 11, 2009. A week later, Steven L. Shrader (Santa Fe, NM - age 56) committed suicide. Gardiner the informant (Holladay, UT - age 52) committed suicide on March 2, 2010. Although Utah Senators Orrin Hatch and Bob Bennett asked U.S. Attorney General Eric Holder to investigate the matter it appears their pleas went for naught.

FWS-OLE Investigation of the Gibson Guitar Company
Woody is carrying over the same overzealous management style from the BLM to the OLE. Under Woody's approach, BLM and OLE Special Agents have labored to justify their next promotion and the next and the next. Woody has energized his employees to pursue high profile vandals with more confidence and with the expectations that said employees are expected to produce results. Although Woody is hoping to garner favorable publicity by initiating high profile investigations by any means; whether through overzealousness or by using unethical employees who have integrity issues or employees who are carrying out sexual relationships with informants or other individuals on the periphery of an investigation history has shown Woody has failed miserably.

On August 24, 2012, Woody executed four federal search warrants at the business offices of Gibson Guitar in Memphis, TN and Nashville, TN, where Henry Juszkiewicz is the Chief Executive. OLE policy requires Special Agents to evaluate the threat level of premises to be searched and only use the appropriate amount of force to safely secure the premises, the individuals present, and to seize the items enumerated in the search warrant. In the instant investigation, the premises of the Gibson Guitar Company consisted of factory floor workers.

In a spectacular show of force, Woody directed case agents John Rayfield, Tim Santel and Hubbard to have the Special Agents who executed the search warrants to brandish high powered long guns, wear bullet proof vests, and to intimidate and coerce the workforce to elicit statements in prosecuting Henry Juszkiewicz and the Gibson Guitar Company.

The seizure netted computers, hard drives, company records, and thousands of guitar fingerboards. The raid caused economic loss to Gibson, created a political firestorm, and has ignited a furious debate around a seminal environmental protection statute, the Lacey Act. Though the Lacey Act was originally designed to combat illegal trafficking in animals, its scope was expanded in 2008 to combat the illegal harvesting of timber, which has contributed to massive deforestation of tropical hardwood forests. The Gibson Guitar Company supported these changes. As a user of tropical woods, the Gibson Guitar Company said it just makes economic sense to buy our materials from sustainable forests, and it makes moral sense to do so in a way that ensures the survival of these resources.

Woody initiated this investigation because neither the Secretary of Interior nor Congress failed to sanction him when, as the BLM Chief, he used the same tactics to frivolously squander tax payer monies and withheld exculpatory information from court/defendants in Operation Christopher Kortlander dba the Custer Battlefield Museum, Inc. and Operation Cerberus Action. Woody's malice, his methods, his star-chamber practices and his decision to punish first and adjudicate later all are at odds with law enforcements ideals of fairness and fair play.

The victims of these raids have not stopped their fight against the federal government's persecution. In 2015, Jay Redd and I attended a hearing in Saint George, Utah. Also in attendance was then House Oversight Committee chairman Jason Chaffetz (R-Utah). Populated by a multitude of protestors, who did not seem to understand what the hearing was about, the initial scene was a madhouse. Armed with a litany of flyers and banners proclaiming allegiance to their favorite national park, the agitators turned the forum into total chaos. After finally being told about the official procedures of the hearing (which entailed allowing speakers to speak) the protestors lost their desire to interrupt and their numbers eventually dissipated.

As the hearing progressed, Jay Redd testified in front of the panel and committee chairman Chaffetz. The panel was very receptive to the story concerning the death of Jay's father. Afterward, Chaffetz promised to address the problem of the federal government's overreach. In the months following the hearing, Chaffetz introduced a bill that would strip the USFWS and BLM of their law enforcement functions, titled the Local Enforcement for Local Lands Act.[1]

Known as H.R. 622, the act proposes to abolish law enforcement units at the Forest Service and Bureau of Land Management. With the abolishment of federal police in these areas, the bill requires state and local law enforcement to police federal lands in their jurisdiction. It also requires the secretaries of the agriculture and interior departments to give grants to those states to fund their enforcement activities. Utah Republican Representatives Rob Bishop, Chris Stewart, and Mia Love are cosponsors of the legislation.

The legislation, if it passes, is intended to de-escalate conflicts between law enforcement and residents like the Redd and Bundy families. The bill would prevent BLM and Forest Service agents from hunting and prosecuting individuals for grazing cattle on public land or for picking up shards of pottery and arrowheads that are just lying on the ground. The law would allow these agents to focus their energies on the stewardship of the land, deterring them from promotional scalp-hunting and destroying people's lives and businesses.

Specifically, the bill would get rid of the Forest Service Law Enforcement and Investigations unit within the U.S. Department of Agriculture and the BLM Office of Law Enforcement at the Interior. It would also require the secretaries of these departments to report to Congress how they are using the grants development program. The states must also demonstrate in an annual report that they're using the funding only for law enforcement purposes.[2]

If successful, there would no longer be a need for a Dan Love, a Brian Cornell, a William Woody, or agents of their ilk. The federal government would no longer need agents seeking high-profile busts and arrests for career enhancement. The ridiculous promotional race would end, and the BLM could return to the purpose it was initially intended to fulfill. No longer would there be incidents like those involving the Bundys, the tragic case of the Redd family, or the abuse of a legitimate and cherished company like Gibson. And people like me who deal in legally acquired artifacts would no longer be suspected felons while running businesses that follow the absolute letter of the law.

Any egregious actions committed by individuals, such as the theft of native burial grounds or illegal trophy-hunting, would be pursued by local law enforcement. I believe, as do many others, that when a massive entity like the federal government tries to regulate local matters and excludes local law enforcement officials who are residents of these communities, it ends up doing much more harm than good.

The Forest Service has proposed adding more law enforcement officers to its ranks. In its fiscal 2017 budget request, the Forest Service asked for roughly $132 million for its Law Enforcement and Investigations unit. Most of those funds would go to additional officers who would work with the agency's growing operations related to illegal marijuana site reclamation and drug trafficking. Unfortunately, this would most likely lead to more nepotism, cronyism, and promotional ladder-climbing.

14

One Nation Under God

As of September 2017, H.R. 622, the Local Enforcement for Local Lands Act, continues to gain momentum in Congress. Representative Chris Stewart, from Utah's second congressional district, was the first sponsor of the bill for the 115th Congress (2017 to 2018).[1] Momentum is growing even with some shameful decisions by the federal government. In August 2017, the government had ample opportunity to pursue charges against Special Agent in Charge Dan Love for several misconduct issues and possible illegal activities.[2] However, it decided to protect its own instead of doing what was right.

The series of events that lead to Love's not being charged began on November 2, 2016. On that day, Love was relieved of duty and directed to turn in his uniforms, badges, and government-issued firearms. Love was also stripped of his law enforcement authority, as he was being investigated by the internal affairs unit of the BLM.[3] Nearly eight years after the death of Dr. James Redd and almost three years following the standoff at the Bundy ranch in Nevada, the U.S. Department of the Interior released a memorandum that read:

> Dan Love, BLM Special Agent in Charge [is] being investigated internally for two extremely heinous acts.
>
> The first offense on record was, that on more than one occasion Love ordered a subordinate to drive a government issued vehicle to run personal errands for [him], and have it washed and cleaned

out. There have been some outside reports that the subordinate also found ancient Indian artifacts in Love's vehicle during this process, but the most egregious allegation [is] still to come.

After a raid on the Redd family of Blanding, Utah, that also involved several other collectors of ancient Indian artifacts in the surrounding area, Love demanded the Utah Department of the Interior evidence custodian to retrieve several of the artifacts from the evidence room so he could display them on his desk. The internal investigation also states that Love gave at least several BLM agents and one private contractor "Moqui Marbles" to keep as a trophy after the 2009 raid he and FBI Special Agent Greg Bretzing called, Operation Cerberus."[4]

This document was signed by the BLM's director of law enforcement security, Salvatore R. Lauro. The "Moqui marbles" mentioned in the document are iron oxide concretions that come from Navajo sandstone that is found across southern Nevada, northern Arizona, northwest Colorado, and Utah. They are believed to represent an extension of Hopi Native American traditions regarding ancestor worship.[5] Possessing these marbles unlawfully is a federal offense and comes with a hefty prison sentence.

Now, if a regular citizen had stolen the Moqui marbles from the federal evidence room, the feds would have raided his house unannounced at gunpoint, arrested him, interrogated him at gunpoint, put him in handcuffs, searched his house for 12 hours or so, and taken anything that they felt looked suspicious. Of course, Love is not a regular citizen; he is protected by an out-of-control federal government.

According to an unnamed BLM officer, Love, on more than one occasion, ordered a subordinate to drive a government-issued vehicle to run personal errands for him, and have it washed and cleaned out. There were some outside reports that the subordinate also found ancient Indian artifacts in Love's vehicle during this process.[6]

This alleged infraction may seem minor, but it gets worse. Congressman and House Oversight and Government Reform Committee chairman Jason Chaffetz, as well as Congressman Blake

Farenthold of Texas, accused Love of having "scrubbed" a multitude of emails, influenced witnesses, and deleted hundreds of documents the day before a congressional investigative committee issued a records request concerning these materials.[7] In the same breath, Love was also accused of using his position to procure tickets to the popular Burning Man music and art festival, which is attended by nearly 65,000 people each year and held in Nevada's Black Rock Desert.[8]

Concerning these accusations of email tampering, Congressman Chaffetz, in a letter to Mary L. Kendall, committee chairwoman, wrote:

> Your report documents that a witness told your investigators that after receiving a congressional request for documents, the witness heard Dan Love "say to [another BLM employee] that [said BLM employee] needed to make sure that he scrubbed the emails before he sent them, you know, flagging anything that looked inappropriate so that [Dan Love] could remove them if needed." In another part of the report, a witness testified about how a BLM employee accessed and "deleted hundreds of documents" from a shared network. The deleted documents were "team documents" which served as the "historical record or administrative record" for a BLM authorized event. The witness also stated the deleted documents were subject to the Federal Records Act, and were required under the law not to be destroyed.[9]
>
> [He] refused to turn over his government-issued laptops, saying they'd been lost which several witnesses revealed that was something he previously told colleagues he planned to do if he ever got in "trouble."[10]

It is not farfetched to assume those emails were "scrubbed" to cover up illegal actions concerning the Redd and/or Bundy cases, in which Love was heavily involved. The scrubbed emails could very well have proven the confiscation of the Redd family's artifacts and that Dan Love was guilty of multiple felonies—felonies, in the case of Operation Cerberus Action, that led to the deaths of four people.

In relation to Operation Cerberus Action, the decision not to prosecute Love came on the heels of the Redd family's wrongful death lawsuit's shamefully being thrown out of court.[11] Sometimes, it really seems there is no justice in the world. Jeanette Redd, the wife of Dr. James Redd, had a personal journal that Dan Love confiscated during the 2009 raids and read with great interest.

In her journal, Jeanette wrote specifically about a collection of "gaming pieces" she legally acquired over the years from several sources. When Love and the other BLM agents confiscated the Redd family's artifacts, along with whatever else they wanted, Jeanette specifically noted that they would never find another collection of "gaming pieces" like hers.[12] These items were most likely Moqui marbles.

A new report concluded that Love misappropriated the strange, naturally occurring globes, which were evidence in an ongoing criminal probe, and instructed a subordinate to conceal his misconduct and thwart a congressional inquiry.

In the wrongful death lawsuit against Love, there is mention of his keeping several crudely fashioned artifacts that Ted Gardiner (the now dead secret informant) had acquired from Jeanette Redd. These artifacts were to have been entered into the evidence locker but evidently never were. After conducting an extensive search for them, the FBI eventually discovered the items in Love's car.[13]

When the FBI agents discovered the artifacts, they generated a document reprimanding Love and "wrote him up" for personally keeping Jeanette Redd's artifacts and not entering them into the evidence locker. When the Redds filed for release of this document, government officials quickly sealed the document.[14] But its existence is unquestioned.

The government still refused to prosecute Love even though he exhibited a pattern of misconduct when it came to several of these artifacts; he acted as if he believed whatever he confiscated from anyone was his and was therefore free for the taking. His conduct in both the Bundy and Redd cases was not only unethical but unlawful. He utilized excessive force, overstepped his authority, persecuted people for minor infractions for his own personal career enrichment, and treated confiscated "evidence" as his own personal treasure trove.[15]

It is perhaps quite fitting that the day before Dr. Redd's funeral, the FOX news affiliate in Utah interviewed then Secretary of the Interior Ken Salazar about the raids. His response about the result of the raids was, "I have frankly no regret about what has happened here. We were simply upholding the law in the name of protecting the cultural and landscape cultures of America.... The law is the law. No man or woman is above the law." This should no doubt include individuals like Love, but the government has made the decision to protect people like him and allow good people like the Redd family to suffer.

With the failure of the investigation involving the conduct of Love, many in the community he has hurt with his illegal actions and egregious conduct will have no justice. According to the reports concerning the investigation into Love's stealing priceless artifacts from the American people, the BLM conducted the investigation and decided not to prosecute.[16] This is yet another example of the federal government's protecting its own.

The BLM has always defended Operation Cerberus Action and its results. In the wake of the operation, as previously noted, Love was named BLM Special Agent of the Year for 2009, and the BLM's year-end review covered the accomplishments of Love concerning Operation Cerberus. He is heralded almost as a conquering hero who brought evildoers to justice. You would have thought he captured Al Capone single-handedly.

The year-end review glowingly states, "Agent Love was selected for the award because of his outstanding work conducting investigations in the protection of renewable and non-renewable resources.... This investigation could not have been completed without the unparalleled dedication of Agent [Love]."

And in regard to Operation Cerberus Action, the year-end review stated, "The many artifacts and other culturally significant pieces that have been recovered in this operation will be returned to the scientific and Native American communities. In addition to returning the stolen properties to their rightful owners, a secondary goal of the operation was to significantly deter the future dealing and illegal excavation of stolen artifacts from public lands. Special Agent Love's exemplary effort on this investigation has brought great credit upon him and the BLM. The cultural significance of the artifacts that were seized is without a doubt of immeasurable value to the scientific, academic, and Native American communities."

According to this review, the BLM seems quite pleased with what happened in Operation Cerberus Action and the major role Love played in it. Yet, according to the memorandum from the Department of the Interior, Love had an evidence custodian retrieve artifacts from the evidence room so he could display them on his personal desk. It does not sound like materials were returned to the "scientific and Native American communities," as they were supposed to have been.

In the greater scope of Love's offenses, Las Vegas attorney Bret Whipple, who represents cattle rancher Cliven Bundy, stated that Love "was [the man who] put together the plan." Whipple went on to add that reports indicate Love has no regard for the rule of law. He stated that federal investigators claim that Love wrongly used his influence as a federal agent with the BLM to gain benefits at Burning Man, and then intimidated other BLM staff into keeping quiet about his misconduct.[17]

Adding to what Whipple had to say about the BLM and Love, Nevada assemblywoman Michele Fiore said about Love, "Scoring a few tickets and having sex with his girlfriend in a BLM trailer at Burning Man is the least of his offenses. This man is the same guy who threatened to use lethal force against American citizens and elected officials—myself included—during the protest at Bundy ranch.... This guy disobeyed the direct order of our state attorney general and beat people up and arrested them when he had no authority to do so.... At this point I think the right thing to do in this situation is to let our men who have been wrongfully accused of threatening the BLM out of jail and put Daniel P. Love, the real criminal, in jail for a very, very long time."[18]

According to the inspector general's report, Love was supposedly on duty for 24 hours of official work, for three consecutive days, but was also in attendance at the Burning Man event. Investigators claim that the agent intimidated coworkers into not cooperating with investigators, coaching them to say, "I don't recall" when asked questions.[19]

In fact, one of Love's BLM coworkers claimed that the agent said, "You know, if you don't side with me, grenades are going to go off and you'll get hit."[20]

Michael Richardson, a spokesman for the BLM, stated, "The Bureau of Land Management takes allegations of misconduct seriously. These types of allegations do not align with our mission or the professionalism and dedication of our 10,000 employees doing essential work for America's public lands every day."[21] At this point, however, it is one thing for BLM officials to say they do not condone this type of behavior, but is a completely different thing when they do not prosecute Love for these actions.

What is most disheartening about all of this is that when the news came out about the investigation of Love, few in the community had any confidence in the U.S. attorneys office to prosecute him. In fact, the attorney's office defended Operation Cerberus Action as vigorously as the BLM did. Neither organization wanted any more scrutiny of their train wreck of an operation, which resulted in no jail time for any of the accused and the deaths of four human beings.[22]

In fact, following the culmination of Operation Cerberus, Deputy Attorney General David Ogden said of the BLM's action, "These archaeological treasures are precious, and protecting them preserves a rich history and heritage. That is why the Justice Department will use all of its tools to vigorously enforce the laws designed to safeguard the cultural heritage of Native Americans."[23]

Adding to that sentiment, U.S. Attorney Brett Tolman commented on Operation Cerberus, saying, "These treasures are the heritage of all Americans, and some of the objects are sacred to American Indians. Those who loot or damage public and American Indian resources for their own personal use or gain take something from all of us. Those engaged in this kind of conduct will be prosecuted."[24] Unless of course it is Love or any other BLM agent who abuses that cultural heritage or loots American Indian resources.

With comments like these, one would think the feds would have proceeded as they did concerning the outcome of Operation Cerberus Action. What was good for the goose would have been good for the gander, but unfortunately it was not meant to be. Love should have faced the same scrutiny and felony charges that were thrust upon the Redd and Bundy families, as well as upon myself after the raids at Garryowen.

Many who were hurt by Operation Cerberus, the Bundy Standoff, the Gibson raid and the Garryowen raids will see no justice. Unfortunately, with the decision to not pursue charges against Love and the dismissal of the Redd family's wrongful death case, many who were involved in these raids feel like there is no hope.

Not surprisingly, there has also been a great deal of pushback concerning Congressman Chaffetz's bill H.R. 622. Opponents of 622 say that federal law enforcement officers, like BLM agents, help protect species and habitats by deterring illegal off-highway vehicle use, patrolling big-game habitats, and curbing waterway pollution.[25]

These opponents say that with 622, Chaffetz appears to be siding with the Bundy family and attaching himself to their cause. They say the bill essentially would force federal agencies to totally cede control of all public lands to local counties. This of course was what Ammon and Ryan Bundy were protesting about in 2016 when they led the armed occupation of Oregon's Malheur National Wildlife Refuge.

Much of the opposition to H.R. 622 comes from environmental groups that, surprisingly, know very little about what the BLM is doing in terms of law enforcement. Many of these "environmentalists" do not exactly occupy the areas that are affected by the BLM tactics used to enforce their brand of "justice." Environmental and conservation groups as well as Brent Fenty, executive director of the Oregon Natural Desert Association, believe that taking away the law enforcement role from the BLM and the Forest Service officers is a part of a trend to "defund public lands, villainize public servants who are managing these lands, and…remove their ability to do their job."[26]

Chaffetz has rightly countered these statements by saying, "Federal agencies do not enjoy the same level of trust and respect as local law enforcement. This legislation [622] will help de-escalate conflicts between law enforcement and residents while improving transparency and accountability." Policing functions are a "distraction" for BLM and Forest Service employees, the statement said, and the bill "is a win all around."[27]

On April 19, 2017, Chaffetz announced he will not seek re-election in 2018.[28] On May 18, 2017, he announced he would leave the House of Representatives.[29] Although Congressman Chaffetz has stepped down from his post, others have championed his cause. The fight must surely continue as it relates to this subject. When it comes to Dan Love and the BLM, the facts are clear, there is a connection between the Bundy Standoff, the Malheur occupation, Operation Cerberus Action, the Gibson Raid, and the raids on Garryowen.

All the raids were perpetrated by agents of the BLM. In the case of Operation Cerberus and the Bundy Standoff, both campaigns were orchestrated and led by Love. He created the plan and commanded its militarized BLM troops in the field to ensure that his instructions were followed to the very letter. Even after reports of abuse of power, of taking extreme measures to punish people for the simplest of infractions, and following the deaths of multiple people, especially in the case of Operation Cerberus, Love was praised for his conduct. Even Secretary of the Interior Ken Salazar heralded him as having done an exemplary job.

Even though there were accusations from the Bundy and Redd families concerning malpractice, they were treated as criminals who had been caught doing the most egregious offense and threatened with federal prison sentences that would have lasted the rest of their natural lives. Dr. Redd died over a $75 bead. I lost almost everything I owned and was nearly given a prison sentence of 80-plus years over a button—a button placed to entrap me. And the Bundys are facing prison terms that will last the rest of their lives over cattle ranching. Not drilling for oil, not fracking, not scarring the land by mining for precious metals, but for ranching on federally owned land in a state that the government just so happens to control 81.1 percent of.

The raids were attacks on civilians' constitutional rights. The BLM orchestrated all of them not to bring down a hardened criminal class bent on committing the most heinous of violent crimes against society, but to further careers and fatten pocketbooks at the expense of American citizens. This, unfortunately, is how the deep state works. It is said, "Power tends to corrupt, and absolute power corrupts absolutely." Nearly unlimited, unaccountable power is given to men and women whom the very system frees to be black-booted thugs. They then use it, beyond all reason, to destroy people's lives.

This aspect of the deep state works in a circle of collusion between intelligence officers and executive branch officials guiding policy through means such as militarization of police[30] or, in this instance, militarization of BLM agents. Luckily for concerned American citizens, people like the Redds and myself have pledged to expose agencies like the BLM for what they have become. Politicians like former congressman Jason Chaffetz have also pledged to expose and eliminate the deep state with legislation like H.R. 622. It is important for all citizens to support these measures that will help end the oppression of the American people.

15

Redemption

In the decade following the raids, I incurred a mountain of debt but strove to keep my head above water and to keep Garryowen open as a functioning town and a nationally important historical site. A quarter of a century ago, when I decided to build the town of Garryowen, I instructed the architect to design the largest building possible for a set amount of money. That he did. However, my instructions had a flaw. Little did I know, to become an accredited museum and to qualify to receive reciprocal loans from the Smithsonian and other accredited museums, the building had to be fireproof, a fact that I did not learn until a few years later. Basically, this means the museum structure must be constructed using stone and steel. The original wood framed structure would not do.

The only way to take Garryowen to the next level would be to have a clean canvas and build a state-of-the-art stone-structure museum on the most famous battlefield in the world, a building designed to be around for 200 years or more.

At the time, I decided the best way to proceed was to put the town up for auction and hope it would appeal to a patriotic philanthropist. I originally teamed up with an auction house in Tulsa, Oklahoma, to auction off the town of Garryowen with a $3 million reserve in place. Not a bad deal for the entire 7.7 acres and the adjoining residences. One of the reasons for the auction was my hope that it would attract a special person who wanted to carry the historic torch, so to speak.[1] I hoped the philanthropist would share my vision and build on the historical foundation I had laid.

So, from that point on, I decided to refocus my efforts and energies toward making Garryowen a site for scholarship and national pride. My current goal is a rebirth of Garryowen, Custer Battlefield Museum Inc., and Elizabeth Custer Library and Museum Inc. (more on that later). This site deserves recognition regionally, nationally, and internationally in perpetuity for its historical significance.

Undeterred by the actions of the United States government to bankrupt me and take my property, I devised a new multimillion-dollar plan to renovate and rebuild the Custer Battlefield Museum. I continue to collect historical materials significant to the Battle of the Little Bighorn, and I hope to find philanthropists to help make the dream of turning Garryowen into the largest first-class museum and research complex in Montana come true.

The unique thing about this philanthropic, patriotic opportunity is that it is not an experiment. The Custer Battlefield Museum has been operating successfully, seeing visitors from dozens of countries annually. The museum is host to thousands of military officers, not only from our great armed forces but from those of our allies around the world. They come here every year to study Custer's mistakes so the same mistakes are not repeated on our battlefields today. Garryowen and the museum complex have a purpose: we are here to teach about the history of how America expanded "from sea to shining sea." The western migration represented a clash of immigrants from the East and local peoples defending their homeland, including their cultures and ideas. Change comes at a price, and the resulting changes still shape our land and society today.

History does matter, and to that end, the National Park Service has been trying to build a new visitors center for the past 60 years, but without success. Now, the earliest the National Park Service will even consider building a new facility is 2025. However, I know the federal government will never be successful in building a new visitors center at the Little Bighorn National Monument. The National Park Service is a bureaucracy manned largely by administrators who are on their way to a healthy government-funded retirement based upon longevity rather than accomplishments. I know these people and understand them to be interested mostly in getting their Department of the Treasury paycheck every two weeks, before and after retirement. Preserving history is at best an incidental goal and most correctly their means to reaching retirement.

Further, it is my belief that a new federal facility will never come to be because the Indian tribes that won the Battle of the Little Bighorn are still enemies with the Crow tribe, whose reservation occupies the battlefield and 200,000 acres surrounding it. At the time of the battle, the Crows were part of the 7th Cavalry and fought side by side with Custer's men. Out of the Plains Indians tribes, only the Crow tribe did not wage war against the United States. And the battlefield is within the exterior boundaries of the Crow reservation, a fact that the tribes who fought in and won the battle are envious of. As a matter of policy, the National Park Service and the Department of the Interior will not build a new visitors center unless *all* the tribes involved in the Battle of the Little Bighorn agree. The tribes will never agree, not only because they are still enemies, but also because the tribes each hold an election for tribal chairman every four years, and the opposing factions within each of the tribes never agree with the previous tribal administration. Sounds all too familiar, doesn't it?

Every few years, the National Park Service votes on doing a feasibility study that costs millions of dollars to justify its budget. Keep in mind, a feasibility study is merely a bunch of paper. Nothing ever comes from these studies, but administrators spend lots of time and millions of our federal tax dollars for these studies. It is a fundamental part of the bureaucratic process that looks good but accomplishes little or nothing (lots of smoke but no fire).

My proposed new museum at Garryowen will provide a 2,000- to 3,000-square-foot mini museum inside the new facility. This will offer a venue for each one of the six tribes who fought in the Battle of the Little Bighorn to tell its own story without federal government intervention because, as we all know, federal government intervention almost never ends well.

Garryowen is a dream location. It occupies ground sacred to the American historical consciousness; it houses a tomb of national importance, and the largest collection of Custer-related documents in the world calls Garryowen home. The site has a dedicated exit from a stretch of interstate highway between the two most popular tourist destinations in the country—Yellowstone Park and Mount Rushmore. Every year, millions of vehicles traverse this stretch of I-90, and 400,000 visitors climb Last Stand Hill.

Over the years, I have examined numerous Sitting Bull items. I have authenticated numerous autographs, the contract he signed with Buffalo Bill's Wild West Show, and artifacts owned by him. One item I encountered was a shield allegedly belonging to Sitting Bull that was apparently a family heirloom passed down through generations. The donor, who gifted it to the Custer Battlefield Museum, stated that it came from his great-great-grandfather, who had homesteaded in Montana and knew Sitting Bull.

As far as provenance goes, it cannot be said for sure if the shield was used in the battle or not. The shield is a spectacular example of Sioux armor. The back of the structure is made from a recycled, painted buffalo hide parfleche, which is a Native American rawhide bag often used to hold dried meats. Inside the muslin, you can see that black feathers were inserted, used as a form of spiritual protection by Native Americans. This aspect makes the item unique; I had never seen feathers inside a shield before.

There are also images on the front of the shield, including a blurred thunderbird, a teepee, a faded crescent moon with two stars, and at the center, a depiction of a buffalo's head. I found an example of this shield in a photograph of Sitting Bull currently owned by the North Dakota Historical Society. The photo shows a thunderbird at the center beneath a crescent moon and three stars along the bottom just like mine.[2]

In years past, I would have been overjoyed when the museum received an item like this. But because of my experiences over the past decade, I tend to treat acquisitions like it more cautiously. I suppose one could say I've been doused with a healthy dose of paranoia. I never know any more if I am accepting something from legitimate donors who mean well and want their items and heirlooms to be enjoyed by the public, or if I am being set up. Is the BLM sending these people to me to test the waters, like it did before? Are the agents trying to reel me in because they feel like I'm the one who got away? I have a hard time really knowing anymore.

At times, when I think about my experiences, I am reminded of a line from the film *The Shawshank Redemption*. Morgan Freeman's character, Red, is released on parole from prison as a very old man, and he sits contemplating the rest of his life in a small apartment room in a halfway house. Narrating the scene, Red relates what he fears while living in the outside world and the meaning of the rest of his life. Through his worry, he says, "Terrible thing, to live in fear." A simple statement, but nothing rings truer.

It is an ugly thing to be afraid every time I sell something from my Historical Rarities Inc. business, not knowing if I have missed something in the provenance of an artifact to cause me to incur the wrath of federal agents. Or if I allow an item to be accessioned into the museum's collection, like the Sitting Bull shield, will it ever be used against me? Is the item an incredible fake that will later be used to humiliate me or discredit my reputation in some fashion? I am not too worried about the latter, having four decades of experience now under my belt, but it's always in the back of my mind.

Through the years I have tried to maintain a good relationship with the Montana tourism board and the communities surrounding Garryowen. Along with living on the Crow reservation, I have also tried to donate my time and resources to worthy causes, reaching out across the nation through other endeavors I have supported. The Shadow Warriors Project, which provides support for private military security contractors and their families, has become a special organization for me in recent years.

I have planned and organized fundraisers in Billings for numerous heroes involved in these operations, along with Mark "Oz" Geist, founder of the Shadow Warriors Project and a survivor of the 2012 attack on the U.S. diplomatic compound in Benghazi, Libya. Mark is also one of the coauthors of the book *13 Hours: The Inside Account of What Really Happened in Benghazi*.

I have also worked with executives at Paramount Pictures, which released the *13 Hours* film based on the book, to arrange a special benefit showing in Billings for several of these military and former military members. As an accompaniment to the Montana premiere of the film, I conducted a silent auction, and Mark was the keynote speaker in a "no-holds-barred question and answer session regarding the horrific events that transpired in Benghazi." All the proceeds went to the Shadow Warriors Project, to help the men and women devastated by events like the Benghazi attack but who are forgotten by our government because they are security contractors hired by the American government but not commissioned or enlisted in the U.S. military.

I am interested in supporting private contractors who were wounded while serving their country in a private capacity. I am not concerned about the politics surrounding any of these events but endeavor to help the men and women who have served our country and have personally paid a great price with their lives and bodies for their courage.

Although these private security contractors may have served in the military, they are considered civilians and do not receive the same support offered to active military personnel or veterans. The Shadow Warriors Project focuses on these contractors and their families.[3] I draw attention to these events and my intentions of rebuilding the Custer Battlefield Museum not to toot my own horn but to demonstrate that after everything I have been through, I still want to be a part of the community in which I live and to give back to that community.

I want to leave behind something that will benefit future generations of Americans. Moving beyond the animosity of the here and now will allow the heirs to this land to make this truly a melting pot of a society that builds on its past successes and its past failures, because history matters.

As I have stated several times throughout this book, I not only want to bring to light the unbridled corruption and malfeasance of many people in overreaching federal agencies that I have experienced. I want to chronicle my efforts and determination to continue to serve the country, state, and community in which I live.

My heart has hardened toward the government and toward organizations like the BLM and the USFWS for the route and lengths that they took to attack and persecute me. They stole a piece of me that will never grow back. I have lain awake for endless nights replaying the scenarios that led to my current position. What if I hadn't just tossed that button in a tackle box? What if I had given better instruction to my employee who pulled them out? What if? What if? What if?

It is enough to drive a person insane. I easily could've insulated myself in a shell and lived my life in depression; however, I decided the best thing for me was to forge ahead and share my experiences with as many people as possible. I want what happened to me to not be experienced by others who find themselves in similar situations.

In a world of unintended, even unexpected, consequences, I want people to be aware of what the potential risks are when they pick up an arrowhead or a pottery shard when hiking around the American West. My goal is to educate citizens on the issues facing people like Jay Redd and his family, or the Bundy family, or myself. If I can bring attention to the injustice perpetrated by the many corrupt individuals in these governmental agencies, then I will feel as though I have accomplished something.

The more people who are aware of these problems, the more there will be opportunities for pressure to be placed on these various government bureaucracies and their employees—employees who act without impunity and who are looking only to further their careers with no remorse for the businesses they destroy or the people they hurt. In the narratives I have presented throughout this book, I detailed the complete disregard that many agents have for the rights of this country's citizens and, in the cases of the Redds and LaVoy Finicum, the very lives of those citizens.

My feelings and views in this volume should not be considered a call to arms or a call for a revolt or coup. Instead, I hope my story serves as motivation for accountability at the highest levels of government operating with no oversight. My hope is that I have been able to shed light on the issues facing a growing number of Americans who find themselves at odds with current policies, destroying the trust between a government and its people.

For many Americans, the relationship with our federal government is "us versus them." It is not to say that bridges cannot be mended and a common understanding between ranchers, artifact dealers, amateur collectors, Boy Scouts picking up arrowheads and the like, and bureaucracies like the BLM and USFWS cannot be reached. First there needs to be a restoration of "we the people" with a government *of*, *by*, and *for* the people.

It is often said in Alcoholics Anonymous meetings that the first step in addressing a problem is admitting there is a problem. And, truly, that is what needs to happen here. The governmental agencies overseeing organizations like the BLM need to stop shirking responsibility for the actions of their agents and stop promoting people who don't understand that they serve the people and not the bureaucracy.

Government agencies exist to protect and to work with their citizens, not to secure record numbers of arrests and prosecutions. These are its fundamental purposes. Much common decency has been lost over time in America. These agencies have been corrupted through the pursuit of convictions of law-abiding citizens simply for agents' own career enhancement.

This is not to say that all arrests made by these agencies are illegitimate. Many people in the trade of historic artifacts have come across their collections by illegal means and deserve to be punished.

But when someone is accused of a crime, there should be due process consistent with the scope and character of the alleged offense. SWAT teams are not needed to issue a parking ticket, nor are SWAT teams needed to reach into museums and businesses already open to the public.

The presumption of innocence does not exist when dealing with a federal agency. There, you are guilty, sometimes even if you can prove your innocence. When incentives are given for securing convictions, it is no wonder that the level of corruption through the zealous pursuit of career enhancement over justice by any means available has reached the point it is at now.

Hopefully this book is not only seen as an exposé but is taken as a serious plea for Congress to make an internal evaluation of the agencies it oversees. All the people and events I have covered in this tome are real. From large companies like Gibson to individuals like Dr. Redd and his family, the damage inflicted by individual agents is stunning and all too real. And there are many more out there. This book is only an attempt to tell my story and the story of some of those I have interacted with. These stories are a grim reminder of what happens when government agents no longer fear or respect the people who put them in power. As Judge Andrew Napolitano says, "When the people fear the government, you have tyranny, but when the government fears the people, the result is liberty!"

Perhaps nothing will come from this book. Perhaps it will be a volume lost to history. But it is undeniable that something is bubbling below the surface in this country. Could it be the deep state? The Bundys are not an isolated case. They are simply at the heart of the most widely covered case because of the controversial tactics they employ to get their points across. But there are many people whose stories I have not touched on who are being persecuted by these out-of-control federal agents.

The good news in all of this is that steps, like the legislation proposed by former congressman Jason Chaffetz to strip the BLM and USFWS of their law enforcement capabilities, are now being taken.

The claims by abused citizens are being given actual credence because of the sheer number of them that are piling up. With more people becoming aware of these situations through greater news coverage, it is at the very least encouraging to see an effort being made to resolve these issues. Perhaps one day, the citizens affected by these policies and raids will be able to find common ground with these government institutions, and the two can work together as they did in the past.

Every generation is critical to our country and our people. We are always on the edge of critical failings and spectacular achievements and successes. Each of us must act knowledgeably and aggressively and responsibly to do something, even many things, each day that are good.

16

Looking Back to the Future

History matters. Not only did our history matter to those who lived it, but it is important to successive generations of Americans. History is more than the simple recitation of events; it is also important to understand the context within which events become our history. We can learn from our history. It has been and remains my goal that the Custer Battlefield Museum should be a resource bringing historical events to life in a meaningful way.

In pursuit of this end, in 2004 I acquired the Elizabeth Bacon Custer Manuscript Archive. It is a collection of thousands of pieces of paper. Its contents cut a great swath through American history, plunging from the Civil War into the Indian Wars, and on through the Gilded Age and World War I. It encompasses a diverse range of materials from the lives of the Custers, both personal and public. It incorporates correspondence to George Armstrong Custer between 1858 and 1870; correspondence to and from Elizabeth "Libbie" Bacon Custer between 1864 and 1933; an immense volume of Elizabeth's notes, drafts, travelogues, and photographs; the Custers' personal collection of stereoviews from the 1874 Black Hills expedition; and hundreds of intact period newspapers relating to Custer's exploits in the Civil War and the Indian campaigns.

This collection has not yet been catalogued. The archive is, for all practical purposes, untouched. To open one of the three dozen thick binders—each bulging with correspondence, original drafts, and voluminous notes—is to reveal a fresh historical treasure every time. These sheaves of original documents are the outcome of Elizabeth's obsession with writing and documentation, the hypergraphia of the wife of the most photographed man of the 19th century.

Elizabeth Custer was complex, intelligent, and beautiful, and she single-handedly and single-mindedly "created" her husband and his legacy for a fascinated American public after he died. She shaped American attitudes about the Indian Wars, the winning of the West, and the legacy of the Little Bighorn for six decades and beyond. In many ways a mysterious figure, she never remarried, but instead gave herself over as an orphan to the care of an American public who venerated her and buoyed her up with the force of their sentiments— particularly the veterans of America's wars.

Remarkable for its many facets, this is an archive of both history and the heart. It represents an important contribution to the understanding of a pivotal moment in American history, and of a battle, a time, a general, and a woman who are still vivid in the American imagination more than 140 years later. Multiple areas of scholarly interest are represented—among them, the rich history of the Western frontier and the extraordinary personalities that shaped it; the Battle of the Little Bighorn and the American reaction to the catastrophe; the social history of the late 19th century; gender studies; veterans' experiences of multiple wars; black Americans during the Civil War.

The collection addresses the great themes of history as well as the smaller, quieter ones: the unwritten lives of Civil War veterans, a father's grief at the death and mutilation of his son in an Indian fight, Elizabeth's joy in her husband and her extreme privation upon his death—all these give the archive an extraordinary emotional depth.

Letters from close family are interleaved with those from Union and Confederate generals. Scrawled, worshipful notes from half-literate men who served under Custer mingle with bawdy yet cultured epistles from his war buddies, who were often decorated heroes. Contemporary correspondence illuminates the Custers' experience of the Civil War, and previously unseen materials relate to the immediate aftermath of the Battle of the Little Bighorn. Letters from potent political figures are mixed with mournful notes from Indian Wars widows. Many letters came from the luminaries of the progressive movement at the end of the 19th century, into whose orbit Elizabeth was absorbed after Custer's death.

There are notes for Elizabeth's extremely popular books, still in print today, and for articles that she wrote, both published and unpublished. There are eloquent travelogues containing detailed firsthand observations of major world events in Europe and Asia; and extraordinary hand-written, unpublished interviews with Buffalo Bill and Custer's black servant Henry during the Civil War. Finally, the collection's true intimacy, and its pathos, comes from the minutiae of two lives that bring home the humanity of the Custers—mortgage receipts, a note from Brooks Brothers saying that a uniform was ready, and the original paid invoice from the newspaper made out to Custer for his father-in-law's (Judge Bacon) obituary.

The great bulk of this archive was in the hands of Custer family members until the mid-1970s. At that time, a California manuscript dealer met Emily Custer, the widow of Custer's grand-nephew and the mother of George Armstrong Custer III. He characterized her as "a delightful, rather elderly lady who loved to shoot pool." Upon meeting her in her home, and in the wake of several games of pool, "which she mostly won," Emily Custer sold the dealer a great mass of Elizabeth Custer's papers. He very soon sold them to a couple who were leading collectors of Custer documents, and who then augmented the collection with materials acquired from the collection of Dr. Lawrence Frost, who was an acknowledged authority on Custer and a collector himself. These combined materials are those now housed at Garryowen as a single archive.

At the time the dealer acquired the material from Emily Custer, it had no order; its second owners seem to have done some minor sorting and placing of some materials in envelopes. The collection is 16 linear feet.

Although the materials were not organized when they were bought from Emily Custer, they were handled and treated as historical items both during Elizabeth's lifetime and immediately afterward; it seems that Elizabeth was constantly cataloguing her papers. Many letters and bundles of manuscripts have pencil notations on their versos indicating their authors or subjects and sometimes their dates.

Many notations are in Elizabeth's handwriting, while others are in a second hand, which is almost certainly that of Marguerite Merington. Merington had been a close friend of Elizabeth's since the late 1890s, when they met at the Catskill literary colony of Onteora, where Elizabeth had a cottage. In Elizabeth's declining years, when neuritis and frailty made it impossible for her to write, she charged Merington with handling her papers and intimate letters, and with the publication of those letters whose content permitted it. Merington's efforts resulted in the book *The Custer Story* (1950).

Merington observes in her preface to *The Custer Story* the condition of the bulk of Elizabeth's papers after she died: "As Mrs. Custer's apartment was closed in a hurry after her death, her loose papers, unsorted, were packed in trunks." Although she notes that they ultimately found a haven at Yale, some of them clearly stayed in the family.

Merington also refers to the purposeful burning of intimate correspondence. Elizabeth seems to have habitually engaged in this practice, and the Custer kin directed that more intimate letters be burned after she died. At least one letter in the present collection has survived: marked "To be destroyed" on the verso, it is a love letter to Elizabeth after Custer's death, and is illustrated in her biographical sketch. Merington, however, made copies of these doomed letters; one of the most fascinating items in the collection is a notebook full of shorthand copies of correspondence, mostly letters written by Custer. A number of them are not published in Merington's book.

To properly house the collections and to display the thousands of historical artifacts and documents pertaining to the Battle of Little Bighorn—including personal items related to Custer, Lewis and Clark, Sitting Bull, the Crow Indians, and the 7th Cavalry—I am prepared to level the existing Custer Battlefield Museum and attached commercial complex to provide a site for new construction. My plans include a 56,000-square-foot Elizabeth Custer Library and Museum of Frontier Women of the West in conjunction with the Custer Battlefield Museum.

I believe the pioneering men of the West could not have made it without the women. The women's stories are an important part of Western history, which is why this museum is so crucial. This new institution will be a haven for important historical artifacts and documents used for public review and scholarly research. The Tomb of the Unknown Soldier would be the only piece of the old Garryowen that would be kept the way it is now.

I believe there is no greater cause than to preserve an important piece of American history for future generations by creating an accredited depository where historical artifacts and documents will be housed. I hope to continue to acquire additional collections and involve others who can enhance or contribute to the preservation of this era in American history.

I estimate the cost of building this new project's needed facility to be between $50 million and $75 million. The existing Custer Battlefield Museum building is insufficient in size to handle the physical demands of the Elizabeth Custer collection. I have helped to finance the Custer Battlefield Museum without any federal funds for a quarter of a century. This is the right time to construct an accredited depository to house these significant collections. But to do that, I need to find that one individual or corporation that will want to fund this project.

I truly believe that the worldwide appeal of the Custer story; the fact that Garryowen is unique, being the only town inside the perimeter of the Little Bighorn Battlefield; and the plan to focus on Elizabeth Custer as well as the history of many other frontier women will boost interest in this historical project. In addition to Custer's widow's vast collection, I also own Annie Oakley's pistol and gambling accoutrements, Calamity Jane's lace-up boots, and some of the rarest books in existence on the Lewis and Clark expedition, which contain references to one of the most famous Native American women in history, Sacagawea.

I find it fascinating that I had possession of Elizabeth's manuscript collection for two years before I discovered the fourth codicil in her will: "Each and every article owned by me, which is or may be considered in any way a souvenir of my late husband, General George Armstrong Custer...I give to my Executor with instructions to deliver the same over to a Public Museum or Memorial which may be erected on the battlefield of the Little Bighorn in Montana." Fate, coincidence, and/or reality? I choose reality, because I will be building the museum someday and her manuscripts are on the battlefield now.

I see the entire Elizabeth Custer acquisition and anticipated new complex as a major boon for Montana and the local area. There would be many outstanding benefits to the community, the county, and the state by building a state-of-the-art depository to house the massive amount of Western Americana.

The extended plan for the museum, however, will be not only to house the Elizabeth Custer Library and materials from the famous pioneer women of the Western plains, but to house a great deal of Indian artifacts, some of which are currently on display in the Custer Battlefield Museum. This collection will also include saddles, eagle feather war bonnets (once confiscated by the feds during the raids and now returned), carbines, battlefield maps, historical battlefield photographs, the largest collection of legally recovered Custer battlefield artifacts (consisting of hundreds of shell casings, ration cans, United States coins, 7th Cavalry equipment, bridles, pistols, arrows shot at the 7th Cavalry command on Last Stand Hill), many newspapers recounting the events of the Battle of the Little Bighorn, and much, much more. Since the museum's construction, the museum has acquired artifacts such as a complete period Crow parade saddle, Little Wolf's war bonnet, and Sitting Bull's death mask, which was created after he was murdered in 1890, just to name a few items. I believe I have seen or dealt with more authentic Sitting Bull signatures than anyone living in the world today.

I know my reputation has been tarnished by these events, but I do not want that to be my legacy. My goal is to tell my story, thus freeing me to go forward, letting bygones be bygones, forgiving but never forgetting, because *history matters*.

Epilogue

This story is far from over. As I wrote this book, many contemporaneous, relevant details emerged, such as the resignation of Jason Chaffetz and the Office of Inspector General investigation of Dan Love. Because of all the emerging details, it was a challenge to decide when to finish writing and submit the manuscript to my publisher.

Over a decade after the raids, I continue to own and operate the town of Garryowen, just as I did before the raids.

The Custer Battlefield Museum and the adjacent trading post receive tens of thousands of visitors from around the world each year, just as they did before the raids. I am the founding director of the museum, just as I was before the raids. The museum attracts many university intern applicants, and I continue to select two or three of them a year, just as I did before the raids.

The point I am making is simple: I may have taken a metaphorical arrow to the heart, but the federal government did not win. The town of Garryowen continues to thrive. It may be where the Battle of the Little Bighorn began in 1876, but it is also where the battle against the Bureau of Land Management, the last battle at the Little Bighorn, was won. This battle has been won, but the war against federal tyranny still goes on. The Bundy family and the Redd family continue to fight for justice every day. The Local Enforcement for Local Lands Act is awaiting its day in the sun. The battle against the federal government's overreach is an uphill one. I hope this book has given each reader the inspiration to keep fighting for what is right.

On September 15, 2017, less than half an hour after I submitted what I thought was my final manuscript to Post Hill Press, I received a text message from Jay Redd, Dr. James Redd's son, with a link to an Associated Press article from *The Salt Lake Tribune* which shared some exciting news. It was officially announced that Special Agent Dan Love, a BLM villain, was fired from the Bureau of Land Management. My wishes are that justice will be served and that he will be prosecuted for the allegedly felonious conduct detailed in the Office of Inspector General's report, as any other United States citizen committing those crimes would be. Jay shared with me that September 15 would have been his dad's birthday. Love's firing was a fitting birthday present for Dr. Redd.

The removal of Dan Love from his post of power, however is only the tip of the iceberg. It was recently revealed that before the Bundy ranch standoff in 2014, the BLM had multiple cameras surveilling the Bundy family.[1] Several sources also divulged that during the standoff agents from the BLM setup sniper positions and attempted to incite a violent confrontation between the Bundy supporters and BLM officials.[2] Larry Wooten, a former BLM employee and current whistleblower, exposed these truths by publishing a memo he had sent to Andrew D. Goldsmith, Associate Deputy Attorney General, concerning the standoff.[3]

In the memo, Wooten exposed the existence of a so-called "kill list" kept by BLM bureaucrats during the standoff containing the names of Bundy family members and their supporters. Wooten also voiced his concern about the BLM agent's actions, unprofessionalism and potential illegal misconduct.[4] He wrote that during the standoff federal agents showed intense religious bigotry against the Bundy family, who are Mormon. These same agents used numerous slurs to describe the Bundy supporters and exhibited an overwhelming desire to create a violent confrontation with them. It was the BLM agents who looked to instigate violence, not the Bundy supporters as was originally reported.[5]

What is even more damning of the federal government in this situation is that during the attempts to prosecute Bundy family members and their compatriots following the standoff, DOJ officials withheld exculpatory evidence from the Bundy's legal defense team. Photographs of BLM snipers, video surveillance of the Bundy family, the existence of the kill list, and recorded conversations between BLM agents were all withheld.[6]

Wooten also revealed that, through conversations with other BLM agents, he was informed that agent Dan Love had a personal "kill book" he kept as a "trophy" to commemorate his role in the death of several people (separate from the kill list). Apparently, this book included the names of Dr. James Redd and the other individuals who committed suicide during the events of Operation Cerberus Action. Love essentially "bragged about getting three people to kill themselves." The fact that a kill book existed with the names of people who had no previous criminal convictions is utterly despicable! People like Dr. Redd were law abiding, tax paying, decent American citizens whose lives were destroyed for nothing.[7]

In a less unlawful but equally disgusting act, it was also revealed that Dan Love sent photos of his girlfriend's genitalia and his feces to other BLM employees. He also kept a doll that he referred to by the name of a Native American BLM employee and called it, "his drunk little Indian."[8] It should be noted that Dan Love is not the only BLM agent who is guilty of this kind of malfeasance. Wooten said, during the Bundy standoff, that even his supervisor, "took photographs in the secure command post area of the Las Vegas FBI Headquarters and even after he was told that no photographs were allowed, he recklessly emailed out photographs of the Arrest Tracking Wall in which Eric Parker, [a Bundy compatriot] and Cliven Bundy had X's through their face and body."[9] This is yet another reason to 'drain the swamp' that is the BLM, eliminating corrupt agents and jailing the worst of the worst.

After these revelations, Federal Judge Gloria Navarro ordered the release of Ammon and Cliven Bundy from prison on November 30, 2017.[10] On December 20, Judge Navarro declared the case against the Bundys a mistrial. The Bundy family members had been incarcerated for the better part of two years for challenging the BLM and the unrestrained and abusive agents they faced in the Bundy ranch standoff. They were held because a completely fabricated Threat Assessment Report identified the men as dangerous terrorists.[11] In the case of Ammon, he was in solitary confinement when he wrote the foreword to this book.

Following the mistrial, in a January 8, 2018 mid-morning hearing to discuss the Bundy Ranch trial, Judge Navarro dismissed the indictment with prejudice due to misconduct by the prosecution for co-defendants Cliven Bundy, Ammon Bundy, Ryan Bundy, and Ryan Payne. What a way to sign off this book—**We the People** have demanded justice and justice has been served. The battle has been won but the war rages on. We must continue to demand justice to be served in all aspects of the federal government until the swamp has been drained!

In January 2016, then presidential candidate Donald J. Trump spoke on the need to bridle and rein in an out-of-control federal government. He talked about the "faceless, nameless bureaucrats [managing] public lands as if the millions of acres were owned by agencies such as the Bureau of Land Management." This, he said, was being done by "a federal government that is more intent on power and control than it is in serving the citizens of the nation."

Once he was elected Donald Trump has been true to his word. It was President Trump's DOJ, led by Attorney General Jeff Sessions, in late December 2017 that ordered an investigation into the prosecution of the Bundy family.[12] This is a step in the right direction that will hopefully begin the process of unraveling the entrenched deep state within agencies like the BLM. Continuing with his government overhaul, President Trump's Interior Department Secretary Ryan Zinke has moved to reverse the Obama-era national monument land grabs that confiscated land to create national monuments. Zinke has also begun the process of reassigning and removing many of the Interior Department agency heads. He has begun what has been referred to as a, "philosophical re-calibration of the Department of the Interior and its branches."[13]

Not all in federal government are corrupt or abusive with the power they wield. Those agents who expose the inner workings of wrongdoing in the federal power system at the expense of its citizens are to be commended. These whistleblowers have seen the abuse and risked their own careers and personal safety to shed a light into very dark corners of our government. These are not men and women putting our national security at risk. They are helping to keep our nation the land of the free.

The problem of government overreach is real, and the challenge is here and now. It is critical for you to demand that all your elected officials remember that they were hired by us to represent us—to serve "we the people" of these United States of America.

Resources

Books

Brust, James S., Brian C. Pohanka, and Sandy Barnard. *Where Custer Fell: Photographs of the Little Bighorn Battlefield Then and Now*. Norman: University of Oklahoma Press, 2007.

Chan, M.A. and W.T. Parry. *Mysteries of Sandstone Colors and Concretions in Colorado Plateau Canyon Country*. PDF version, 468 KB, Public Information Series no. 77. Utah Geological Survey, Salt Lake City, Utah.

Donovan, James. *A Terrible Glory: Custer and the Little Bighorn—The Last Great Battle of the American West*. New York: Little Brown, 2008.

Fox, Allen. *Archaeology, History, and Custer's Last Battle: The Little Bighorn Reexamined*. Norman: University of Oklahoma Press, 1993.

Hyde, George E. *Life of George Bent: Written from His Letters*. Edited by Savoie Lottinville. Norman: University of Oklahoma Press, 1968.

Miller, David Humphreys. *Custer's Fall*. Lincoln: University of Nebraska Press, 1985.

Monnett, John H. *The Battle of Beecher Island and the Indian War of 1867–1869*. Boulder: University Press of Colorado, 1992.

Utley, Robert. *Custer: Cavalier in Buckskin*. Norman: University of Oklahoma Press, 2001.

Wagner, Frederic C. *The Strategy of Defeat at the Little Bighorn: A Military and Timing Analysis of the Battle*. Jefferson: McFarland and Company, Inc., 2014.

Windolph, Charles, Frazier Hunt, Robert Hunt, and Neil Mangum. *I Fought with Custer: The Story of Sergeant Windolph, Last Survivor of the Battle of the Little Bighorn—With Explanatory Material and Contemporary Sidelights on the Custer Fight.* Lincoln: University of Nebraska Press, 1987.

Articles and More

Ahtone, Tristane. "Paying attention to the Native American vote." *Rocky Mountain PBS*, accessed July 1, 2017. pbs.org/frontlineworld/election2008/2008/11/paying-attention-to-the-n.html.

American History USA. "Battle of the Little Bighorn." Accessed July 12, 2016 americanhistoryusa.com/topic/battle-of-the-little-bighorn/.

Andrews, Evan. "10 Things You May Not Know about Sitting Bull." *History*, December 15, 2015. history.com/news/10-things-you-may-not-know-about-sitting-bull.

Baldwin, Tyler. "Custer's Legacy Lost." Accessed May 10, 2016. custermuseum.org/Battlefield percent20News/100329 percent20Custer's percent20legacy percent20lost percent20article.pdf.

Big Horn County. "Big Horn County Abstract of Votes, 2006 General Election." Accessed September 13, 2017. sos.mt.gov/portals/142/Elections/archives/2000s/2006/general/BIG_HORN.2006.pdf?dt=1505314613474.

Billings Gazette. "Montana Supreme Court disbars Billings attorney." *Billings Gazette*, June 12, 2014. billingsgazette.com/news/state-and-regional/montana/montana-supreme-court-disbars-billings-attorney/article_03768053-3f8d-5104-bdf7-f267195438e5.html.

Bird and Exotic Clinic of Seattle. "California Desert Tortoise." Accessed June 20, 2017. birdandexotic.com/becs-veterinary-care-animals/california-desert-tortoise/.

Brown, Matthew. "Custer dealer seeks return of seized artifacts." *Missoulian*, January 29, 2012. missoulian.com/news/state-and-regional/custer-dealer-seeks-return-of-seized-artifacts/article_37148b50-4aec-11e1-a76a-0019bb2963f4.html.

Brown, Matthew "Feds: Some Custer museum artifacts were stolen." *San Diego Tribune*, March 19, 2012. sandiegouniontribune.com/sdut-feds-some-custer-museum-artifacts-were-stolen-2012mar19-story,amp.html.

Brown, Tim. "Bundy Ranch Special Agent in Charge Dan Love Facing More Allegations of Misconduct that led to Suspension." *The Washington Standard*, May 19, 2017. thewashingtonstandard.com/bundy-ranch-special-agent-charge-dan-love-facing-allegations-misconduct-led-suspension/.

Brown, Tim. "If You Think the BLM and Daniel P. Love were Bad at Bundy Ranch Look What They did to this Man over Indian Artifacts." *The Washington Standard*, February 22, 2017. thewashingtonstandard.com/think-blm-daniel-p-love-bad-bundy-ranch-look-man-indian-artifacts/.

Burr, Thomas. "Utah's Stewart: BLM doesn't need a SWAT team." *The Salt Lake Tribune*, April 30, 2014. archive.sltrib.com/article.php?id=57881083&itype=CMSID.

Byas, Steve. "BLM Agent in Bundy Case Accused of Misconduct." *The New American*, February 13, 2017. thenewamerican.com/index.php?option=com_k2&view=item&id=25370:blm-agent-in-bundy-case-accused-of-misconduct-in-bundy-case&Itemid=632.

City of Columbia. "Dr. Robert Daniel Goerdeler." Accessed July 11, 2016. city-of-columbia.wikia.com/wiki/Dr._Robert_Daniel_Goerdeler.

Coinforce. "Challenge Coins." Accessed June 26, 2017. coinforce.com/challenge-coins/.

Conserve Energy Future. "What is Overgrazing?" Accessed June 20, 2017. conserve-energy-future.com/causes-effects-solutions-overgrazing.php.

Custer Battlefield Museum. "Custer Battlefield Museum Press Release." July 22, 2014. custermuseum.org/press-releases/CusterMuseum-Hearing2014-07-24.pdf.

Custer Battlefield Museum. "Garryowen, Montana." Accessed 7 January 2017. custermuseum.org/Garryowen.htm.

Custer Battlefield Museum. "OIG complaint." Accessed October 4, 2017. custermuseum.org/press-releases/DepartmentoftheInteriorOfficeofInspectorGeneralReportMuseumGarryowenMT.pdf.

Darcy, Oliver. "U.S. Officials End Tense Standoff Between Nevada Rancher, Federal Government." *theblaze*, April 12, 2014. theblaze.com/news/2014/04/12/nevada-rancher-wins-battle-with-feds-after-tense-standoff/.

Denver Post. "Report: Artifacts source blamed self for suicides." *Denver Post*, April 1, 2010. denverpost.com/2010/04/01/report-artifacts-source-blamed-self-for-suicides/.

Department of the Interior. "Federal Agents Bust Ring of Antiquity Thieves Looting American Indian Sites for Priceless Treasures." June 10, 2009. doi.gov/news/pressreleases/2009_06_10_releaseA.

Dovale, Shari. "BLM and FBI Exposed or How the Bundy's Got Out Of Prison." *redoubtnews*, November 29, 2017. redoubtnews.com/2017/11/blm-fbi-exposed-bundys-released/.

Egan, Timothy. "In the Indian Southwest, Heritage Takes a Hit." *New York Times*, November 2, 1995. nytimes.com/1995/11/02/us/in-the-indian-southwest-heritage-takes-a-hit.html?pagewanted=all.

Egelko, Bob. "Judge Richard Cebull sent hundreds of racist e-mails, panel says." *San Francisco Chronicle*, January 20, 2014.

Email from Jay Redd to Christopher Kortlander, received May 26, 2017.

Federal Bureau of Investigation. "Jason Dean Pitsch Sentenced in U.S. District Court." last modified May 9, 2012. archives.fbi.gov/archives/saltlakecity/press-releases/2012/jason-dean-pitsch-sentenced-in-u.s.-district-court.

Forest Legality Initiative. "U.S. Lacey Act." Accessed June 21, 2017. forestlegality.org/policy/us-lacey-act.

Fox News. "Fed Raid Targets Guitars Made from Endangered Trees." *Fox News*, August 26, 2011. foxnews.com/politics/2011/08/26/feds-environmental-enforcement-on-guitars-leaves-musicians-in-fear.html.

Fund, John. "United States of SWAT?" *National Review*, April 18, 2014. nationalreview.com/article/376053/united-states-swat-john-fund.

Garryowen, Montana. "List for Crypt." Accessed September 10, 2017. townforsale.net/images/Crypt_List.jpg.

Geni. "First Lt. William W. Cooke, 7th U.S. Cavalry." Accessed June 16, 2017. geni.com/people/First-Lt-William-W-Cooke-7th-U-S-Cavalry/6000000018271497532.

Gibbs, John. "Voter Fraud Is Real. Here's the Proof." *The Federalist*, October 13, 2016. thefederalist.com/2016/10/13/voter-fraud-real-heres-proof/.

Gold, Hadas. "Jason Chaffetz signs with Fox News." *Politico*, June 28, 2017. politico.com/story/2017/06/28/jason-chaffetz-fox-news-240045.

Great Nonprofits. "Custer Battlefield Preservation Committee, Inc." Accessed November 14, 2016 greatnonprofits.org/org/custer-battlefield-preservation-committee-inc_.

Greenfield, Daniel. "Gibson Commemorates Obama's Raid With Government Series Guitars." *Front Page Magazine*, January 30,

2014. frontpagemag.com/point/217649/gibson-commemorates-obamas-raid-government-series-daniel-greenfield.

Gunderson, Laura. "LaVoy Finicum shooting: What happened when." *The Oregonian*, January 26, 2017. oregonlive.com/oregon-standoff/2016/02/post_6.html.

Hammond, Dwight. "Oregon ranchers reject Cliven Bundy family occupation." *CBS*, January 3, 2016. cbsnews.com/news/oregon-ranchers-reject-cliven-bundy-family-occupation/.

Haun, Marjorie. "Zinke moves to Drain the Swamp at Interior Department." *redoubtnews*, June 20, 2017. redoubtnews.com/2017/06/zinke-drain-swamp-interior-department/.

Hayward, John. "The Gibson Guitar Raid." *Human Events*, August 26, 2011. humanevents.com/2011/08/26/the-gibson-guitar-raid/.

Henetz, Patty. "The Source: the inside story of the key player in Fed's Indian artifacts case." *Salt Lake Tribune*, February 23, 2017.

History Channel. "1994 Northridge Earthquake." *History*, Accessed August 11, 2016. history.com/topics/1994-northridge-earthquake.

Huffingtonpost. "Garryowen, Montana, Site Of Custer's Last Stand, For Sale For $250,000." *Huffingtonpost*, last modified August 7, 2012. huffingtonpost.com/2012/08/07/garryowen-montana-custer-for-sale_n_1751962.html.

Indianz. "DOJ denies US Attorneys were fired for Indian work." *Indianz*, June 22, 2007. indianz.com/News/2007/003577.asp.

Indianz. "Native vote in Montana favors Democrat Tester." *Indianz*, accessed July 1, 2017. indianz.com/News/2006/016837.asp.

Indianz. "US Attorneys targeted for Indian Country work." *Indianz*, September 30, 2008. indianz.com/News/2008/09/30/us_attorneys_targeted_for_indi.asp.

Ingraham, Christopher. "Voter Fraud Commission wants to Know the Voting History party ID and address of every voter in America." *Washington Post*, June 29, 2017. washingtonpost.com/news/wonk/wp/2017/06/29/trumps-voter-fraud-commission-wants-to-know-the-voting-history-party-id-and-address-of-every-voter-in-america/?utm_term=.87f2c3de2c25.

Jalonick, Mary Clare. "Mercer top candidate to become No. 3 at Justice Dept." *Independent Record*, August 18, 2006. helenair.com/news/state-and-regional/mercer-top-candidate-to-become-no-at-justice-dept/article_718003b8-8063-58d1-8974-ef0de2f6a63d.html.

Jawort, Adrian. "President Obama's Adoptive Crow Father, Sonny Black Eagle, Walks On." *Indian Country Media Network*, Last modified

November 29, 2012. indiancountrymedianetwork.com/news/native-news/president-obamas-adoptive-crow-father-sonny-black-eagle-walks-on/.

Jay Redd, email to author, May 26, 2017.

Johnson, Theodora. "Ranchers face added jail time for BLM fire." *Tri-State Livestock News*, July 17, 2015. tsln.com/news/ranchers-face-added-jail-time-for-blm-fire/.

Jordan, Deb. "BLM Agent Daniel P. Love Under Fire By Bundy Case Attorney After Inspector General Probe Finds Him Guilty Of Misconduct." *The Pete Santilli Show*, February 2, 2017. thepetesantillishow.com/blm-agent-daniel-p-love-under-fire-by-bundy-case-attorney-after-inspector-general-probe-finds-him-guilty-of-misconduct.

Jordan, Deb. "More Allegations of BLM Agent Dan Love Misconduct." *redoubtnews*, May 19, 2017. redoubtnews.com/2017/05/allegations-agent-love-misconduct.

Justia. "Estate of James D. Redd, M.D. v. Love et al., No. 2:2011cv00478 - Document 55 (D. Utah 2012)." June 11, 2012. law.justia.com/cases/federal/district-courts/utah/utdce/2:2011cv00478/80481/55/.

Kane, Jenny and Robert Anglen. "BLM misconduct probe may derail Bundy Ranch standoff trial." *USA Today*, February 3, 2017. azcentral.com/story/news/local/arizona-investigations/2017/02/03/blm-misconduct-probe-impacts-bundy-ranch-trial-dan-love-cliven-bundy-bunkerville/97450944/.

Kanigher, Steve. "An abbreviated look at rancher Cliven Bundy's family history." Accessed January 1, 2018. lasvegasnow.com/news/an-abbreviated-look-at-rancher-cliven-bundys-family-history/70830238.

Kelleher, Kathleen. "Malibu Is Not Liable for Road, Judge Rules: Litigation: Rambla Pacifico is deemed county's responsibility. Action means city won't be a party to $6-million suit by 6 landowners who lost their homes in firestorm." *Los Angeles Times*, June 2, 1994. articles.latimes.com/1994-06-02/news/we-64873_1_rambla-pacifico.

Kemmick, Ed. "Sunday events will support Shadow Warriors Project." *Last Best News*, June 2, 2016. lastbestnews.com/site/2016/06/sunday-events-will-support-shadow-warriors-project/.

Kortlander, Christopher. "OIG complaint." September 19, 2011.

Kortlander, Christopher. Personal collection. Letter from Thomas J. Stusek, attorney at law to Wilma A. Lewis, Office of Inspector General, BLM. October 30, 1995. Also includes letter of receipt from Susanne A. Gorey, director, Division of Operations and Special

Investigations and references complaint sent to Walter Johnson, chief law enforcement officer.

Kudialis, Chris. "Why Cliven Bundy tried to pay grazing fees to Clark County, not BLM." *Las Vegas Sun*, November 7, 2017. lasvegassun.com/news/2017/nov/07/why-cliven-bundy-sent-grazing-fees-clark-county/.

Legal form provided by the court for temporary protection (eventually full protection) filled out and signed by Cathy Lingard, produced by Montana 13th Judicial District Court, Yellowstone County, Montana Case Number DR 95-278. Filed October 23, 1995.

Loesch, Dana. "The Real Story Behind The Bundy Ranch Harassment." *The Dana Show*, last modified April 10, 2014. danaloeschradio.com/the-real-story-of-the-bundy-ranch.

Los Angeles Fire Department Historical Archive. "Official Report: Old Topanga Incident." November 2-11, 1993. lafire.com/famous_fires/1993-1102_OldTopangaFire/1993-1102_OfficialReport_OldTopangaIncident.htm.

Maffly, Brian. "New report faults controversial BLM agent for mishandling evidence." *The Salt Lake Tribune*, August 25, 2017. sltrib.com/news/environment/2017/08/25/new-report-faults-controversial-blm-agent-for-mishandling-evidence/.

Malibu Complete. "Malibu Disasters, 1970-1991." Accessed January 8, 2017. malibucomplete.com/mc_history_dev_1970s-91_disasters.php.

Manta. "Reno Battlefield Museum, Inc." Accessed June 16, 2017. manta.com/c/mm5xb98/reno-battle-field-museum-inc.

McAllister, Bill. "The $7 billion offer that never was." *Native Times*, September 23, 2008. nativetimes.com/archives/22/293-the-7-billion-offer-that-never-was.

McNeel, Jack. "Native Vote is Big in Montana." *Indian Country Media Network*, last modified November 22, 2006. indiancountrymedianetwork.com/news/native-vote-is-big-in-montana/.

Meiner, Scott Alexander. "Kortlander's Stand." Custer Battlefield Museum, February 1, 2012. thelbha.proboards.com/thread/1363/kortlanders-stand-more-museum-info.

Montana Office of Tourism. "Tomb of the Unknown Soldier." Accessed January 7, 2017. visitmt.com/listings/general/landmark/tomb-of-the-unknown-soldier.html.

Monzingo, Joe. "A Sting in the Desert." *Los Angeles Times*, September 21, 2014. graphics.latimes.com/utah-sting/.

MTGenWeb Project. "The Tribal Nations of Montana." Accessed July 1, 2017. mtgenweb.com/native.html#tribal.

Nature and Wildlife Pictures. "American Bald Eagles—Don't Go to Jail for One." Last modified February 25, 2015. natureandwildlifepics.com/2015/02/25/american-bald-eagles-dont-go-to-jail-for-one/.

Newman, Alex. "Whistleblower: Federal Thug Behind Bundy Fiasco Had "Kill Book." *The New American*, December 19, 2017. thenewamerican.com/usnews/crime/item/27612-whistleblower-federal-thug-behind-bundy-fiasco-had-kill-book.

Notarianni, John. "An Occupation in Eastern Oregon." *Oregon Public Broadcasting*, December 20, 2017. opb.org/news/series/burns-oregon-standoff-bundy-militia-news-updates/.

Nottage, James H. "The Bohlin Brand." *Edward H. Bohlin*, accessed June 13, 2017. bohlinmade.com/history.

Ogrysko, Nicole. "Forest Service, BLM could lose law enforcement units under new bill." *Federal News Radio*, March 28, 2016. federalnewsradio.com/legislation/2016/03/forest-service-blm-lose-law-enforcement-units-new-bill/.

Oral History Of The Dakota Tribes 1800's – 1945. "Oral History of the Dakota Tribes: As told to Colonel A.B. Welch, the First White Man Adopted by the Sioux Nation." Accessed January 7, 2017. welchdakotapapers.com/2011/08/50th-anniversary-of-the-little-big-horn-fort-yates-june-26-1926.

Patrick, Neil. "Surviving examples of warbonnets worn by respected American Plains Indians." *The Vintage News*, August 7, 2016. thevintagenews.com/2016/08/07/would-love-to-see-these-surviving-examples-of-warbonnets-worn-by-american-plains-indians-2/.

Perez-Pena, Richard. "Attorney General Sessions Orders Investigation After Bundy Mistrial." *New York Times*, December 21, 2017. nytimes.com/2017/12/21/us/attorney-general-sessions-bundy.html.

Petabox. "Montana Governor Brian Schweitzer's speech to the annual trial lawyers' convention in Philadelphia." Accessed July 1, 2017. ia801407.us.archive.org/29/items/MontanaGov.BrianSchweitzerSpeechToTrialLawyersConvention7142008/Gov_Schweitzer_speech_to_trial_lawyers_convention_14_July_2008_64kb.mp3.

Redoubtnews. "Dan Love Will Not Be Prosecuted." Accessed September 6, 2017. redoubtnews.com/2017/08/dan-love-not-prosecuted/.

Reptile Gardens. "The REAL Story of an Eagle." Last modified September 5, 2015. reptilegardens.com/scales-and-tales/article/the-real-story-of-an-eagle.

Resource Party. "Richard M. Stephens Groen Stephens," and "Amended Complaint for Declaratory and Injunctive Relief." Accessed July 1, 2017. theresourceparty.org/index.php?option=com_content&view=article&id=77%20percent3Aamendedcomplaint&catid=1%20percent3Aissues&Itemid=2.

Revolvy. "Bundy Standoff." Accessed June 20, 2017. revolvy.com/main/index.php?s=Bundy percent20standoff.

Right in the Rockies. "Voter Intimidation, fraud and frank talk on both sides!" Accessed July 1, 2017. rightintherockies.wordpress.com/2008/10/09/voter-intimidation-fraud-and-frank-talk-on-both-sides/.

Roche, Lisa Riley. "Chaffetz says he won't seek re-election but his plans remain unclear." *Deseret News*, April 19, 2017.

Santa Monica Mountains Conservancy. "Who We Are and What We Do." Accessed November 8, 2016. smmc.ca.gov/mission.html.

Sepulvado, John and Amelia Templeton. "Militant Says Foster Children Were Pulled From His Home." *Oregon Public Broadcasting*, January 16, 2016. opb.org/news/series/burns-oregon-standoff-bundy-militia-news-updates/militant-says-foster-children-were-pulled-from-his-home-lavoy-finicum-burns-oregon/.

Shay, Beck. "Crow Tribe endorses Indian slate." *Billings Gazette*, November 3, 2006. billingsgazette.com/news/state-and-regional/montana/crow-tribe-endorses-indian-slate/article_7bc4b0f2-0920-5db1-b532-f0a27cb41e09.html.

Smith, Christopher. "Burial ruling stuns Indians and Scientists." *Salt Lake Tribune*, March 1, 1998.

Sottile, Leah. "The Plan to Stop Federal Law Enforcement of Public Lands." *Outside*, accessed June 10, 2017. outsideonline.com/2154531/law-enforcement-public-land.

Stevens, Jay. "Someone tell Chuck Denowh the election is over." *Wordpress*, accessed July 1, 2017. 4and20blackbirds.wordpress.com/2006/11/17/.

Straub, Noelle. "Mercer wrote job provision into Patriot Act." *Montana Standard*, May 2, 2007. mtstandard.com/news/national/mercer-wrote-job-provision-into-patriot-act/article_4bd53aa3-6b83-58d8-8bac-5dff482ba098.html.

Taub, Amanda and Max Fisher. "As Leaks Multiply, Fears of a Deep State in America." *New York Times*, February 16, 2017. nytimes.com/2017/02/16/world/americas/deep-state-leaks-trump.html?_r=1.

Taylor, Phil. "Why LaVoy Finicum spurned the government." *Environment and Energy Publishing*, February 5, 2016. eenews.net/stories/1060031902.

Turck, Andrew. "Shield donated to Battlefield Museum may have belonged to Sitting Bull." *Big Horn County News*, June 11, 2015. bighorncountynews.com/news/uncertain-treasure.

Tuttle, Greg. "Billings lawyer accused of having sexual relations with client." *Billings Gazette*, January 19, 2011. billingsgazette.com/news/local/crime-and-courts/billings-lawyer-accused-of-having-sexual-relations-with-client/article_1b98a740-421d-54b7-9b00-f47514e85952.html.

U.S. Congress. "H.R.622 - Local Enforcement for Local Lands Act." Accessed September 6, 2017. congress.gov/bill/115th-congress/house-bill/622.

U.S. Department of Justice. "Arrests Made in Operation Targeting Network Selling Stolen Native American Artifacts." June 10, 2009. justice.gov/opa/pr/arrests-made-operation-targeting-network-selling-stolen-native-american-artifacts.

U.S. Department of Justice. "Eastern Oregon Ranchers Convicted of Arson Resentenced to Five Years in Prison." October 7, 2015. justice.gov/usao-or/pr/eastern-oregon-ranchers-convicted-arson-resentenced-five-years-prison.

U.S. Department of Justice. "Fact Sheet: Protecting Voting Rights and Prosecuting Voter Fraud." October 31, 2006. justice.gov/archive/opa/pr/2006/November/06_crt_738.html.

U.S. Department of Justice. "Justice Department Announces Policy on Tribal Member Use of Eagle Feathers." Last modified October 12, 2012. justice.gov/opa/pr/justice-department-announces-policy-tribal-member-use-eagle-feathers.

U.S. Fish and Wildlife Service. "Federal Laws that Protect Bald Eagles." Last modified April 20, 2015. fws.gov/midwest/eagle/protect/laws.html.

U.S. Fish and Wildlife Service. "Possession of Eagle Feathers and Parts by Native Americans." February 2009. fws.gov/eaglerepository/factsheets/PossessionOfEagleFeathersFactSheet.pdf.

U.S. Office of the Clerk: U.S. House of Representatives. "Current Vacancies." Accessed June 10, 2017. chaffetz.house.gov/news/documentsingle.aspx?DocumentID=458.

U.S. Office of Inspector General, Department of the Interior. "Investigative Report of Ethical Violations and Misconduct by Bureau of Land Management Officials." Accessed January 30, 2017. doioig.gov/sites/doioig.gov/files/EthcialViolationsAndMisconductBy-BLMOfficials_Public.pdf.

U.S. Office of the Inspector General. "An Investigation into the Removal of Nine U.S. Attorneys in 2006." September 2008. oig.justice.gov/special/s0809a/final.pdf.

United States History. "Little Wolf." Accessed June 17, 2017. u-s-history.com/pages/h3883.html.

Walker, Carol. "BLM Continues Lack of Transparency in Adobe Town Wild Mare Radio Collar Study." *Wordpress*, February 28, 2017. reclaimourrepublic.wordpress.com/2017/02/28/blm-continues-lack-of-transparency-in-wild-mare-radio-collar-study-blm-agent-in-bundy-case-accused-of-misconduct.

Whitehurst, Lindsay. "APNewsBreak: Investigators say US land agent took evidence." *Washington Post*, August 24, 2017. washingtonpost.com/national/energy-environment/apnewsbreak-investigators-say-federal-agent-took-evidence/2017/08/24/99539a92-8900-11e7-96a7-d178cf3524eb_story.html?utm_term=.e2e9620313cb.

Wikipedia. "Alberto Gonzales." Last modified December 24, 2017. en.wikipedia.org/wiki/Alberto_Gonzales.

Wikipedia. "Crow Indian Reservation." Last modified October 5, 2017. en.wikipedia.org/wiki/Crow_Indian_Reservation.

Wikipedia. "Richard F. Cebull." Last modified December 10, 2017. en.wikipedia.org/wiki/Richard_F._Cebull.

Wikipedia. "United States Senate election in Montana, 2006." Last modified December 20, 2017. en.wikipedia.org/wiki/United_States_Senate_election_in_Montana,_2006.

Wikipedia. "William W. Mercer." Last modified November 17, 2017 en.wikipedia.org/wiki/William_W._Mercer.

Wilson, Jenny. "Letter names BLM agent in charge of Bundy case as target of federal ethics probe." *Las Vegas Review Journal*, February 18, 2017. reviewjournal.com/news/bundy-blm/letter-names-blm-agent-in-charge-of-bundy-case-as-target-of-federal-ethics-probe/.

Wooten, Larry. "BLM Memo." *redoubtnews*, December 2017. redoubtnews.com/wp-content/uploads/2017/12/Larry-Wooten-Communication_77PI.pdf.

Wordpress. "Case 1:07-cv-00074-RFC. Document 26." November 5, 2007. rightintherockies.files.wordpress.com/2008/10/order-on-motion-to-dismiss.pdf.

York, Arnold G. "From the Publisher: 1993 Fire Sweeps Malibu." *The Malibu Times*, April 28, 2016. malibutimes.com/opinion/article_08995756-0d8e-11e6-9cc7-032a5949af62.html.

YouTube. "Footage of LaVoy Finnicum's Death." Last modified January 29, 2016. youtube.com/watch?v=_5J9NHAiC4E.

YouTube. "Fox News: SOS Brad Johnson on Schweitzer's election scandal." Last modified September 21, 2008. youtube.com/watch?v=xdHVGBqTtVM.

Endnotes

Foreword
1. John Fund, "United States of SWAT?" *National Review*, April 18, 2014, nationalreview.com/article/376053/united-states-swat-john-fund. Thomas Burr, "Utah's Stewart: BLM doesn't need a SWAT team," *The Salt Lake Tribune*, April 30, 2014, archive.sltrib.com/article.php?id=57881083&itype=CMSID.
2. "Estate of James D. Redd, M.D. v. Love et al., No. 2:2011cv00478 - Document 55 (D. Utah 2012)," Justia, accessed October 4, 2017, law.justia.com/cases/federal/district-courts/utah/utdce/2:2011cv00478/80481/55/.

Chapter 1
1. Robert Utley, *Custer: Cavalier in Buckskin*, (Norman: University of Oklahoma Press, 2001), 143.
2. James Donovan, *A Terrible Glory: Custer and the Little Bighorn—The Last Great Battle of the American West*. (New York: Little Brown, 2008), 205.
3. Ibid.
4. Donovan, *A Terrible Glory*, 206.
5. Ibid.
6. Evan Andrews, "10 Things You May Not Know about Sitting Bull," *History*, December 15, 2015, history.com/news/10-things-you-may-not-know-about-sitting-bull.
7. Charles Windolph, Frazier Hunt, Robert Hunt, and Neil Mangum, *I Fought with Custer: The Story of Sergeant Windolph, Last Survivor of the Battle of the Little Big Horn—With Explanatory Material and Contemporary Sidelights on the Custer Fight* (Lincoln: University of Nebraska Press, 1987), 86.
8. David Humphreys Miller, *Custer's Fall* (Lincoln, NE: University of Nebraska Press, 1985), 158.
9. Allen Fox, *Archaeology, History, and Custer's Last Battle: The Little Big Horn Reexamined* (Norman: University of Oklahoma Press, 2007), 255–59.
10. "Dr. Robert Daniel Goerdeler." City of Columbia, accessed July 11, 2016, city-of-columbia.wikia.com/wiki/Dr._Robert_Daniel_Goerdeler.

11 "Battle of the Little Bighorn," American History USA, accessed July 12, 2016, americanhistoryusa.com/topic/battle-of-the-little-bighorn/.
12 Donovan, *A Terrible Glory*, 92.
13 James S. Brust, Brian C. Pohanka, and Sandy Barnard, *Where Custer Fell: Photographs of the Little Bighorn Battlefield Then and Now* (Norman: University of Oklahoma Press, 1993), 82–89.
14 "Who We Are and What We Do," Santa Monica Mountains Conservancy, accessed November 8, 2016, smmc.ca.gov/mission.html.
15 Tyler Baldwin, "Custer's Legacy Lost," Custer Battlefield Museum, accessed May 10, 2016, custermuseum.org/Battlefield%20News/100329%20Custer's%20legacy%20lost%20article.pdf.
16 Ibid.
17 "Tomb of the Unknown Soldier," Montana Office of Tourism, accessed January 7, 2017, visitmt.com/listings/general/landmark/tomb-of-the-unknown-soldier.html.
18 "As Told to Colonel A.B. Welch, the First White Man Adopted by the Sioux Nation," Oral History of the Dakota Tribes 1800's – 1945, accessed January 7, 2017, welchdakotapapers.com/2011/08/50th-anniversary-of-the-little-big-horn-fort-yates-june-26-1926.
19 "List for Crypt," Garryowen, Montana, accessed September 10, 2017, townforsale.net/images/Crypt_List.jpg.
20 "Garryowen, Montana," Custer Battlefield Museum, accessed January 7, 2017, custermuseum.org/Garryowen.htm.
21 "Official Report: Old Topanga Incident," Los Angeles Fire Department, November 2 - 11, 1993, lafire.com/famous_fires/1993-1102_OldTopanga-Fire/1993-1102_OfficialReport_OldTopangaIncident.htm.
22 "Malibu Disaster, 1970-1991," Malibu complete, accessed January 8, 2017, malibucomplete.com/mc_history_dev_1970s-91_disasters.php.

Chapter 2

1 Arnold G. York, "From the Publisher: 1993 Fire Sweeps Malibu," *The Malibu Times*, April 28, 2016, malibutimes.com/opinion/article_08995756-0d8e-11e6-9cc7-032a5949af62.html.
2 Ibid.
3 Ibid.
4 Ibid.
5 Ibid.
6 Ibid.
7 Ibid.
8 Ibid.
9 James H. Nottage, "The Bohlin Brand," Edward H. Bohlin, accessed June 13, 2017, bohlinmade.com/history.
10 Ibid.
11 "1994 Northridge Earthquake," *History*, accessed August 11, 2016, history.com/topics/1994-northridge-earthquake.
12 Ibid.

13 Kathleen Kelleher, "Malibu Is Not Liable for Road, Judge Rules: Litigation: Rambla Pacifico is deemed county's responsibility. Action means city won't be a party to $6-million suit by 6 landowners who lost their homes in firestorm," *Los Angeles Times*, June 2, 1994, articles.latimes.com/1994-06-02/news/we-64873_1_rambla-pacifico.
14 Ibid.
15 Ibid.
16 Ibid.
17 Ibid.
18 Ibid.

Chapter 3

1 Legal form provided by the court for temporary protection (eventually full protection) filled out and signed by Cathy Lingard, produced by Montana 13th Judicial District Court, Yellowstone County, Montana Case Number DR 95-278, October 23, 1995.
2 Frederic C. Wagner, *The Strategy of Defeat at the Little Big Horn: A Military and Timing Analysis of the Battle,* (Jefferson: McFarland and Company, Inc., 2014), 69.
3 "Custer Battlefield Preservation Committee, Inc.," Great Nonprofits, accessed November 14, 2016, greatnonprofits.org/org/custer-battlefield-preservation-committee-inc.
4 Matthew Brown, "Custer dealer seeks return of seized artifacts," *Missoulian*, January 29, 2012, missoulian.com/news/state-and-regional/custer-dealer-seeks-return-of-seized-artifacts/article_37148b50-4aec-11e1-a76a-0019bb2963f4.html.
5 "Reno Battlefield Museum, Inc.," Manta, accessed June 16, 2017, manta.com/c/mm5xb98/reno-battle-field-museum-inc.
6 Chris Kortlander, "OIG Complaint," *Wordpress*, last modified September 19, 2011, turtletalk.files.wordpress.com/2012/02/kortlander-v-us-complaint.pdf.
7 Ibid.
8 Brown, "Custer dealer."
9 Ibid.
10 Ibid.
11 Ibid.
12 "First Lt. William W. Cooke, 7th U.S. Cavalry," Geni, accessed June 16, 2017, geni.com/people/First-Lt-William-W-Cooke-7th-U-S-Cavalry/6000000018271497532.
13 Evan S. Connell, *Son of the Morning Star: Custer and the Little Bighorn* (New York: Harper and Row, 1984), 289-90.
14 Ibid.
15 Brown, "Custer dealer."
16 Ibid.
17 Ibid.
18 Ibid.

19 Kortlander, "OIG complaint."
20 Kortlander, Christopher. Personal collection. Letter from Thomas J. Stusek, attorney at law to Wilma A. Lewis, Office of Inspector General, BLM, October 30, 1995. Also includes letter of receipt from Susanne A. Gorey, director, Division of Operations and Special Investigations and references complaint sent to Walter Johnson for further investigation.
21 "Jason Dean Pitsch Sentenced in U.S. District Court," Federal Bureau of Investigation, last modified May 9, 2012, archives.fbi.gov/archives/saltlakecity/press-releases/2012/jason-dean-pitsch-sentenced-in-u.s.-district-court.
22 Brown, "Custer dealer."

Chapter 4

1 Ibid.
2 "Federal Laws that Protect Bald Eagles," U.S. Fish and Wildlife Service, last modified April 20, 2015, fws.gov/midwest/eagle/protect/laws.html.
3 George E. Hyde, *Life of George Bent: Written from His Letters*, Edited by Savoie Lottinville (Norman: University of Oklahoma Press, 1968), 390.
4 John H. Monnett, *The Battle of Beecher Island and the Indian War of 1867–1869* (Boulder: University Press of Colorado, 1992), 46–48.
5 Neil Patrick, "Surviving examples of warbonnets worn by respected American Plains Indians," *The Vintage News*, August 7, 2016, thevintagenews.com/2016/08/07/would-love-to-see-these-surviving-examples-of-warbonnets-worn-by-american-plains-indians-2/.
6 "Little Wolf," United States History, accessed June 17, 2017, u-s-history.com/pages/h3883.html.
7 "Possession of Eagle Feathers and Parts by Native Americans," U.S. Fish and Wildlife Service, February 2009, fws.gov/eaglerepository/factsheets/PossessionOfEagleFeathersFactSheet.pdf.
8 "The REAL Story of an Eagle," Reptile Gardens, last modified September 5, 2015, reptilegardens.com/scales-and-tales/article/the-real-story-of-an-eagle.
9 "Justice Department Announces Policy on Tribal Member Use of Eagle Feathers," U.S. Department of Justice, last modified October 12, 2012, justice.gov/opa/pr/justice-department-announces-policy-tribal-member-use-eagle-feathers.
10 "American Bald Eagles – Don't Go to Jail For One," Nature and Wildlife Pics, last modified February 25, 2015, natureandwildlifepics.com/2015/02/25/american-bald-eagles-dont-go-to-jail-for-one/.
11 Timothy Egan, "In the Indian Southwest, Heritage Takes a Hit," *New York Times,* November 2, 1995, nytimes.com/1995/11/02/us/in-the-indian-southwest-heritage-takes-a-hit.html?pagewanted=all.
12 Ibid.
13 Ibid.
14 Ibid.
15 Kortlander, "OIG complaint."

Chapter 5
1. Greg Tuttle, "Billings lawyer accused of having sexual relations with client," *Billings Gazette*, January 19, 2011, billingsgazette.com/news/local/crime-and-courts/billings-lawyer-accused-of-having-sexual-relations-with-client/article_1b98a740-421d-54b7-9b00-f47514e85952.html.
2. "Montana Supreme Court disbars Billings attorney," *Billings Gazette*, June 12, 2014, billingsgazette.com/news/state-and-regional/montana/montana-supreme-court-disbars-billings-attorney/article_03768053-3f8d-5104-bdf7-f267195438e5.html.

Chapter 6
1. Scott Alexander Meiner, "Kortlander's Stand," Custer Battlefield Museum, February 1, 2012, thelbha.proboards.com/thread/1363/kortlanders-stand-more-museum-info.
2. Ibid.
3. Ibid.
4. Matthew Brown, "Feds: Some Custer museum artifacts were stolen," *San Diego Tribune*, March 19, 2012, sandiegouniontribune.com/sdut-feds-some-custer-museum-artifacts-were-stolen-2012mar19-story,amp.html.
5. Ibid.
6. Ibid.
7. Ibid.
8. Ibid.
9. Ibid.
10. Meiner, "Kortlander's Stand."
11. Ibid.
12. Ibid.
13. Ibid.
14. Adrian Jawort, "President Obama's Adoptive Crow Father, Sonny Black Eagle, Walks On," *Indian Country Media Network*, last modified November 29, 2012, indiancountrymedianetwork.com/news/native-news/president-obamas-adoptive-crow-father-sonny-black-eagle-walks-on/.

Chapter 7
1. "The Tribal Nations of Montana," The following information is taken from the booklet, "The Tribal Nations of Montana - A Handbook for Legislators," published in 1995, the booklet was prepared by The Committee on Indian Affairs and published by the Montana Legislative Council, Helena, MT, and is in the public domain, mtgenweb.com/native.html#tribal.
2. "United States Senate election in Montana, 2006," Wikipedia, last modified December 20, 2017, en.wikipedia.org/wiki/United_States_Senate_election_in_Montana,_2006.
3. Ibid.
4. Ibid.

5 Tristane Ahtone, "Paying attention to the Native American vote," *Rocky Mountain PBS*, accessed July 1, 2017, pbs.org/frontlineworld/election2008/2008/11/paying-attention-to-the-n.html.
6 "Voter Intimidation, fraud and frank talk on both sides!" Right in the Rockies, accessed July 1, 2017, rightintherockies.wordpress.com/2008/10/09/voter-intimidation-fraud-and-frank-talk-on-both-sides/.
7 "Richard M. Stephens Groen Stephens," and "Amended Complaint for Declaratory and Injunctive Relief," Resource Party, accessed July 1, 2017, theresourceparty.org/index.php?option=com_content&view=article&id=77 percent3Aamendedcomplaint&catid=1 percent3Aissues&Itemid=2.
8 "Crow Indian Reservation," Wikipedia, last modified October 5, 2017, en.wikipedia.org/wiki/Crow_Indian_Reservation.
9 Ibid.
10 Ibid.
11 Beck Shay, "Crow Tribe endorses Indian slate," *Billings Gazette*, November 3, 2006, billingsgazette.com/news/state-and-regional/montana/crow-tribe-endorses-indian-slate/article_7bc4b0f2-0920-5db1-b532-f0a27cb41e09.html.
12 Stephens, "Amended Complaint."
13 Ibid.
14 Ibid.
15 Ibid.
16 Ibid.
17 Shay, "Crow Tribe."
18 "Big Horn County Abstract of Votes, 2006 General Election," Big Horn County, accessed June 3, 2017, sos.mt.gov/portals/142/Elections/archives/2000s/2006/general/BIG_HORN.2006.pdf?dt=1505314613474.
19 Jay Stevens, "Someone tell Chuck Denowh the Election is Over," *Wordpress*, last modified November 17, 2006, 4and20blackbirds.wordpress.com/2006/11/17/.
20 Jack McNeel, "Native Vote is Big in Montana," *Indian Country Media Network*, last modified November 22, 2006, indiancountrymedianetwork.com/news/native-vote-is-big-in-montana/.
21 "Native vote in Montana favors Democrat Tester," *Indianz*, November 9, 2006, indianz.com/News/2006/016837.asp.
22 Ibid.
23 Ibid.
24 Ibid.
25 Ibid.
26 Ibid.
27 Ibid.
28 Stephens, "Amended Complaint."
29 "Fact Sheet: Protecting Voting Rights and Prosecuting Voter Fraud," U.S. Department of Justice, October 31, 2006, justice.gov/archive/opa/pr/2006/November/06_crt_738.html.
30 Ibid.

Endnotes   **259**

31 "Case 1:07-cv-00074-RFC. Document 26," *Wordpress*, November 5, 2007, rightintherockies.files.wordpress.com/2008/10/order-on-motion-to-dismiss.pdf.
32 Ibid.
33 "William W. Mercer," Wikipedia, last modified November 17, 2017, en.wikipedia.org/wiki/William_W._Mercer.
34 Bob Egelko, "Judge Richard Cebull sent hundreds of racist e-mails, panel says," *San Francisco Chronicle*, January 20, 2014.
35 "Richard F. Cebull," Wikipedia, last modified December 10, 2017, en.wikipedia.org/wiki/Richard_F._Cebull.
36 Montana Governor Brian Schweitzer's speech to the annual trial lawyers' convention in Philadelphia on July 14, 2008, in which Schweitzer boasted (to the cheers of the trial lawyers) of his misuse of official powers to interfere with the voting and vote-counting process to tip the 2006 Montana election for a U.S. Senate seat to his favored candidate, Jon Tester (listen at 10:30 to 12:00 about the plan Schweitzer carried out to use threats of false arrest to force Republican poll watchers to abandon their posts, and at 12:45 to 14:30 about Schweitzer's directive to the clerk of Silver Bow County to delay the release of vote counts for many hours so as to give Tester a tactical advantage in resisting a recount), accessed July 1, 2017, ia801407.us.archive.org/29/items/MontanaGov.BrianSchweitzerSpeechToTrialLawyersConvention7142008/Gov_Schweitzer_speech_to_trial_lawyers_convention_14_July_2008_64kb.mp3.
37 "Fox News: SOS Brad Johnson on Schweitzer's election scandal," YouTube, last modified September 21, 2008, youtube.com/watch?v=xdHVGBqTtVM.
38 John Gibbs, "Voter Fraud Is Real. Here's the Proof," *The Federalist*, October 13, 2016, thefederalist.com/2016/10/13/voter-fraud-real-heres-proof/.
39 Christopher Ingraham, "Voter Fraud Commission wants to Know the Voting History party ID and address of every voter in America," *Washington Post*, June 29, 2017, washingtonpost.com/news/wonk/wp/2017/06/29/trumps-voter-fraud-commission-wants-to-know-the-voting-history-party-id-and-address-of-every-voter-in-america/?utm_term=.87f2c3de2c25.

Chapter 8

1 "Alberto Gonzales," Wikipedia, last modified December 24, 2017, en.wikipedia.org/wiki/Alberto_Gonzales.
2 Ibid.
3 Ibid.
4 "DOJ denies US Attorneys were fired for Indian work," *Indianz*, June 22, 2007, indianz.com/News/2007/003577.asp.
5 "US Attorneys targeted for Indian Country work," *Indianz*, September 30, 2008, indianz.com/News/2008/09/30/us_attorneys_targeted_for_indi.asp.
6 Ibid.

7 Bill McAllister, "The $7 billion offer that never was," *Native Times*, September 23, 2008, nativetimes.com/archives/22/293-the-7-billion-offer-that-never-was.
8 "An Investigation into the Removal of Nine U.S. Attorneys in 2006," U.S. Office of the Inspector General, September 2008, oig.justice.gov/special/s0809a/final.pdf.
9 Noelle Straub, "Mercer wrote job provision into Patriot Act," *Montana Standard*, May 2, 2007, mtstandard.com/news/national/mercer-wrote-job-provision-into-patriot-act/article_4bd53aa3-6b83-58d8-8bac-5dff482ba098.html.
10 Mary Clare Jalonick, "Mercer top candidate to become No. 3 at Justice Dept.," *Independent Record*, August 18, 2006, helenair.com/news/state-and-regional/mercer-top-candidate-to-become-no-at-justice-dept/article_718003b8-8063-58d1-8974-ef0de2f6a63d.html.

Chapter 9

1 "Footage of LaVoy Finnicum's Death," YouTube, last modified January 29, 2016, youtube.com/watch?v=_5J9NHAiC4E.
2 Laura Gunderson, "LaVoy Finicum shooting: What happened when," *The Oregonian*, January 26, 2017, oregonlive.com/oregon-standoff/2016/02/post_6.html.
3 John Sepulvado and Amelia Templeton, "Militant Says Foster Children Were Pulled From His Home," *Oregon Public Broadcasting*, January 16, 2016, opb.org/news/series/burns-oregon-standoff-bundy-militia-news-updates/militant-says-foster-children-were-pulled-from-his-home-lavoy-finicum-burns-oregon/.
4 Phil Taylor, "Why LaVoy Finicum spurned the government," *Environment and Energy Publishing*, February 5, 2016, eenews.net/stories/1060031902.
5 Jenny Kane and Robert Anglen, "BLM misconduct probe may derail Bundy Ranch standoff trial," *USA Today*, February 3, 2017, azcentral.com/story/news/local/arizona-investigations/2017/02/03/blm-misconduct-probe-impacts-bundy-ranch-trial-dan-love-cliven-bundy-bunkerville/97450944/.
6 "What is Overgrazing?" Conserve Energy Future, accessed June 20, 2017, conserve-energy-future.com/causes-effects-solutions-overgrazing.php.
7 "California Desert Tortoise," Bird and Exotic Clinic of Seattle, accessed June 20, 2017, birdandexotic.com/becs-veterinary-care-animals/california-desert-tortoise/.
8 Dana Loesch, "The Real Story Behind The Bundy Ranch Harassment," *The Dana Show*, last modified April 10, 2014, danaloeschradio.com/the-real-story-of-the-bundy-ranch.
9 Ibid.
10 Oliver Darcy, "U.S. Officials End Tense Standoff Between Nevada Rancher, Federal Government," *theblaze*, April 12, 2014, theblaze.com/news/2014/04/12/nevada-rancher-wins-battle-with-feds-after-tense-standoff/.

11 Ibid.
12 Chris Kudialis, "Why Cliven Bundy tried to pay grazing fees to Clark County, not BLM," *Las Vegas Sun*, November 7, 2017, lasvegassun.com/news/2017/nov/07/why-cliven-bundy-sent-grazing-fees-clark-county/.
13 Steve Kanigher, "An abbreviated look at rancher Cliven Bundy's family history," accessed January 1, 2018, lasvegasnow.com/news/an-abbreviated-look-at-rancher-cliven-bundys-family-history/70830238.
14 Ibid.
15 Darcy, "U.S. Officials."
16 "Bundy Standoff," Revolvy, accessed June 20, 2017, revolvy.com/main/index.php?s=Bundy%20standoff.
17 Dwight Hammond, "Oregon ranchers reject Cliven Bundy family occupation," *CBS*, January 3, 2016, cbsnews.com/news/oregon-ranchers-reject-cliven-bundy-family-occupation/.
18 "Eastern Oregon Ranchers Convicted of Arson Resentenced to Five Years in Prison," U.S. Department of Justice, October 7, 2015, justice.gov/usao-or/pr/eastern-oregon-ranchers-convicted-arson-resentenced-five-years-prison.
19 Theodora Johnson, "Ranchers face added jail time for BLM fire," *Tri-State Livestock News*, July 17, 2015, tsln.com/news/ranchers-face-added-jail-time-for-blm-fire/.
20 Ibid.
21 Ibid.
22 Ibid.
23 John Notarianni, "An Occupation in Eastern Oregon," *Oregon Public Broadcasting*, December 20, 2017, opb.org/news/series/burns-oregon-standoff-bundy-militia-news-updates/.

Chapter 10

1 Joe Monzingo, "A Sting in the Desert," *Los Angeles Times*, September 21, 2014, graphics.latimes.com/utah-sting/.
2 Christopher Smith, "Burial ruling stuns Indians and Scientists," *Salt Lake Tribune*, March 1, 1998.
3 Patty Henetz, "The Source: the inside story of the key player in Fed's Indian artifacts case," *Salt Lake Tribune*, February 23, 2017.
4 Ibid.
5 "Report: Artifacts source blamed self for suicides," *Denver Post*, April 1, 2010, denverpost.com/2010/04/01/report-artifacts-source-blamed-self-for-suicides/.
6 Tim Brown, "If You Think the BLM and Daniel P. Love were Bad at Bundy Ranch Look What They did to this Man over Indian Artifacts," *The Washington Standard*, February 22, 2017, thewashingtonstandard.com/think-blm-daniel-p-love-bad-bundy-ranch-look-man-indian-artifacts/.
7 Ibid.
8 "Challenge Coins," coinforce, accessed June 26, 2017, coinforce.com/challenge-coins/.

Chapter 11

1 "Fed Raid Targets Guitars Made From Endangered Trees," *Fox News*, August 26, 2011, foxnews.com/politics/2011/08/26/feds-environmental-enforcement-on-guitars-leaves-musicians-in-fear.html.
2 "U.S. Lacey Act," Forest Legality Initiative, accessed June 21, 2017, forestlegality.org/policy/us-lacey-act.
3 John Hayward, "The Gibson Guitar Raid," *Human Events*, August 26, 2011, humanevents.com/2011/08/26/the-gibson-guitar-raid/.
4 Daniel Greenfield, "Gibson Commemorates Obama's Raid With Government Series Guitars," *Front Page Magazine*, January 30, 2014, frontpagemag.com/point/217649/gibson-commemorates-obamas-raid-government-series-daniel-greenfield.

Chapter 12

1 "Custer Battlefield Museum Press Release." Custer Battlefield Museum, July 22, 2014, custermuseum.org/press-releases/CusterMuseumHearing2014-07-24.pdf.

Chapter 13

1 Nicole Ogrysko, "Forest Service, BLM could lose law enforcement units under new bill," *Federal News Radio*, March 28, 2016, federalnewsradio.com/legislation/2016/03/forest-service-blm-lose-law-enforcement-units-new-bill/.
2 Ibid.

Chapter 14

1 "H.R.622 - Local Enforcement for Local Lands Act," U.S. Congress, accessed September 6, 2017, congress.gov/bill/115th-congress/house-bill/622.
2 "Dan Love Will Not Be Prosecuted," *redoubtnews*, accessed September 6, 2017, redoubtnews.com/2017/08/dan-love-not-prosecuted/.
3 Deb Jordan, "More Allegations of BLM Agent Dan Love Misconduct," *redoubtnews*, May 19, 2017, redoubtnews.com/2017/05/allegations-agent-love-misconduct.
4 Tim Brown, "Bundy Ranch Special Agent in Charge Dan Love Facing More Allegations of Misconduct that led to Suspension," *The Washington Standard*, May 19, 2017, thewashingtonstandard.com/bundy-ranch-special-agent-charge-dan-love-facing-allegations-misconduct-led-suspension/.
5 M.A. Chan and W.T. Parry, *Rainbow of Rocks: Mysteries of Sandstone Colors and Concretions in Colorado Plateau Canyon Country* (Utah Geological Survey, 2002), 11.
6 Jordan, "More Allegations."
7 Jenny Wilson, "Letter names BLM agent in charge of Bundy case as target of federal ethics probe," *Las Vegas Review Journal*, February 18, 2017, reviewjournal.com/news/bundy-blm/letter-names-blm-agent-in-charge-of-bundy-case-as-target-of-federal-ethics-probe/.
8 Ibid.

9 Jay Redd, email to author, May 26, 2017.
10 Lindsay Whitehurst, "APNewsBreak: Investigators say US land agent took evidence," *Washington Post*, August 24, 2017, washingtonpost.com/national/energy-environment/apnewsbreak-investigators-say-federal-agent-took-evidence/2017/08/24/99539a92-8900-11e7-96a7-d178cf3524eb_story.html?utm_term=.e2e9620313cb.
11 Brian Maffly, "New report faults controversial BLM agent for mishandling evidence," *The Salt Lake Tribune*, August 25, 2017, sltrib.com/news/environment/2017/08/25/new-report-faults-controversial-blm-agent-for-mishandling-evidence/.
12 Jay Redd, email to author, May 26, 2017.
13 Ibid.
14 Ibid.
15 "Investigative Report of Ethical Violations and Misconduct," U.S. Office of Inspector General, Department of the Interior, January 30, 2017, doioig.gov/sites/doioig.gov/files/EthcialViolationsAndMisconductByBLMOfficials_Public.pdf.
16 Jay Redd, email to author, May 26, 2017.
17 Carol Walker, "BLM Continues Lack of Transparency in Adobe Town Wild Mare Radio Collar Study," *Wordpress*, February 28, 2017, reclaimourrepublic.wordpress.com/2017/02/28/blm-continues-lack-of-transparency-in-wild-mare-radio-collar-study-blm-agent-in-bundy-case-accused-of-misconduct.
18 Deb Jordan, "BLM Agent Daniel P. Love Under Fire By Bundy Case Attorney After Inspector General Probe Finds Him Guilty Of Misconduct," *The Pete Santilli Show*, February 2, 2017, thepetesantillishow.com/blm-agent-daniel-p-love-under-fire-by-bundy-case-attorney-after-inspector-general-probe-finds-him-guilty-of-misconduct.
19 Steve Byas, "BLM Agent in Bundy Case Accused of Misconduct," *The New American*, February 13, 2017, thenewamerican.com/index.php?option=com_k2&view=item&id=25370:blm-agent-in-bundy-case-accused-of-misconduct-in-bundy-case&Itemid=632.
20 Kane and Anglen, "BLM misconduct."
21 Steve Byas, "BLM Agent."
22 Ibid.
23 "Arrests Made in Operation Targeting Network Selling Stolen Native American Artifacts," U.S. Department of Justice, June 10, 2009, justice.gov/opa/pr/arrests-made-operation-targeting-network-selling-stolen-native-american-artifacts.
24 "Federal Agents Bust Ring of Antiquity Thieves Looting American Indian Sites for Priceless Treasures," U.S. Department of the Interior, June 10, 2009, doi.gov/news/pressreleases/2009_06_10_releaseA.
25 Leah Sottile, "The Plan to Stop Federal Law Enforcement of Public Lands," *Outside*, accessed June 10, 2017, outsideonline.com/2154531/law-enforcement-public-land.
26 Ibid.

27 "Current Vacancies," U.S. Office of the Clerk U.S. House of Representatives, accessed June 10, 2017, chaffetz.house.gov/news/documentsingle.aspx?DocumentID=458.
28 Lisa Riley Roche, "Chaffetz says he won't seek re-election but his plans remain unclear," *Deseret News*, April 19, 2017.
29 Hadas Gold, "Jason Chaffetz signs with Fox News," *Politico*, June 28, 2017, politico.com/story/2017/06/28/jason-chaffetz-fox-news-240045.
30 Amanda Taub and Max Fisher, "As Leaks Multiply, Fears of a Deep State in America," *New York Times*, February 16, 2017, nytimes.com/2017/02/16/world/americas/deep-state-leaks-trump.html?_r=1.

Chapter 15

1 "Garryowen, Montana, Site Of Custer's Last Stand, For Sale For $250,000," *Huffingtonpost*, last modified August 7, 2012, huffingtonpost.com/2012/08/07/garryowen-montana-custer-for-sale_n_1751962.html.
2 Andrew Turck, "Shield donated to Battlefield Museum may have belonged to Sitting Bull," *Big Horn County News*, June 11, 2015, bighorncountynews.com/news/uncertain-treasure.
3 Ed Kemmick, "Sunday events will support Shadow Warriors Project," *Last Best News*, June 2, 2016, lastbestnews.com/site/2016/06/sunday-events-will-support-shadow-warriors-project/.

Epilogue

1 Alex Newman, "Whistleblower: Federal Thug Behind Bundy Fiasco Had "Kill Book", *The New American*, December 19, 2017, thenewamerican.com/usnews/crime/item/27612-whistleblower-federal-thug-behind-bundy-fiasco-had-kill-book.
2 Ibid.
3 Larry Wooten, "BLM Memo," *redoubtnews*, December 2017, redoubtnews.com/wp-content/uploads/2017/12/Larry-Wooten-Communication_77PI.pdf.
4 Newman, "Whistleblower."
5 Ibid.
6 Shari Dovale, "BLM and FBI Exposed or How the Bundy's Got Out of Prison," *redoubtnews*, November 29, 2017, redoubtnews.com/2017/11/blm-fbi-exposed-bundys-released/.
7 Newman, "Whistleblower."
8 Ibid.
9 Ibid.
10 Dovale, "BLM and FBI."
11 Ibid.
12 Richard Perez-Pena, "Attorney General Sessions Orders Investigation After Bundy Mistrial," *New York Times*, December 21, 2017, nytimes.com/2017/12/21/us/attorney-general-sessions-bundy.html.
13 Marjorie Haun, "Zinke moves to Drain the Swamp at Interior Department," *redoubtnews*, June 20, 2017, redoubtnews.com/2017/06/zinke-drain-swamp-interior-department/.

Acknowledgments

While writing this book, I received guidance and support from numerous people, too many to list here. To everyone who helped with this book in any capacity who is not listed here, please know that I am infinitely grateful to have received your help. First and foremost, I would like to thank my publisher, Anthony Ziccardi, my editor, Billie Brownell, and the entire team at Post Hill Press for helping me to tell the world this story.

I would like to extend many special thanks to the following people:

Special thanks to my mother, Patricia Kortlander, for an incredible childhood and education. Without her, the historic Town of Garryowen and the Custer Battlefield Museum never would have been realized.

Penny Strong, Esq., to whom I owe my freedom, liberty, and sanity; who did not let me melt under the pressure from the over-handedness of the U.S. Attorney's office and would not let me plead guilty to a crime I did not commit; who stood by me through thick and thin and believed in my innocence. I will be forever appreciative of her expertise and knowledge of federal criminal law.

Charles "Timer" Moses, Esq., and his wife, Betty, for opening their home to me on all the occasions that I went to him seeking legal guidance, help, and direction; for his hundreds of pages of legal memos to me; for encouraging me to stand up for my Constitutional guarantees and giving me encouragement through some of the darkest days.

Kellen Cutsforth, for all the hundreds of hours and dedication that he has put into this book. This book project could not have been done without him, and I will be forever grateful for his contributions and his writing and editing skills.

Tyler Baldwin, who's been a friend, confidante, and a remarkable editor for this book; for keeping me focused and organized throughout the many decades I have known her.

Amy Schaffer, for her dedication and devotion to this project; for keeping me on track and organized to see this book through to its completion; for being willing and able to go with the flow of the ins and outs of the daily running of the town of Garryowen.

Rich Solberg, Esq., for being a good friend, confidant, and counselor; for sticking with me through every difficulty and obstacle, from the day of the raid to the completion of this book. I am forever grateful.

Bill Reynolds, for decades of an enduring friendship, through trials and tribulations; for sharing the passion of the American West; for his guidance and mentoring, I will always be appreciative.

Jerry and Gail Schneider, for their love; for always believing in me; for being there for me through all of the peaks and valleys. Garryowen and the Custer Battlefield Museum would not be here today if it was not for their support and contributions, of which there are too many to name.

A very special thank you to Ammon Bundy for writing the foreword to this book. His willingness and determination, as well as that of his family, to do whatever it takes has inspired countless Americans to join the fight against federal overreach.

Kimberly and Clinton Kortlander, and my dearly beloved brother, Shawn, for all of their unconditional love, emotional support, and understanding throughout this difficult period of my life.

For emotional support and always believing in me, I am grateful to Dr. Donald Couch, Dr. Curtis Couch, and Christopher Couch, who have always been in my life.

Acknowledgments

Special thanks to:

Gina Cannan, Esq., at Mountain States Legal Foundation
Chris Enss
Larry Grubbs, Esq.
Jason Harkins, Esq.
Jon and Christie Matovich
Andrew T. Miltenberg, Esq.
Steve and Marcia Nikolich
William Perry Pendley, Esq., president of Mountain States Legal Foundation
Michael Plank
Dr. Shannon Plank
Dr. Jay Redd and family
Jeff and Donna Robertson
Peter Stanley, Esq.
Harold Stanton, Esq.
Jim Vogel, Esq.